Rum & Reggae's Rio de Janeiro

Rum & Reggae®'s

Rio de Janeiro

Jonathan Runge &
Sam Logan

Rum & Reggae Guidebooks, Inc.
Boston, Massachusetts • August 2008

While every effort has been made to provide accurate information, the prices, places, and people do change rather frequently in Rio de Janeiro. Just a couple years ago, Rio was in the process of reconfiguring its phone system to add an eighth digit (usually a 2 or 3 in front of the first digit) to its seven-digit local phone numbers. So, among other exciting traits, Rio is a city of rapidly changing contact information, including Web sites and e-mail addresses. We've put forth our best effort to provide up-to-the-minute information, but if there are still some inaccuracies, we do apologize for any inconvenience this may cause to our valued readers.

Typographical errors also occasionally occur. Thus, please keep in mind that there may be discrepancies between what you find and what is reported here. In addition, some of the recommendations have been given by individuals interviewed by the authors and may not represent the opinion of the authors or publishers of Rum & Reggae Guidebooks, Inc. The reader assumes all responsibility when participating in the activities or excursions described in this book.

First Edition

ISBN 13: 978-1893675-16-2
ISBN 10: 1-893675-16-5
ISSN: 1941-0530

Edited by Jonathan Runge and Joe Shapiro

Book design by Valerie Brewster, Scribe Typography
Cover design by Jonathan Runge

Cover and Interior Illustrations by Eric Orner
Front cover photo of Copacabana Beach by Sam Logan
Back cover photos: Leblon Beach by iStockphoto.com/OSTILL; Christ statue by iStockphoto.com/luoman
Maps by Regner Camilo, Rodrigo Fleury, and Luiz Fernando Martini

Printed in the United States on 30% PCW recycled FSC certified paper.

Mixed Sources
Product group from well-managed forests, controlled sources and recycled wood or fiber
FSC www.fsc.org Cert no. SW-COC-002283
© 1996 Forest Stewardship Council

For Aunt Lil

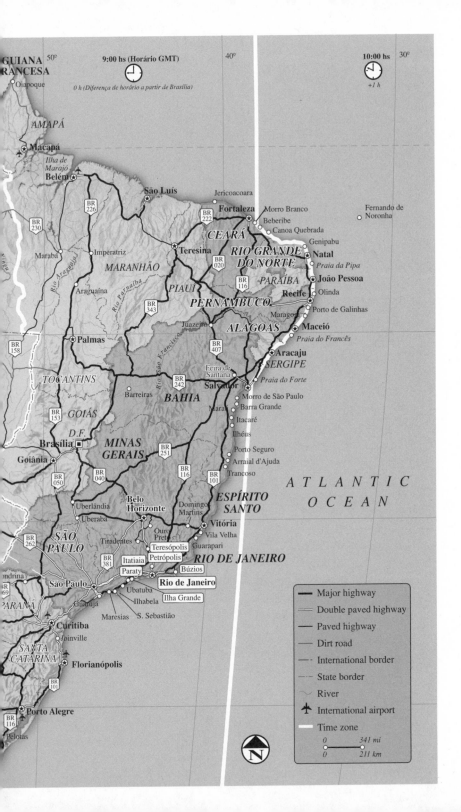

CONTENTS

Before You Go 3

Rio de Janeiro State 25

TOURISTO SCALE:

Rio de Janeiro City 29

👤👤👤👤👤👤👤👤👤 (9)

Búzios   147   TOURISTO SCALE: 👤👤👤👤👤👤👤👤 (8)

Ilha Grande   169   TOURISTO SCALE: 👤👤👤👤👤👤 (6)

Paraty   179   TOURISTO SCALE: 👤👤👤👤👤👤 (6)

Petrópolis   195   TOURISTO SCALE: 👤👤👤👤👤 (5)

Teresópolis   205   TOURISTO SCALE: 👤👤👤👤👤 (5)

Itatiaia   215   TOURISTO SCALE: 👤👤👤 (3)

LIST OF MAPS

Lodging and Restaurant Key

A note about this guide: We have used a number of symbols and terms to indicate prices and ambiance. Here are the code breakers.

Lodging Symbols

ℭ telephone number

✆ fax number

🖳 Web site URL and/or e-mail address

💲 room rates

🍴 meal plan

[CC] major credit cards

Be sure to ask if your credit card is accepted when making reservations

★ This is a Rum & Reggae "best of category" establishment.

Lodging Rates

- Prices are *rack rates* for the least expensive double (two people) in high season — generally mid-December through mid-April — unless otherwise noted. Rio de Janeiro winter rates are often as much as 30 percent cheaper. Unless otherwise noted, prices for singles are the same or slightly less.

Dirt Cheap	under $50
Cheap	$51–$100
Not So Cheap	$101–$150
Pricey	$151–$200
Very Pricey	$201–$300
Wicked Pricey	$301–$400
Ridiculous	$401–$500
Beyond Belief	$501–$600
Stratospheric	$601 and up!

- Hotels in *Rum & Reggae's Rio de Janeiro* are separated by neighborhood (where applicable) and are listed in order of most to least expensive (Stratospheric to Dirt Cheap), and then alphabetically within each category.

- *Rum & Reggae's Rio de Janeiro* covers hotels and inns (*pousadas*), but we have deliberately omitted motels. In Rio, motel rooms are offered at hourly rates only (wink, wink). For more information on motels, see the short piece on page 70 in Rio City's "Where to Stay" section.

Lodging and Meal Codes 🕈

All hotel prices are assigned a corresponding code that relates to the meals that are included in the rates.

EP   **European Plan** — No meals included.

CP   **Continental Plan** — Continental breakfast (bread, cereal, juice, coffee) included.

BP   **Breakfast Plan** — Full hot breakfast included.

MAP   **Modified American Plan** — Full breakfast and dinner included.

FAP   **Full American Plan** — Full breakfast, lunch, and dinner included (sometimes with an afternoon "tea" or snack as well).

All-Inclusive All meals, beer, wine, and well drinks (house brands) are included, most or all on-site activities, and usually tax and service charges.

Restaurant Prices

Prices represent per-person cost for the average meal, from soup to nuts. Restaurants are separated by neighborhood (where applicable) and are listed alphabetically.

$	Under $15	$$$$	$36–$50
$$	$15–$25	$$$$$	Over $50
$$$	$26–$35		

Note: s/n means *sem número* ("without number") and is often used in Brazilian street addresses. *Loja* means "store" or "shop" and is sometimes used in addresses to indicate a specific room or store number within a small building or mall.

Touristo Scale 🕈

You'll find the key to our Touristo Scale on the last page of the book.

ACKNOWLEDGMENTS

Contrary to what you might think, writing a book on Rio de Janeiro is not very glamorous. We've always said that the most glittering part about this business is answering the "So what do you do?" question at cocktail parties. It's all uphill from there. We do not spend our days on the beach or by the pool sipping a *caipirinha*. Well, okay, sometimes we do (and New Year's Eve *was* a blast). But most of the time we are running around, coordinating bus schedules, trying to communicate in Portuguese, checking out this or that, and complaining about the heat. Just when we start to get comfortable in a place, it's time to uproot ourselves and start all over again. Try doing that at least every other day, and you'll begin to know what we mean.

Fortunately, some wonderful people helped us out during our travels through Rio. We'd like to take this opportunity to sincerely thank them. First and foremost are: Ricardo Ramalho, Cristiano Moreira, Anderson Lopes, Richard Hanson, and Vinícius and Andrea Monteiro. And, of course, we will never forget that woman in the green and yellow hat who guided us out of Itatiaia National Park when the weather closed in on us. We didn't get her name, but thanks so-o-o-o much!

Rum & Reggae's Rio de Janeiro is published by Rum & Reggae Guidebooks, Inc. We are not exactly an industry behemoth, but we have many helpers, and all deserve hearty thanks. Our warmest gratitude goes to the following: our fabulous and wonderfully easygoing book designer, Valerie Brewster of Scribe Typography; our very talented Web designer, Michael Carlson; our corporate illustrator and Disney animation megastar, Eric Orner; our amazing travel agent, Flávia Almeida; our cartographers, Regner Camilo, Rodrigo Fleury, and Luiz Fernando Martini; our very patient distributor, Independent Publishers Group—its chief, Curt Matthews, the incomparable Mary

Rowles, and the rest of IPG's great staff; our legal team at Sheehan, Phinney, Bass & Green of Maria Recalde and Doug Verge; our printer, McNaughton & Gunn; and our meticulous copy editor and indexer, Judith Antonelli.

There were several people who helped in other ways. Many thanks to Lynn Clark, Barbara Carneiro Logan, Iris Carneiro Logan, Nadine Banks, Dorothy Shapiro, Jordan Shapiro, Gail Shapiro, Andy Shapiro, Ruth Bonsignore, Kevin Moore, F. James Meaney, Wilmar Silveira, Kendall Dudley, Paul and Jill Boudreau, Waldirene Almeida, Adriana Knackfuss, Roberto Caldera, Duncan Donahue and Tom Fortier, Nan Garland, Elvis Jiménez-Chávez and Chris Lawrence, Bucky Parker, Brendan Hickey and Judith Wright, Martin Merle, Matt Wilhelm, Megan McElheran, Nicole Riddle and the rest of the Stanford gang, Rubens Taveira, Tony Lulek, Jeffrey Runge, and Gregory Runge.

Finally, a wicked thanks to Rum & Reggae's president, Joe Shapiro, whose enthusiasm, dedication, and hard work helped to push this book to completion.

As always, a can of dolphin-safe tuna to the Rum & Reggae cat and guardian angel, Jada.

To all who helped, *muito obrigado*!

Jonathan Runge and Sam Logan
Authors
Rum & Reggae Guidebooks, Inc.
Boston, Massachusetts
August 1, 2008

WRITE TO RUM & REGGAE

Dear *Rum & Reggae's Rio de Janeiro* Readers,

We really do appreciate and value your comments, suggestions, or information about anything new or exciting in Rio de Janeiro. We'd love to hear about your experiences, good and bad, while you were there. Your feedback will help us to shape the next edition. So please drop us a line.

Visit our Web site at www.rumreggae.com, e-mail us at yahmon @rumreggae.com, or write to:

Mr. Yah Mon
Rum & Reggae Guidebooks
P.O. Box 130153
Boston, MA 02113

Sincerely,

Joe Shapiro
President

P.S. We often mention cocktails, drinking, and other things in this book. We certainly do not mean to upset any nondrinkers or those in recovery. Please don't take offense—rum and its relatives are not a requirement for a successful vacation in Rio.

INTRODUCTION

Travel with an Opinion.® That's how we describe our distinct point of view. *Rum & Reggae's Rio de Janeiro* is not your typical tourist guide to this immensely beautiful, diverse, and fascinating land. We like to say that the Rum & Reggae series is written for people who want more out of a vacation than the standard tourist fare. Our reader is sophisticated and independent. He's livelier—be it exploring, beaching, art seeking, hiking, festivities seeking, or just pure partying. She's more particular, in search of places that are secluded, cerebral, or spiritual.

This book differs from other guidebooks in another way. Instead of telling you that everything is "nice"—nice, that is, for the average Joe and Jane—*Rum & Reggae's Rio de Janeiro* offers definitive opinions. We will tell you what's fantastic and what's not, from the point of view of someone who loathes the tourist label and the other bland and tired travel books whose names we won't mention.

We'll take you throughout the best parts of Rio de Janeiro and its surroundings and share our recommendations of where to go (and where not to go). More important, we filter out all the crap for you so you can have fun reading the book while enjoying your vacation and keeping the decision making to a minimum.

So mix yourself a *caipirinha* (we even provide the recipe), put on some bossa nova, and sit back and let *Rum & Reggae's Rio de Janeiro* take you on your own private voyage to feel *maravilhoso*.

Rum & Reggae's Rio de Janeiro

BEFORE YOU GO

Climate

The state of Rio de Janeiro is located in the southeast of Brazil, where you'll find some temperature fluctuation with the seasons. Daytime temperatures in Rio city and the other coastal areas often reach the 90s (32°C), with high humidity in the summer months (December through March). Things cool off in the evenings, but not much. The mountain regions of Rio state offer a respite from the summer heat, with daytime temperatures in the 80s (26°C) and nighttime temperatures in the low 70s (20°C). This is why Petrópolis and Teresópolis are particular favorites for the Rio de Janeiro crowds. The summer can bring a fair amount of rain, but long stretches of rainy weather are not common.

The winter months (June through September) bring temperatures that fluctuate between 45°F/7°C at night and 85°F/29°C during the day. Occasional cold fronts coming from the southeast do occasionally pelt the region with days of cold weather, wind, and rain. The coldest day in Rio, however, is generally about as warm as an average summer day in many North American cities!

Travel Necessities

Brazil maintains a reciprocal **visa** policy with all countries. In the case of U.S. citizens, whose country requires that Brazilians obtain a tourist visa before entering the country, Brazil requires that U.S. citizens do the same. We've found that you can apply for a simple 90-day tourist visa that allows you to enter and exit the country at will for 90 days from the day you first enter Brazil.

You can extend this visa, with a good excuse, for another 90 days. Keep in mind, however, that foreigners on a simple tourist visa can stay in Brazil for only up to 180 days every year. So if you extend your visa early in the year, for instance, to stick around after *Carnaval*, you won't be able to reenter the country until the next calendar year, once you leave. Most forms of tourist visas are good for five years. Those with family in the country can get a visa for up to 10 years.

There are many companies that specialize in visa services. Just Google it. Usually they take a week to 10 days to process your visa, use FedEx to ship, and charge you a premium for speedy service, which can get you a turnaround in under one business week.

Visa forms can be found on the Brazilian embassy Web site (www .brasilemb.org) or at your nearest consulate. Although it can save cash to go directly to the consulate or embassy yourself, it's often a time-consuming process and can be a pain in the butt if an officer subjects you to a random interview. Visa agencies, on the other hand, have established relationships and, in our experience, have never failed to obtain a simple 90-day visa with professionalism and efficiency.

Aside from a visa, there is little else absolutely necessary—that is, besides some street smarts, a photocopy of your passport and visa, an ATM card, and a major credit card; actually, bring at least two credit cards—it is common in Brazil for some companies not to accept certain ones. We find that money exchange posts charge a healthy commission. ATM machines charge less and give you the best possible exchange rate up to the second. Citibank is particularly friendly. HSBC will also accept your U.S. ATM card.

The general **health** concerns about travel to Brazil and acquiring one of its mosquito-carrying viruses are largely blown out of proportion. However, if you are heading deep into the Amazon, you might want to get vaccinated for yellow fever. Malaria could also be a concern, but more so in parts of the Amazon and northern Brazil. In recent years, dengue has become more prevalent in Rio. Hepatitis A—transmitted through contaminated food and water—is another disease against which it would be wise to take precautions (there is a vaccine). That being said, the majority of our friends who have traveled and lived in Brazil have never been vaccinated for any of these diseases, and they have never had any problems. To be safe, consult your family doctor prior to travel.

What to Wear and Take Along

Less is more. That is always the motto to remember when packing to go to Rio de Janeiro. Bring only what you can carry for 10 minutes at a good clip, because you'll often be schlepping your luggage for at least that time, and it's hot. If you haven't already done so, invest in a piece of luggage with wheels.

What you really need to take along are a bathing suit, shorts, T-shirts or tank tops, a cotton sweater, a pair of sandals, sunglasses, and an iPod. After all, you are on vacation. However, this is the new millennium and people are dressing up for no reason, so you might want to bring some extra togs to look presentable at the dinner table. Rio de Janeiro is a contemporary city, so feel free to bring a pair of nice pants and a comfortable (but chic) shirt. Jeans are still the universal language and are worn in almost every club and restaurant throughout Rio. To help you be totally prepared (and to make your packing a lot easier), we've assembled a list of essentials for a week.

The Packing List

Clothes

- [ ] bathing suit (or two)
- [ ] T-shirts (4) — you'll end up buying at least one
- [ ] polo shirts (2)
- [ ] dress shirts (2)
- [ ] shorts (2)
- [ ] nice, compatible lightweight pants
- [ ] jeans — two pairs (one casual, one chic)
- [ ] sandals — those that can get wet, like Tevas, are best (You can buy a pair of flip-flops once you're in Brazil.)
- [ ] shoes for going out
- [ ] cotton sweater or sweatshirt
- [ ] light coat, especially for São Paulo winter months
- [ ] undergarments (if you so choose)
- [ ] sneakers (or good walking shoes)

☐ Women: lightweight dress (or a couple of dresses for evening)

☐ Men: If you must have a lightweight sport coat, wear it (with appropriate shoes) on the plane.

Essentials

☐ toiletries and any necessary meds

☐ sunscreen (at least SPF 30, and lip protector)

☐ moisturizer

☐ pure aloe gel for sunburn

☐ some good books—don't count on finding a book in English there

☐ Cutter's or Woodsman's insect repellent, or Skin So Soft (oh, those nasty bugs)

☐ sunglasses (We bring two pairs!)

☐ hat or visor!

☐ iPod

☐ camcorder, digital camera, or pocket camera (Disposables are great for the beach.)

Sports Accessories (Where Applicable)

☐ hiking shoes

☐ fins, mask, snorkel, regulator/BC, and C-card (certification card)

And...

☐ ATM card and credit cards

☐ valid passport with visa (Keep in hotel safe and carry around a photocopy in your wallet.)

☐ driver's license

Rio de Janeiro Superlatives ⊛

Best *Caipirinha*—Academia da Cachaça, Leblon, Rio de Janeiro

Best *Chopp*—Bracarense, Leblon, Rio de Janeiro

Best Samba School — Mangueira, Rio de Janeiro

Best *Carnaval* — Rio de Janeiro! (Hey, what else are we going to put here?!)

Best Large Luxury Resort (over 50 rooms) — Copacabana Palace, Copacabana, Rio de Janeiro

Best Small Luxury Resort (under 50 rooms) — Sítio do Lobo, Ilha Grande

Best Resort for Kids — Hotel Le Canton, Teresópolis

Best Romantic Lodging — Casas Brancas Boutique Hotel & Spa, Búzios

Best Boutique Hotel — Fasano Hotel, Ipanema, Rio de Janeiro

Best *Pousada*/Inn — Pousada do Ouro, Paraty

Best Eco-Friendly "Green" Hotel — Vrindávana Pousada & Spa, Teresópolis

Best Room with a View — Best Western Sol Ipanema, Ipanema, Rio de Janeiro

Best Brazilian Cuisine Restaurant — Brasileirinho, Ipanema, Rio de Janeiro

Best International Cuisine Restaurant — Fasano Al Mare (in Fasano Hotel), Ipanema, Rio; Nam Thai, Leblon, Rio

Best Lunch Spot — Gula Gula, Ipanema & other locations, Rio; Felice Café, Ipanema, Rio

Best Kilograma ("Pay per kilo") — Frontera, Ipanema, Rio de Janeiro

Best Place for a Sunset Cocktail — Fasano Hotel (roofdeck bar), Ipanema, Rio de Janeiro

Best Sunset — Praia da Tartaruga, Búzios

Best Nightclub — Carioca da Gema, Lapa, Rio; The House Bar, Leblon, Rio

Best Bar — Devassa, Leblon, Rio de Janeiro

Best Neighborhood for Nightlife — Leblon, Rio de Janeiro

Best Spa — Copacabana Palace, Copacabana, Rio; Casas Brancas Boutique Hotel & Spa, Búzios

Best-Kept Secret — Sitio do Lobo, Ilha Grande

Best Place to Meet Women (Straight) — The House Bar, Leblon, Rio; Baronetti, Ipanema, Rio

Best Place to Meet Men (Straight) — Melt, Leblon, Rio de Janeiro

Best Place to Meet Women (Gay) — La Girl, Copacabana, Rio de Janeiro

Best Place to Meet Men (Gay) — Le Boy, Copacabana, Rio; Bar Bofetada, Ipanema, Rio

Best Gay-Friendly Accommodation — Fasano Hotel, Ipanema, Rio; Visconti Residence, Ipanema, Rio; Ipanema Plaza Hotel, Ipanema, Rio

Best Romantic Restaurant — Tartaruguinha, Búzios

Best Helicopter Tour — Rio de Janeiro (Use Helisight's Lagoa helipad)

Best Diving — Ilha Grande

Best Golf Course — Gávea Golf & Country Club, Gávea, Rio de Janeiro

Best Hiking — Teresópolis

Best Surfing — Búzios (less crowded)

Best Windsurfing — Cabo Frio

The 10 Best Beaches in Rio de Janeiro

The state of Rio de Janeiro has tons of great beaches, and it was no easy task to narrow down the list. After some heated debate, the following *praias* made the grade, in no particular order.

Praia Lopes Mendes, Ilha Grande

Rated one of the top 10 beaches in the world by *Vogue* magazine, this splendor of white sand and clear blue water rests on the southern shores of Ilha Grande, a 45-minute walk from Vila do Abraão. Arrive early for that special privilege of being the only one on the sand!

Ipanema, Rio de Janeiro

This long stretch of city sand is quite possibly the world's most famous beach. It has a kickin' daytime and nighttime social scene. With Dois Irmãos and other mountains as a backdrop, it is also a stunning spot.

Copacabana, Rio de Janeiro

Much like Ipanema Beach, Copa has it all—parties, soccer, volleyball, kiosks, hot bods, and beautiful vistas. The only thing it lacks is a song as good as "The Girl from Ipanema."

Praia de Geribá, Búzios

This spanning beach is the Ipanema of Búzios. At low tide, the wide beach offers an excellent scene for beach soccer, frisbee, or just about any sport, and at high tide, the currents are not too strong for a good swim. When the right swell hits, this beach becomes an ideal surf spot for beginners.

Prainha, Rio de Janeiro

This little gem of a beach is just past Recreio, the last suburb of Rio de Janeiro. It is a surfer's haven and accessible only by car, so don't expect to find people bused in from the center of town here. Get there early to enjoy the day's sun before it tucks behind the mountains around 3 p.m. Just behind the beach is a well-kept national park (Parque da Prainha), and at the far end you'll find a dirt-floor restaurant (named Mirante da Prainha) with the best fish and bean dish around.

Praia do Pepê, Rio de Janeiro (in the Barra da Tijuca neighborhood)

At the beginning of Rio's famous neighborhood, Barra da Tijuca, rests a magnet for beautiful people and famous actors. If you're a Brazilian soap opera buff or simply a fan of Brazilian models, soccer players, or musicians, check out this bumpin' beach spot, especially on a hot day in the summer. You'll likely find Preta Gil (Gilberto Gil's daughter), Leonardo DiCaprio, or Gisele Bundchen with her latest boyfriend (who, at press time, happens to be Tom Brady, and still going strong).

Praia da Tartaruga, Búzios

Before you get too far into Búzios, and a little way after the entrance to Praia Geribá, a little dirt road leads away from the asphalt, seemingly into jungle. Once you summit the little hill and pass a few curves, you'll arrive at the Pousada da Tartaruga, which sits on one extreme end of Praia da Tartaruga. This beach is one of the best spots for a sunset, and it is very peaceful compared to Praia Geribá.

Praia Ferradura, Búzios

This beach is protected by a semicircular formation of rocks, making the waters here ideal for swimming with children.

Praia Caxadaço, Ilha Grande

What used to be a receiving point for slaves became one of Ilha Grande's best-kept secrets, until a little-known trail that led to this paradise cove was discovered. Straight from your favorite island movie, this little cove is the ideal spot for a peaceful picnic or some of the state's best snorkeling.

Praia Dois Rios, Ilha Grande

The site of one of Rio's most infamous prisons, this beautiful beach is loaded with history. Just inland from the sand are stacks of ruins, making for an interesting archaeological outing. If that's not your thing, keep in mind that this beach is one of the more isolated spots on Ilha Grande. If you're willing to make the one-hour walk, you just might be rewarded with solitude on the sand.

About Money and Tipping

The Brazilian form of currency is the *real* (pronounced "hay-OW" by Brazilians), but feel free to just say "real," like the English "real"). The Brazilian *real* generally trades at a 2-to-1 ratio to the U.S. dollar. However, due to the fickle nature of the world currency markets, the spectrum usually fluctuates between 2.4 to 1 and 1.6 to 1. Unless you're particularly mathematical, an easy division by 2 on all printed prices will give you a good idea of what you're spending. (Note: At press time, the exchange rate was 1.7 to 1.)

When preparing for travel to Brazil, you should consider a few things. First, commission booths on the street will charge you much more than the bank, but they are convenient and don't have the long lines you'll find in most Brazilian banks. If you choose to save some money and use a bank, be sure you ask for small bills when receiving *reais* (pronounced "hay-EYESH"; this is the Portuguese plural of *real*, but feel free to just say "reals"). Banks generally want to give you large bills, which don't often go over well with street vendors, taxis, bartenders, or beach merchants, especially in small towns or rural areas. (It's amazing how few people have change in this country.) You will mostly deal with the 1, 2, 5, 10, 20, and 50 *real* notes. Coins are useful for bus rides, street vendors, and market merchants.

If you decide to play it safe with traveler's checks, the commission is even higher in the exchange booths, and banks will require that you present your passport. Unfortunately, a photocopy or a driver's license will not do the trick. Brazilian bank tellers, especially in the larger branches such as Itaú, Banco do Brasil, or Unibanco, are notorious for being annoyingly detail oriented. They don't cut corners.

We've found that the best route to go is an ATM. Upon arrival, exchange some money in the airport, enough to get to your hotel, *pousada* ("inn"), or house. Then, during *daylight* hours, visit an ATM and get your cash. Depending on the service charge, which is never too much (remember the division by 2), you might want to take out enough for a week or two, but you won't be able to take out more than 1,000 *reais* per card per day. WARNING: Frequent trips to ATMs in a busy city like Rio are not advised. Local thieves keep a close eye on the comings and goings. A foreigner who takes out money daily, or every other day, is an easy target. We recommend that you not visit the same ATM more than two or three times a week. *Most important: Do not visit ATMs in the evening.*

Another point to keep in mind about ATMs is that some might not accept your Visa check card or credit card simply because many Brazilian banks, especially the smaller branches, are not linked to an international system. Citibank and HSBC are almost always a good bet, and Banco Santander, a Spanish-owned bank, usually works for European bank account access. American Express card owners should note the AmEx office locations throughout Rio.

Credit card use has become more widely accepted outside the city of Rio de Janeiro, but there are still many pockets where only cash will pay for your meal or trinket. Brazilians are charged quite a bit more for late fees and interest than Americans or Europeans are, so many Brazilians don't use credit cards in the countryside, such as at small restaurants outside Itatiaia or on the way to Paraty. Don't expect restaurants in these areas to accept your Diner's card or AmEx Blue. These areas are almost strictly cash based. City locations usually accept Visa or AmEx, and many of the better restaurants, hotels, and nightclubs will accept Visa, Master Card, AmEx, and Diner's.

A few words about **tipping** are in order. Almost all restaurants will add a 10 percent service charge to the bill. Although it is not expected that you leave anything else, it is acceptable (and appreciated) to toss a few extra *reais* on the table. A similar charge is added to bar tabs at nightclubs, so most *cariocas* (natives of Rio) don't feel the need to tip bartenders. When standing up and eating at a streetside café or juice bar, it is common to leave a few coins on the counter for whoever served you. We usually just leave the change. Taxi drivers don't expect much from their riders. People often round up to the nearest *real*. We've seen some *cariocas* actually round *down* and receive no gripe from their *taxista*. However, what goes around comes around, so don't expect change from your 10 *real* note if the meter reads R$8.70. And, of course, no *taxista* will complain if you "over" tip. In hotels, it is customary to give porters a *real* or two.

Sex and Social Mores

The social mores concerning sex are not at all aligned with what you might expect from a Catholic country. Unlike their Latino cousins, Brazilians view sex with an open mind and a liberal attitude. Promiscuity is not socially frowned upon; rather, it's celebrated. Some women go out expecting to kiss at least a handful of men a night. Foreign men might find some Brazilian women, or men, very aggressive. Foreign women will feel the same. Among the young heterosexual crowd, women may expect to be kissed within a half hour of meeting a new man. Guys who don't step up to the plate will find themselves alone at the end of the night, which usually doesn't end until the morning, in most places. Attitudes toward gays and lesbians in Rio (and São Paulo and Salvador, for that matter) are more tolerant than in other Latin American countries.

Music and Dance

A vibrant selection of music and dance facilitates the unabashed social habits mentioned above. The national music, **samba**, is energetic and spunky, and it comes in a variety of genres. *Pagode* is improvisational in nature and usually accompanied by street parties. *Chorinho* is melancholic, with slower beats and sultry lyrics. **Bossa nova**, referred to as the "grandfather" of lounge music, is a slower, jazzy version of samba. **Funk** is very energetic and popular with younger men and women, as is *música popular brasileira* (**MPB**), the catchall term for Brazilian-made music that doesn't fall into any other category. *Forró*, a Portuguese term derived from the English words "for all," is Brazil's version of folk music. Couples dancing is encouraged! And, of course, there's rock, electronic, reggae, *reggaetón*, and classical. Take your pick, Brazil's musicians do it all!

Food and Drink

Brazilian food is more varied than the music, and you will find almost all of it in Rio de Janeiro. From all areas of the country come distinct dishes, each with its own history and story behind it. Through restaurateurs from the South, near Uruguay and Argentina, Rio de Janeiro has established some of the country's best *churrascos* (the Brazilian barbeque), where the meat is considered more tender and rich than that of the neighboring Argentines, of course! The state of Rio de Janeiro is also home to some of the best *feijoadas* in the country. This multicourse meal is a combination of black beans, a stew that includes beef and pork, and collard greens. It is very good and extremely filling. But be sure to ask for *carne nobre*, or "noble meat," to avoid ears, tongues, and other body parts!

The dry, poor regions of Rio Grande do Norte yield some of the best beef jerky and *carne seca* ("dried meat") dishes in all of Brazil. Black beans, or *feijão*, are ubiquitous and easily the most widely available Brazilian dish. From Brazil's northeast, in Bahia, comes a rich seafood stew made with chili peppers and *dendê* ("palm") oil, called *moqueca*. As much as we love this dish, it is hard to find *moqueca* in Rio that will compare to the *moqueca* you'll eat in Bahia or even Espírito Santo. It's kind of like the decline in quality you might find when you order crab cakes outside Maryland.

No talk of Brazilian food would be complete without mention of the **tropical fruit and juice bars.** In almost any corner of Rio de Janeiro (and all of Brazil, for that matter) you can find a juice bar. For more information on fruit and juices, see page 97 in "Where to Eat."

Finally, **guaraná**, usually found in soft-drink form, is something akin to a Brazilian root beer, only sweeter. It's a digestive aid and stimulant that is widely believed to enhance sexual performance. No wonder the sexually progressive Brazilians have made *guaraná* a national soft drink that's more ubiquitous than the ever present Coca-Cola!

"Football" in Brazil

"*Brasil é penta! Brasil é penta!*" It was July 2002, and this was the celebratory cry of a soccer-crazed nation that had just captured its record fifth World Cup. Some of you might remember your Brazilian neighbors dancing in the streets while waving their recognizable green, yellow, and blue flags. For those of you who are out of the loop, Brazil is the greatest *football*-playing nation in the world. (Note: The grace period of calling the sport "soccer" will end for the time being.) It is the only team to have qualified for all 18 quadrennial World Cup tournaments, holding records for most games played, most games won, and most goals scored. Italy holds four World Cups and Germany two, but no country can claim a more proud history of football greatness than Brazil.

In addition, no country has provided us with more flamboyant teams and players. Notorious for a potent and relentless attacking style, Brazil has produced the top two goal scorers of all time, and the creator of the "bicycle" kick—the mind-boggling, inverted, aerial ball strike. The list of one-named icons is endless: Friedenreich, Leônidas, Jairzinho, Zico, Sócrates, Romário, Ronaldo, Rivaldo, Ronaldinho, and of course, Pelé. Argentina, the chief rival of Brazil, answers with the immensely talented Diego Maradona. However, he has a reputed legacy of abusing cocaine, alcohol, women, authority, and the press. His rumored ties to organized crime, his ejection from the 1994 World Cup for use of banned performance-enhancing drugs, and his verbal assaults on Pelé have certainly not elevated his role-model status.

By contrast, the incomparable Pelé (Edson Arantes do Nascimento), besides being the game's all-time greatest goal scorer and sharing the Player of the Century Award (with Maradona), has remained a worldwide goodwill ambassador of the sport. He has won the International Peace Award, received honorary British knighthood, and been an author, a movie actor, and a successful business owner. In 1980, the National Olympic Committee awarded him the title of

Athlete of the Century even though he never actually competed in the Olympics! That's not a bad résumé for a guy whose nickname, derived from Portuguese and Turkish words, means "foot fool." (Apparently, the young Edson was dubbed Pe-Le after trying to control a ball with his hand during a match with a group of Turkish kids.)

Despite Brazil's perennial dominance of the sport, football did not originate here. As early as the year 200, precursors of the game existed in China, Rome, and Greece. England took up interest in football in the Middle Ages; the rumor is that it used the head of a dead Danish bandit as the first ball. Those crazy Brits! By the 19th century, England had revolutionized football into a sport very similar to what we see today, forming official leagues in the 1860s. It was in 1904 that the Federation Internationale de Football Association (FIFA) was created to govern all worldwide competition. FIFA initiated the first World Cup in 1930.

The British influence reached Brazil in 1894, when the first match took place in São Paulo. From this match, football's popularity spread rapidly throughout the country, and it was not long before Brazil's abilities were showcased on an international scale. By 1950, Brazil had its chance to host the World Cup. People packed into Rio's newly built Maracanã stadium—the world's largest, at 130,000 seats. Unfortunately, the high expectations of the crowd literally ended in tears, heart attacks, fights, and suicide attempts as the powerful Brazilian squad was squelched by Uruguay in the finals. This loss was truly indicative that, to Brazilians, football had become all-consuming.

It was not until 1958 that Brazil's World Cup prayers were answered in the form of Pelé. At 17, he was the youngest player ever to compete on a World Cup stage. He did not disappoint, notching a hat trick in the semis and tallying twice in the final match against Sweden to snare Brazil's first-ever World Cup. In 1962, despite an injured Pelé in the finals, Brazil became a repeat champion. The 1966 campaign was marred by dirty tactics on the part of the competition, placing Pelé and a few others on the bench with injuries, thus eliminating their World Cup hopes. However, the 1970 squad was considered to be the greatest team ever. Again led by Pelé, it proved victorious in its quest for a third World Cup. For the next five competitions, Brazil entered many highly touted teams, but all of them came up short. It was not until 1994 that Brazil, anchored by

Romário's brilliance, was able to win its then record fourth World Cup. Its triumph at the 2002 World Cup served to solidify to the world what Brazil already knew: It is simply the best!

The success on the world stage has proliferated throughout the national scale. Brazil has so many professional leagues and national competitions that football has become a year-round sport. For fans in Rio state, there was once nothing more intense than a match between blood rivals Flamengo and Fluminense in a jammed Maracanã stadium. Of late, a somewhat weakened *carioca* talent pool has diminished the passion over these famous "Fla" versus "Flu" battles, but they are still probably the most exciting soccer matches a foreigner will see in Rio de Janeiro, except for a game between the national team and archrivals Uruguay or Argentina. The energy created by fan fervor, the rhythmic beat of drums, flag waving, and chanting is still a spectacle worth seeing. Unfortunately, due to a recent upsurge in fan violence, we would advise you not to wear the shirt of any rival teams. Also, we recommend traveling to a match with a reputable tour group (ask at your hotel), since it will know the safest way to get gringos in and out of the stadium.

Beyond the professional game, football has become ingrained in the cultural and social fabric of Brazil. People of all ages play it *everywhere*! From remote clearings in the Amazon forest to back alleys in the city, and from empty basketball courts to busy beaches, football is played by all types and at all hours. They even play volleyball with their feet, a sport known as *futevôlei*. (Here in the States, we would just call it crazy folks trying to play volleyball with their feet.) Indeed, it is nearly impossible to walk along Rio's Copacabana Beach without getting bonked on the head by an errant ball. A word to the wise: If this happens to you, please *kick* the ball back to the players. *Never throw it*, lest you be laughed off the beach. That faux pas might have worked out well for the original Pelé, but you should prepare yourself for a different fate.

Crime in Rio de Janeiro

First and foremost, crime in Rio de Janeiro happens to Brazilians 10 times more often than to foreigners. There are three levels of crime in Brazil. Level one, you'll never see on the street. Level two, you might read about but would most likely hear about from a local. Level three, you'll see from time to time, but it's the level that cops target the most.

Let's start with level three. Beggars, street bums, men and women hard on their luck, or a snotty-nosed brat might decide to snatch your purse and run as far as they can before a socially conscious local or a cop trips them. A deal might actually be cut to split the contents of your purse, but be assured that your safety is not in question, only the attractive contents of your wallet. Professional thieves work in pairs on the beach during the summer, on buses and the metro during the winter, and on almost any other day that they're not having luck on the beach. It's the classic distract-and-retract method. One gets you looking the other way, or thinking you're getting somewhere, while the other pulls out your wallet, slips your watch off your wrist, or cuts a purse strap so they can pull it away with minimal effort. In all cases, common street smarts will keep your wallet and your wits about you.

Level two involves a deadly weapon. A shank, a knife, or a pistol will be used to scare you into instant submission. Scared or not, you should do what the robbers say. Life is cheap in Rio, and armed robbers will not hesitate to stick you or to shoot you in the stomach, leg, or chest to subdue you. Tourists with brand-name backpacks, camera cases, laptop cases, or nice clothes, shoes, or watches are targeted. These guys will most likely not stick you up in daylight; they prefer the dusk hours and nighttime. Again, keep your wits about you, and if you're out after dark, get in a cab if you're spooked; walk in pairs or groups; walk with pace and purpose; and don't flash a bunch of cash in front of people you don't know. After all, they might know someone who is willing to make you a target.

Level one involves organized crime, politicians, highly trained policemen, and teenagers armed to the teeth. Conflict between these people, if it's not in a high-tower office building over a money laundering mishap, will happen far, far away from where tourists reside. These guys are interested in one thing, making money. They are in positions of power and influence, so they will not waste time on petty crime. Ironically, however, the most visible and violent face of this level is what scares many tourists away from visiting Rio de Janeiro. The truth is, as a tourist, you're simply not that important. And if you do find yourself in the middle of a shootout between cops and robbers, well, we suggest you duck.

A Not-So-Brief History of Brazil

Upon his return from the New World, Christopher Columbus beseeched Pope Alexander IV to settle a boiling land dispute between the Portuguese and the Spanish. The good pope decided upon a line drawn north to south through the new world, 100 leagues west of the Cape Verde Islands. In 1494, the Portuguese and Spaniards found reason to agree on an official demarcation line. The Treaty of Tordesillas decreed that all lands to the east of the demarcation line would be Portuguese; to the west, Spanish. The Spaniards ended up with most of the New World, but the Portuguese got Brazil.

Under Portuguese rule, Brazilian indigenous tribes were relatively subdued, although a few still exist in the far interior of the Amazon, and a vibrant slave trade supported a growing agrarian economy of sugar and coffee. Brazil's thousands of miles of coast facilitated trade, as well as pirating, so many forts were installed to protect Portuguese lands from French, British, and Spanish pirates and other similarly motivated parties.

When gold was discovered in the mountains outside present-day Belo Horizonte, the Brazilian capital (which was in Salvador da Bahia and had grown with the slave trade), slowly moved to Rio de Janeiro, and most of the gold was exported back to Europe. The early 1700s brought many riches and fanfare to Rio de Janeiro, but the French sacked the city in 1710 and demanded a ransom of gold, sugar, and cattle in exchange for not razing the most beloved Portuguese city in the New World. The Portuguese capitulated. However, justice was somewhat served because the French ships, loaded down with all these spoils, lost much of it on the voyage home.

In 1808, a grip of Portuguese sailing vessels brought Dom João VI, his family, and his court to Rio de Janeiro. (As alluring as Rio was, it is likely that his motive for coming here was to avoid an ensuing confrontation with Napoleon, who was about to invade the Iberian peninsula. Heck, we'd pick Rio, too!) If there had been any doubts before about the capital of Brazil, all were erased when Dom João oversaw massive beautification efforts and a vast modernization of the city. Meanwhile, the rest of Brazil, especially the interior, was basically ignored, and growth was focused on the coast. Think present-day China.

Brazil won its independence when the Brazilian-born son of Dom João, Pedro, simply declared it so. Pedro's father had left a few years before to take care of political matters in Portugal. Father and son agreed not to cause bloodshed, so Brazil is the only Latin American country to have won its independence without war. Maybe that's why Brazilians are so laid-back! Pedro's 50-year reign is widely considered Brazil's first golden age. Slavery was abolished, and geopolitical dominance of the region was established.

As the decades passed, Brazil went through a political modernization process: It industrialized, moving most business matters to São Paulo, and built a shiny new city in the middle of nowhere. Brasília, Brazil's current capital, replaced Rio de Janeiro as the country's capital in 1960. The country suffered from a brutal military coup in 1964, and it wasn't until 1984 that the military dictators handed over power to the democratic process.

In 2002, after three tries at the post, impoverished-born Luis Inácio Lula da Silva (or Lula, for short), won the presidency. Despite quite a bit of controversy, scandal, and accusations of misconduct against Lula's government, his balance of progressive social programs with fiscal austerity has ushered Brazil back into the number one slot in South America. Today Brazil is the largest trading partner with most of its neighbors; it deals with Russia, China, and the European Union over matters of trade and geopolitics; and it is a leading dissenting voice to U.S.-led matters of geopolitical influence. Despite the Brazilian government's resentment of U.S. foreign policy, you'll not find a more visitor-friendly country in the Western Hemisphere. Come and enjoy.

Getting to Brazil

Delta, American, and Continental all service Brazil from major hubs at Houston, Miami, Atlanta, New York, and Washington, D.C. You'll find direct shots from Los Angeles and Miami to São Paulo, and a direct shot on Delta from Atlanta to Rio's Galeão Airport (a.k.a. Antônio Carlos Jobim Airport); most other hubs will require a layover. Flights to Rio de Janeiro usually will stop off in São Paulo before making the 45-minute jump to the coast. Direct flights to Rio de Janeiro are most likely found in New York, Atlanta, and Miami, but the

Brazil: Key Facts

Location	10° S by 55° W; South America, bordering 10 countries
Size	3,285,618 square miles/8,511,965 square kilometers, about the size of the continental United States
Highest Point	Pico de Neblina: 9,886 feet/3,014 meters
Population	186 million
Language	Portuguese
Time	GMT minus 5 hours in the far interior, near Rio Branco on the border with Bolivia, extending to GMT minus 3 hours on the Atlantic Coast
Area Code	To call Brazil from the U.S., dial 011 (the international dialing code), then 55 (the country code for Brazil), then the city code for the town you're calling, such as 21 for Rio de Janeiro, followed by the eight-digit local number.
Electricity	110 volts or 220 volts; two round-pin plugs are standard. Most standard U.S. plugs for cell phones, laptops, CD players, etc., will work.
Currency	The Brazilian *real* (plural, *reais*), BRL (US$1 = R$1.71 as of this writing)
Driving	On the right; a valid U.S., Canadian, or international driver's license is acceptable. (Note: Some rental car companies do not like international drivers' licenses and prefer one recognized by a country.)
Documents	Valid passport (Note: It is a good idea to keep a copy with you at all times.); a tourist visa obtained from a Brazilian consulate, embassy, or accredited visa service (www.brasilemb.org). A driver's license or some form of ID is necessary to get into sophisticated clubs.
Departure Tax	Sometimes included in your ticket. Otherwise expect it to be between $40 and $50.
Beer to Drink	Skol, Bohemia, or *chopp* (draft beer)
Rum to Drink	*Cachaça* (a close equivalent to Brazilian rum)
Music to Hear	Samba, *forró, chorinho*
Extra Numbers	For police, dial 190; fire or ambulance, 193; time, 130; temperature and weather, 131 (all in Portuguese); 24-hour physician's referral service (in English), 21-2325-9300, ext. 44; U.S. Consulate, 21-2292-7117.

number of weekly direct flights diminishes in the off-season. We've found that the cheapest tickets from Miami to São Paulo will run around $800. BACC Travel has decent deals. One of the Brazilian airlines, Tam, also operates flights out of Miami. From Europe, Air France offers direct flights from Paris to Rio de Janeiro. British Airways flies from London to São Paulo. You can also find flights from Lisbon, Portugal, to Rio. Occasionally there are flights from Porto, Portugal, to Rio. Flights on Iberia from Madrid are common year-round.

For travel within Brazil, its national operators Tam and Gol offer flights to all major cities in the country. Visit www.voegol.com for the cheapest domestic flights, and be prepared to use an American Express card. We've found Brazilian operators to be particularly ornery with Visa and MasterCard. Other airlines require that you have a Brazilian social security number to purchase online. Gol is your best bet for e-tickets with no hassle. Although Varig still operates some commuter flights between Rio and São Paulo, it is a largely extinct airline (unless something changes real quickly), and most of its flights are listed as canceled, every day. Uh, no thanks!

Rum & Reggae's Brazilian Cocktails

Rum & Reggae's Caipirinha

The *caipirinha* is the most widespread typical Brazil-ian cocktail. The name means "little country girl." The quantities of sugar, ice, and lime in relation to the *cachaça* vary widely. (Note that *cachaça* is basically the Brazilian version of rum, although Brazilians are quick to point out that *cachaça* is *not* rum—it just stands alone as *cachaça*.) Brazilians in general have a sweet tooth and use a lot of sugar. In a restaurant or bar, we always ask for only a little lime and sugar and lots of ice. If we don't, we usually receive a glass one quarter full of semi-dissolved sugar and a chopped whole lime or two. The mixture reminds us of lime syrup with a kick.

One of the best widely available *cachaças* is Ypioca. Use the *prata* ("silver") or clear variety. A cheaper substitute is 51. You may substi-tute the *cachaça* with vodka, in which case the name changes to *caipi-roska*. White rum may also be used—the name for this is *caipirissima*.

This is our recipe and you may vary it to your taste.

1 half lime, thinly sliced
1 heaping teaspoon of granulated sugar
5 ice cubes
cachaça

Place the lime and sugar in a thick whiskey glass or a mortar. Crush the lime with a pestle or stick until the juice has dissolved the sugar. Pour the mixture into a whiskey glass or tumbler or leave it in the whiskey glass you used to crush the lime. Add the 5 ice cubes (crush them, if you prefer). Pour the *cachaça* over the ice, almost fill-ing the glass. Stir with a spoon or a wooden spatula and serve with a couple of short straws. Use the straws to mix the drink occasionally.

If you use a shaker to mix the ingredients once all is crushed and dissolved, it makes for a much smoother delivery—less harsh for those who don't like straight liquor.

Rum & Reggae's Melzinho ("Little Honey")

This drink has long been a standard for Brazil's generation of elderly men who have graduated from weak beer to harder liquor and now spend more time leaning against a bar in Speedos than anywhere else. *Cachaça* poured into a bottle, half filled with honey, and then left to sit for days was the old-school recipe. Simple and sweet. After years in Brazil, and almost as long drinking the old-school version, Sam Logan—our half-Brazilian, half-American author—took an old dog's drink and gave it a zesty twist. The modified version, called a *melzinho*, involves the same *cachaça* one would use for a *caipirinha*, some natural lime juice (preferably lime juice produced with sugar found at grocery store such as Zona Sul), and, of course, honey. This drink is perfect for those folks who have a sweet tooth. But be careful—it's powerful—Sam once mixed a number of these drinks for his friend Guilherme, and by the end of the night, Guilherme had proposed to his girlfriend! Fortunately, he's happily married and still drinks Sam's *melzinhos*, but it could have been a disaster.

1 half cup of natural lime juice (not squeezed, but purchased)
2 tablespoons of honey (vary, depending on desired sweetness)
5 ice cubes
cachaça

Using a highball glass, pour in the half cup of natural lime juice and add honey. Stir until the honey has dissolved in the juice, fill the glass with *cachaça* until two-thirds full, and add ice. If you have a shaker, use it. If not, just stir the contents with a spoon until the ice melts a little. Add a leaf of mint to garnish (if you're really trying to impress). Enjoy!

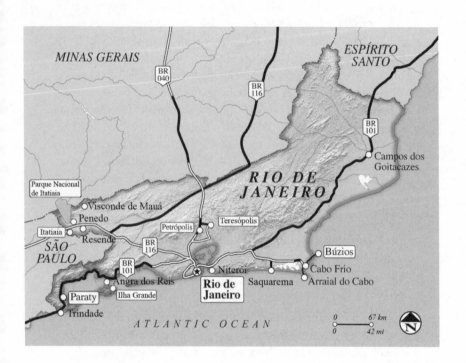

Rio de Janeiro State

Many years ago, when we first came to Brazil, we were like the average traveler who expected Rio de Janeiro to be one of the most alluring cities in the world. Indeed, the city of Rio is just that. What we also came to learn, and what many people do not know, is that this city is contained within an extraordinary state by the same name, albeit with a somewhat different flavor. The state of Rio de Janeiro blends spectacular mountains, stellar shorelines, and a seductive city of 12 million people into a region that is steeped in history, culture, and a way of life not easily replicated in other parts of the world.

Anyone who has made the trip to Rio will bring home countless tales of parties, culture, dance, music, food, fruit juices, and wildlife. The stories may be as varied as their owners, but they will all have one common factor—the Brazilians. Of course, you cannot avoid having a run-in or two with the locals. From the moment you meet your first few Brazilians to the last time you see them, their easygoing nature, quickness to laugh, vibrating energy, and, above all, beautiful language will put you at ease, make you laugh, and just maybe convince you to come back.

Brazilians consider themselves Brazilian first, Latino second. Portuguese sets them apart from their Latin American cousins. African influences in Brazil have forever altered the language, separating it from the Portuguese spoken in Portugal. Nowhere is this more notice-able than in Rio, where new words, phrases, expressions, and body language all combine to create a form of communication that is as simple as a thumbs-up, as positive as the ever present *tudo bem* ("it's all good"), and as direct as the finger wag, performed by extending your index finger and wagging your fist back and forth at the wrist to say "no."

Folks from Rio embrace life. Here you will find that a majority can laugh, dance, and sing despite earning less than $2 a day. Whether it's all-night dancing, singing in the street with friends, getting fired up for a soccer match, or simply sitting in the sun on the beach, Brazilians put everything they have into the moment. If you dare to go along, it's all you can do not to be swept up in the current. Almost every moment here is full of energy, and if you let it take you, it will seem as if time has been suspended. Suddenly your two-week vaca-tion feels like a month, especially if you find a local who takes a par-ticular interest in you.

OK, OK, we gush too much. What's wrong with this place? Well, plenty, actually. Our biggest issue is the disparity between the haves and the have-nots. There's a small class of ultra-rich who rival any of the moneyed classes anywhere in the world. There is a large but strug-gling middle class, with whom such luxuries as English lessons and overseas travel are rare, and who can barely make ends meet (sounds too familiar these days). Then there are the masses—millions and millions of them, trying to lift themselves out of the poverty mire but finding the ability and resources with which to do so almost impos-sible and nonexistent—hence the twice-elected leftist-leaning and Worker's Party candidate Luis Inacio da Silva, known as Lula, as Brazil's president. Something has got to give, or things are going to get very tense around these parts.

With this huge gap between rich and poor, crime can rear its ugly head—Rio (and many of the large cities in Brazil) is no stranger to this. Rio has had and will continue to experience some dangerous periods. In Rio, a recent power struggle between the cities' drug lords (who rule the *favelas*, or slums) and Rio's law enforcement has encroached on Zona Sul, usually impervious to such battles.

Despite its socioeconomic problems, Rio de Janeiro is still a fas-cinating state and is an excellent place for tourism. It offers diversity in food, music, culture, language, people, and topography. Beyond containing the famous city of Rio itself, this state has dozens of miles of coastline that is home to many small villages, some discovered, others forgotten. Foremost on this list is Búzios, located to the northeast of Rio. It is one of the discovered stretches of land and has established itself as a getaway for the rich and famous, who seek to escape what they consider crowded (and hoi polloi) beaches elsewhere. (Note that neither we, nor the many young up-and-comers who often find their way here on summer weekends, are rich or famous, but we all fit in just fine here — and so will you). The hillsides on this peninsula are peppered with homes worth millions and *pousadas* that range from Dirt Cheap to Very Pricey. To the southwest of Rio, the small, low-key village of Paraty contrasts the glitz and glamour of Búzios with sublime beauty and a relaxing atmosphere. An old *cachaça* repository has evolved into a sleepy fisherman's village with a few high-brow tourist installations. Tom Cruise and Mick Jagger have graced the cobbled streets (although we have seen *only* the photos). So who knows, you might have a star sighting on the wharf or rub elbows with someone famous in the fort ruins. Also southwest of Rio sits Ilha Grande (the Big Island), just off the coast. What used to be Brazil's version of Alcatraz has been transformed into a tourist-friendly deposit in the middle of luscious Atlantic tropical rainforest. These beach towns and the island retreat provide a weekend's worth of respite from the sweaty beat of the incredibly energetic capital city, Rio de Janeiro.

For those in search of a cooler, mountainous escape, the former royal retreat of Petrópolis is a about a 50-minute drive, yet worlds away, from Rio. A little farther from Rio and about an hour from Petrópolis is the town of Teresópolis, which is an ideal spot for relaxing within the surroundings of its beautiful mountains. This is also a great place to take advantage of many outdoor activities like hiking, rock climbing, white-water rafting, horseback riding, or even ziplining on canopy tours. (Ah, yes, there was so much to choose from here that most of our gang got overwhelmed and pretty much chose to just relax.) Finally, tucked away in Rio's southwestern corner, near São Paulo state and Minas Gerais, is Itatiaia, another mecca for adventurous outdoor activities.

Clearly, the grand prize of the state is the city of Rio de Janeiro. Once the capital city of Brazil, Rio has always evoked passion, has earned a reputation for beauty and debauchery, and, more recently, has become one of the top tourist destinations in the world. We sometimes think of Rio as a much more exotic version of Miami Beach, only set in some of the world's most stunning surroundings. Although it's not the cultural capital of Brazil (our vote goes to Salvador), the nightlife in this city is among the best in the Americas. Rio rivals any city in Latin America for its cosmopolitan atmosphere, clubs, bars, food, and, of course, its energetic brew of locals (called *cariocas*) who keep the flame torching well into the wee hours. But Rio de Janeiro pulls away from the pack because it has scenic beaches with miles of sand whose beckoning call seduces tourists and locals alike, any time of day, all year long. Rio is beach culture and the big city. Yet it's easy to separate the two—a stroll along Praia de Ipanema (Ipanema Beach) as the sun sets over the abutting mountains will take you to a place far removed from the chaos of this huge metropolis.

Rio de Janeiro City

WE LIKE TO THINK WE'RE PRETTY GOOD AT THIS TRAVEL thing. Rio begs to differ. Whenever we come here, we end up throwing our plans out the window because Rio always has its own plans for us. We kind of like that. Life in this city moves at its own sultry rhythm, and no *one* or no *thing* is going to change that. There is no reason to rush, push, or force-feed your vacation here. We always try to avoid that temptation while in this sensuous city. When we find ourselves in a hurry, we soon become very impatient and frustrated —not to mention hot and sweaty. Rushed or not, we spend easily a third of our time here waiting on someone or something. It just doesn't make sense to hurry up and wait. In other words: Relax, enjoy, and work *with* Rio, not *against* it, and before you know it, you'll be swept up in all the fun and energy that this amazing city has to offer.

Lazer, the Brazilian Portuguese word for "leisure," would not accurately describe how Rio's inhabitants actually live. It describes how they prefer to live, as much as possible. Although those who live here work most of the time, leisure is a daily pursuit of Rio's denizens from all levels of society. If you run an Internet café, you have computer games; if you drive a bus, you bullshit with the fare collector; if you run a Copacabana beachfront kiosk from 7 p.m. to 7 a.m. five days a week, you sell beer, liquor, and drugs, you smoke at least four or five joints a shift, and you get to know an array of prostitutes.

Rio is a town with an incredible amount of human energy packed into a very small space. Copacabana and Ipanema are two of the most densely populated neighborhoods in the world. The rest of Rio is just as jammed with people, animals, and nature. All of them contribute to an energy that is raw, sensual, and powerful. It's like a sticky pheromone that envelops.

Rio de Janeiro: Key Facts

Location	22° S by 42° W
	261 miles/420 kilometers northeast of São Paulo
	202 miles/325 kilometers south of Belo Horizonte
	575 miles/925 kilometers southeast of Brasília
	8-hour flight from Miami
	12-hour flight from Los Angeles
Size	485 square miles/1,256 square kilometers
Highest Point	Pedra da Gávea (2,526 feet/770 meters)
Population	12 million
Language	Portuguese
Time	Brazil Eastern Time. Also considered GMT minus 2 hours (or EST plus 1 hour) during Rio's Daylight Savings Time from mid-October through mid-March; the time zone switches to GMT minus 3 hours (or EDT plus 1 hour) from mid-March until mid-October. Note: Rio's Daylight Savings Time occurs during U.S. standard time, and vice versa.
Area Code	To call Rio de Janeiro from the U.S., dial 011 (the international dialing code), then 55 (the country code for Brazil), then 21 (the city code for Rio de Janeiro), followed by the eight-digit local number.
Electricity	110 volts or 220 volts; two round-pin plugs are standard. Most standard U.S. plugs for cell phones, laptops, CD players, etc., will work in the city. Some 220-volt plugs are not so marked. If in doubt, ask before something implodes in a thin, acrid fume of smoke.
Currency	The Brazilian *real* (plural, *reais*), BRL (US$1 =R$1.7 as of this writing)
Driving	On the right; a valid U.S., Canadian, or international driver's license is acceptable. (Note: Some rental car companies do not like international driver's licenses and prefer one recognized by a country.)
Documents	Valid passport with visa. (Note: It is a good idea to keep a copy with you at all times. Keep the real thing in the hotel safe.) A driver's license or some form of ID is necessary to get into sophisticated clubs.
Departure Tax	Sometimes included in your ticket. Otherwise expect to pay up to US$45 in reais, or R$90.

Beer to Drink	*Chopp* ("draft beer"); Skol; Bohemia; Devassa; Cerpa
Rum to Drink	*Cachaça*
Music to Hear	*Pagode*, samba, *forró, chorinho*
Extra Numbers	For police, dial 190; fire or ambulance, 193; time, 130; temperature and weather, 131 (all in Portuguese); 24-hour physician's referral service (in English), 2325-9300, ext. 44; U.S. Consulate, 2292-7117.
Tourism	Riotur is Rio's best mainstream tourism agency, with a hotline (English spoken), 2542-8080; multilingual Web site, www.rio.rj.gov.br/riotur; and an office in Copacabana, 2541-7522, 183 Avenida Princesa Isabel, open from 8 a.m. to 8 p.m. The Web site www.Ipanema.com, run by our friend Marcos Prado, is a great source of information for just about anything you need to know about Rio.

By day and by night, Rio pulsates with the life of 12 million inhabitants. The energy from such a high density is intoxicating and can cause sensory overload. We find that the longer one stays in Rio de Janeiro, the more its magic spellbinds. Many of us who choose to remain here never hear of visitors who didn't like it.

However, there is also a downside to all this seething humanity. Like many of Brazil's big cities, Rio is loaded with poverty, and it can be dirty and dangerous—reminders of that are everywhere. Fortunately, the area most visitors stay in and frequent, Zona Sul, is well patrolled by the local police, because tourism is big business.

This is a huge city, but what makes Rio most charming are the long stretches of beach that are embraced by jagged (and iconic) green mountains. The setting is so beautiful that it is enough to soften the city's tough edge. Stroll down to the water on Ipanema Beach and look back toward the city—you will see buildings, cars, and people, but you will hear only the surf and the city's hum. We find it enchanting.

OK, here's more of what makes Rio so special. For men and women alike, eye candy abounds. You can't help but see a gorgeous man or woman every five minutes. *Cariocas* are preoccupied with their looks, which makes for a great show for the rest of us who like to look at them. (Hair salons stay open until 10 p.m., and plastic surgery is nearly ubiquitous amongst the over-40 crowd—and trending younger by the day). The hard bodies that sunbathe, swim, and play *futebol* along Ipanema Beach will make your head spin. When these same people get souped up for a night out on the town, they leave all competitors in the dust.

Eventually we all must leave Rio—only the *cariocas* can handle this lifestyle. If you give your stay a week, you'll leave perhaps wanting more. If you give it two weeks, you'll leave exhausted but satiated. However, if you try to leave after having spent a month in this city, you probably won't want to go home, and you'll begin to understand in a very personal way why those who live here consider Rio de Janeiro the *Cidade Maravilhosa*. It truly is the "Marvelous City."

So when you come to Rio, don't be scared to try it, smell it, feel it, or taste it, because whether you like it or not, the essence that swirls in this place will invade your body, mind, and soul. We recommend that you jump into Rio head first.

A Not-So-Brief History

It is believed that indigenous tribes have inhabited Rio's Guanabara Bay for some 50,000 years. Known as the Tomio, they first encountered crusading Europeans when a Portuguese sailor, Pedro Alvaro Cabral, came upon the bay in January 1502. Mistaking the entrance to the bay for a river mouth, he named the region Rio de Janeiro (River of January), and continued to make more discoveries elsewhere to the South.

In 1555, three French ships seeking to claim a French colonial beachhead in South America established the first European settlement in Rio de Janeiro, on an island in Guanabara Bay. For some strange reason the French called their settlement "Antarctic France." The colony didn't last long, and Portuguese soldiers, led by Rio's recognized founder, Estacão de Sá, finally expelled both the French and their Indian friends—the Tomio—in 1567, after two years of fierce fighting.

Soon after, the Portuguese settled a fortified town, honoring their king by naming it São Sebastião do Rio de Janeiro. Some consider the 500 or so founders as Rio's first *cariocas*, a title bestowed upon people born and bred in Rio de Janeiro. An excellent harbor and arable lands fueled Rio's growth into the 17th century. By the 1700s, Rio de Janeiro was the Brazilian colony's third most important settlement. The city blossomed in 1704, when a road from the interior Brazilian state of Minas Gerais facilitated the export of gold through Rio's ports. Such a slew of gold attracted the French, who in 1710 made two attempts to take the city. The second attempt won the French their prize, and they threatened to raze the adolescent city if the Portuguese didn't pay a handsome ransom of gold, sugar, and cattle. A deal was struck and the French split, leaving Rio intact, but the French never enjoyed their ill-gotten wealth. On the way back to Europe, they lost two overloaded ships and most of their gold (poetic justice?).

By 1763, Rio replaced Salvador da Bahia as Portugal's most important city in the New World. It was home to some 50,000 *cariocas*, Africans, pacified Indians, and a host of Catholic priests, monks, and scholars. Steaming into the 19th century, the city expanded south toward Botafogo and north toward São Cristovão. Roads were paved and swamps filled to make more room for expansion.

Rio became the most important city within the Portuguese empire in 1808, when 40 Portuguese ships, carrying the prince regent, Dom João VI, and some 15,000 members of his court, first landed on Brazilian soil. The newcomers had left Portugal to avoid certain subjugation under Napoleon, who was having his way with the Iberian peninsula. As an enlightened ruler, Dom João modernized Rio. He founded the Botanical Gardens, built the palace at Quinta da Boa Vista, and established the School of Medicine, the Bank of Brazil, legal courts, the Naval Academy, and the Royal Printing Press.

Even after Napoleon's defeat at Waterloo in 1815, Dom João did not want to leave Rio. When his mother, Dona Maria I, died, Dom João became the first European king to rule his empire from the new world. By 1820, King João relented to political pressure and returned to Portugal, leaving his son Pedro in Rio de Janeiro as prince regent. Taking full advantage of his father's favor, Pedro declared Brazil's independence in 1822 and became Brazil's first emperor when Portugal, and Pedro's father, simply let him have Brazil. No blood was shed in Brazil's independence, certainly an anomaly in South America (if not the world).

Perhaps the first, and certainly not the last, Brazilian man to sire more than a score of children, Pedro's greatest legacy is not the legend of his spawn, but a clear inability to govern. It seems he set a party-hard pace (which *cariocas* have maintained ever since!). After nine years of leadership, Brazil's first emperor abdicated the crown in 1831, turning it over to his five-year-old son. Easy come, easy go. A loosely tied band of regents took the reins until 1840, when a young Dom Pedro II rallied his supporters and the country at 14 years of age. The 50-year reign of Brazil's second emperor was a time of prosperity and peace. During this time, Pedro II abolished slavery, ushered in the birth of Brazil's modern-day democracy, established geopolitical dominance of the region surrounding Brazil, installed plumbing and sewage, and initiated the use of modern technology by being the first Brazilian to communicate by telephone. He was also the first Brazilian to be photographed.

By 1860, Rio de Janeiro boasted a population of some 250,000 citizens. It was the biggest city in South America, capital of the biggest country. Yet two-thirds of the population was enslaved. The very tardy abolition movement finally became a widely supported social cause in Rio by the mid-1880s, and in 1888 the National Assembly formally abolished slavery. All of this change eventually led to the proclamation of a new Brazilian Republic in 1889.

Soldiers returning to Rio from the War of the Canudos in the northeastern state of Bahia founded Rio's first shanty town in the late 1880s on Providência Hill. In return for their bravery and patriotism, the government gave the soldiers permission to "temporarily" squat on the hill. To this day, that is probably the longest "temporary" in Brazilian history.

By 1890, Rio was bulging with more than a million residents. Former slaves migrated en masse from the north, and immigrants poured in from Europe. The city expanded rapidly, and so did its *favelas* ("slums"). The year 1904 saw a face-lift in the center of town when demolition cleared room for Rio's central promenade, Avenida Rio Branco. In 1920 and again in 1940, tunnels were built, opening expansion into Copacabana and eventually the remaining neighborhoods of Rio's Zona Sul. Tourism was steadily on the rise.

The Copacabana Palace and Hotel Glória, in Flamengo, attracted many high-profile tourists from the United States and Europe. Not long after, Rio de Janeiro became a playground for the rich and famous. Three landfill projects created space for Flamengo Park, Santos Dumont airport, and the famous Avenida Atlântica stretch at

Copacabana. *Cariocas* and foreigners alike consider the 30 years between 1920 and 1950 as Rio's golden age.

Rio lost center stage when Juscelino Kubitschek, the president in 1960, realized his dream of a modern city and moved the capital of Brazil to Brasília in the center of the country. As a city, Rio suffered greatly at the hands of the military generals who took Brazil by force in 1964.

The generals largely considered Rio de Janeiro a hotbed of liberal activists and insurgent sympathizers. For most of the military's 21-year grip on power, Rio fell out of favor and received little funding for city maintenance. The mammoth growth of São Paulo has taken the country's financial assets from Rio's streets. By 1985, Rio was missing two-thirds of what had supported its strong ego and festive ways, but it was not enough to dampen the *carioca* spirit.

Rio de Janeiro is now a city with more than 12 million inhabitants (sadly, 1 million of them live in a *favela*), and almost everyone here makes time to enjoy life. Rio de Janeiro is today the capital of the state of Rio de Janeiro, the cultural center of Brazil, and the weekend getaway for politicians and business executives from Brasília and São Paulo. It is believed by many to be the most sophisticated, fast-paced, and feverishly fun city in the Western Hemisphere. (For more history on Brazil itself, see the section at the beginning of this book.)

Rio's Slums and Some Safety Issues

Anyone who travels to Rio de Janeiro must pass through an unfolding scene of what is obviously a disorganized series of red-brick housing, oxidized tin roofs, and spray-paint decoration. The slums of Rio de Janeiro, known here as *favelas*, are the first to greet all who arrive to Rio by way of its international airport at Galeão. These *favelas* harbor some of the most violent urban battles in the Western Hemisphere, but with some understanding of their history, people, and nature and with some street smarts, you can avoid any and all trouble caused by those *favela* denizens who venture out in desperation to rob Brazilians and tourists alike.

The War of the Canudos, fought in the northern Brazilian state of Bahia in 1897, required that Rio de Janeiro, the capital city at that time, send troops north to quell the uprising. When the soldiers returned, they requested that the state reward them with the right to build on state-owned land on the hills of Providência, overlooking present-day Copacabana. The state allowed temporary squatting, promising that permanent space would soon be provided.

By the early 1920s, it became apparent that the state would neither provide the promised land nor take action to forcibly remove the hundreds of poor Brazilians who had built permanent housing on Providência and the surrounding hills. Thus, through government apathy, the early *favelas* of Rio de Janeiro became a permanent fixture, even as the city rapidly grew around them on the land developed below between the hills and beaches.

By the 1960s, during Brazil's third military dictatorship, the *favelas* had become so numerous, and their denizens so frowned upon, that the military leadership decided to build a series of low-income housing projects. Called *complexos*, these projects were designed to encourage *favela* communities to move to the outskirts of Rio de Janeiro, where their "undesirable" existence could be ignored by the majority of *cariocas*. The idea worked, but not for long.

The money used to build *complexos* such as Cidade de Deus ("City of God") quickly dried up as the Brazilian economic miracle of the late '60s imploded in the early '70s, forcing a surge by the rural poor to move to Rio de Janeiro and other cities to look for work, food, and a place to live—or squat, as was the case. Massive urbanization saw hundreds of thousands of rural poor find space on the hills overlooking Rio de Janeiro. After years of state apathy, these communities have no political representation, no consistent police presence, and little protection from the urban battles that rage among the three prominent drug gangs in town, as well as between the drug gangs and an aggressive, often corrupt military police force.

Most of the violence and death you read about in Rio de Janeiro happens in the Northern Zone, or Zona Norte, where *favelas*, grouped in tremendous projects, offer protection and hiding for gang members running from invading police or rival gang soldiers. In the Southern Zone, or Zona Sul, there are *favelas*, but they are relatively calm compared to those to the north. All together, there are more than a million Brazilians living in the 800-plus *favelas* in greater Rio de Janeiro. In fact, some *favelas* in the Zona Sul have received a large amount of attention from the state, which has invested in a limited number of infrastructure and community policing projects. These efforts have greatly reduced the violence in the *favelas* overlooking the Rio neighborhoods that are most attractive to tourists. One *favela* in particular allows foreigners to take a tour of its lower levels, where one can see poverty up close and personal. We do not recommend that you take such a tour, however. Poverty in Rio de Janeiro is everywhere, nearly on every corner, and will greet you for free, in the form of a begging street child, a pregnant mother, or a three-legged dog. There is no need to pay someone to put you in the back of a truck to take a ride through a less desirable part of town. We also feel that the idea of touring a slum is disrespectful to its inhabitants — these are not zoos.

For some reason, more Brazilians than tourists fall victim to street violence outside the *favelas*. Many are targets of a simple robbery, in which a young man often pulls a gun on an unsuspecting individual who either is carrying no cash or refuses to acquiesce to the demand for it. Hesitation to comply wins one a lead bullet in the head or chest and, if the crime is brutal enough, mention in the evening newscast.

If you happen to find yourself on the wrong end of a shank or pistol, do *not* hesitate! Empty your pockets. Carrying a substantial amount of cash in your sock is a good idea, especially at night, on the off-chance that you are mugged. Those intent on survival might simply kill you if you have nothing to offer. Losing US$100, or roughly 200 *reais*, is worth your life any day.

Do not carry your wallet or anything of value, like a passport or an ATM card, with you at night or to the beach. Taking the bus in Zona Sul or downtown is fine during the day, but you should stick to taxis at night. We repeat, do *not* ride the bus at night. Don't wander around at night, either. If you must walk alone at night, walk with a pace and a purpose, and stay in well-lit areas. Most tourists visit Rio de Janeiro without a hitch or even a close call. If you keep simple street smarts about you, there is little chance that you will become another statistic.

Getting There

The Antônio Carlos Jobim International Airport (formerly, but still referred to as, Galeão) welcomes all international travelers to Rio de Janeiro. Tam, a domestic airline, offers direct and nonstop service to and from London, New York, Miami, Los Angeles, and Paris. Daytime direct flights from Miami can be purchased for $850 and up. United, American, Delta, and Continental Airlines offer service to and from the same cities, plus Houston, for a comparable price, but the service is not nearly as pleasant. For a comfortable seat, consider Lan Chile's service from New York, Miami, or Los Angeles. Air France offers direct service from Paris.

Domestic flights arriving in Rio de Janeiro land at Jobim/Galeão. Santos Dumont, Rio's original international airport, services flights only to and from São Paulo. Tam and Gol fly to all major cities in Brazil. Gol (www.voegol.com.br) tends to offer the most competitive rates, but don't expect domestic flights to be cheap!

Getting Around

Galeão and St. Dumont present you with many choices to make your way into Rio's concrete jungle. Taxis are fast and cheap—depending on where you want to go. It's best to pay for a radio taxi (these are generally the white taxis). Pick any stand and purchase a one-way ticket. Prices range from $25 to $45, depending on the size of the taxi you require. Each normally fits four, but we've crammed up to seven in a cab for a longer trip. Make sure your cabby turns on the meter. Moto taxis are the most daring public transportation and the most fun. They hang out at the bottom of hills, such as Santa Teresa, to score a fare. You don't get a helmet unless it's a long ride. The price is a third of the rate of car taxis. Oh, and be sure to hang on tight!

Buses roll all over the city, run intuitive routes, and have easy-to-read insignia on the front windshield and "forehead," above the windshield. Figure where you want to go—Leblon, Ipanema, Copacabana, Praça XV—and simply get on the bus with your destination stenciled across its banner. The small placard to the bottom left of the windshield lists the stops the bus makes along its route. Prices fluctuate with the price of oil but normally run between $1 and $1.50 (R$2 and R$3) for a city bus and $3 to $10 (R$6 to R$20) for a direct-line bus.

The best direct-line bus company is Real. It runs down the main *avenidas* of Zona Sul or on the beachside avenues on the way to

---

Helpful City Bus Routes

433, 434	Leblon–Copacabana
172	Leblon–Jardim Botânico
438	Praça XV–Leblon
512	Ipanema–Urca (Pão de Açúcar)
523	Ipanema-Gávea
123	Leblon–Rododoviária

Regional Bus Companies

Facil Unica	Petrópolis ℭ 21-2263-8792
Costa Verde	Paraty ℭ 21-2233-5295
1001	Búzios ℭ 21-4004-5001
Util	Belo Horizonte (Minas Gerais) ℭ 21-2622-1582

Galeão, Santos Dumont, or the Rodoviária Novo Rio. From Galeão, take the Real bus straight to Avenida Atlântica in Copacabana, and ride the beach stretch all the way into town. It's only $3 (R$6) — much cheaper than the $23 to $35 (R$45 to R$70) you'll pay for a cab. Then again, the cab will get you there in half the time and with twice the excitement! Use a city bus or a Real bus to get to the central bus station, or Rodoviária Novo Rio — the price is normally $1 for a regular bus and $1.50 for an air-conditioned bus (R$2 and R$3).

There's no reason to rent a car in Rio de Janeiro. Driving is dangerous and frustrating in this town unless you live here. (Also, many highway maps are out of date.) Taxis are much cheaper, and the driver, more often than not, knows where to go. If you still want to rent a car, try Avis, Hertz, Interlocadora, Localiza Rent a Car, or Unidas, all located at Galeão and Santos Dumont. A number of other rental agencies are strung along Avenida Princesa Isabel, just before the tunnel between Copacabana and Botafogo. The rates at these offices will probably be a little lower than the airport-based rental offices.

Bicycles are an ideal way to get around Zona Sul. The best rental deals can be found along the promenade at Copacabana and Ipanema beaches. There is also a bike rental spot in Ipanema at the corner of Teixera de Melo and Avenida Visconde de Pirajá, just in front of the taxi stand and catty-corner to the Shenanigan's Pub that overlooks Praça General Osório.

Note that almost all your time will be spent in Zona Sul, which comprises the neighborhoods of Ipanema, Copacabana, Leblon, Lagoa, Leme, Gávea, Botofogo, Flamengo, and Urca. We also recommend exploring the Centro and Lapa neighborhoods, as well as some parts of Zona Oeste (West Zone) such as Barra da Tijuca (known as just Barra). There is very little reason for you to go into Zona Norte unless you're headed to the airport or to a soccer game at Maracanã (something we strongly recommend doing with a tour group that can guide you safely in and out of the stadium). Thus, all our hotel, restaurant, and club or bar recommendations are located within the neighborhoods that make up Zona Sul (with just a few spots in Centro and Barra).

Focus on Rio de Janeiro: The Beach Culture

By 10 a.m. Ipanema beach is full of Brazilians sunning, surfing, playing *futebol*, weight-lifting, hustling, drinking natural juice, smoking grass, or simply standing in the sun taking it all in. Beach life in Rio de Janeiro takes precedence over most activities. The beach is, for all *cariocas*, a place to get tan, show off one's physique, make money, meet friends, and, above all, relax. It should be central to your visit.

Rio de Janeiro city planners (if you can call Rio "planned") squeezed the city's densely populated Southern Zone, or Zona Sul, between beautiful beaches and a chain of steep, rainforest-covered mountains. It is as if the mountains in the interior force human spillage out onto the sand to relieve the pressure from such a densely packed urban environment. So by noon on almost any day of the week in the Southern Hemisphere summer (December–March), there is little room to sit. Winter months (June–September) offer more space, but not much. Year-round hustlers, who sell fried cheese (*queijo quente* or *queijo coalho*), soda, beer, and tourist trinkets, manage to weave in and out of the crowd without stepping on too many toes or fingers.

There are five beaches that you are most likely to visit in Rio de Janeiro: Copacabana, Ipanema, Leblon, Barra da Tijuca, and Prainha.

Copacabana

Copacabana Beach, bordered by the celebrated Avenida Atlântica, is the preferred destination for most of Rio's middle-class denizens. The beach is organized by a series of lifeguard towers, referred to as *postos* (pronounced "PÓSH-toos"), that are evenly punctuated along the beach side of Avenida Atlântica. Between the small neighborhood of Leme at the downtown end of Copacabana and the small fish market at the other end, where Avenida Atlântica makes a right on its way past the Forte Copacabana naval base toward Ipanema, *Postos* 1 through 6 define Copacabana. Kiosks, which sell anything from food and drink to trinkets, sex, and drugs, are placed near each *posto*, and sometimes at the halfway point between two *postos*. Most kiosks are open 24/7 and will serve you anything you want at any time. Ahead of the 2006 Pan-American games, the city installed shiny new kiosks along Copacabana Beach, replacing the old, and in some cases, cockroach-infested stands, with bright tourist beacons. These new kiosks are grouped in pairs and come complete with cold beer on tap, a full kitchen, and, down the steps, a complete bathroom and changing area. Besides drawing tourists, these kiosks attract well-heeled locals who, until recently, perhaps thought they were too good for those who frequent Copacabana's sands. The beach crowd is a mixture of Brazilians and tourists who are easy on the eyes. The gay crowd hangs out in front of the Copacabana Palace hotel—look for the flag. (However, most head for the area halfway between Ipanema's *Postos* 8 and 9 in front of Rua Farme de Amoedo; it's much more happening there.)

Ipanema

Postos 7 through 10 define Ipanema Beach, by far the most densely packed beach in Rio de Janeiro. Well-to-do *cariocas* from the neighborhoods of Ipanema, Leblon, and Lagoa visit Ipanema daily. Beginning with the large Arpoador lookout rock, a promontory situated just before *Posto* 7 and next to Garota de Ipanema Park, Ipanema Beach yawns forth until coming to an abrupt stop at the canal that drains the interior lagoon, or *lagoa*, just after *Posto* 10. The Arpoador rock is an excellent place to take in an awe-inspiring view of Ipanema in the evening, a must-do for any fan of beautiful sunsets. It is well lit and safe, as long as you don't cut through the Praça do Arpoador (just next to Garota de Ipanema Park), where a lack of public lighting attracts

A Salute to Rio's Beach Vendors

The sands of Rio's beaches are usually loaded with scantly covered bodies baking in the sun. Some choose to play volleyball, soccer, that annoying paddleball game called kadima, or some other sport, whereas others opt to socialize or do absolutely nothing (not that there's anything wrong with that — we're always up for a good dose of doing nothing!). There is a beachtime working class that provides the critical support functions for those "do-nothing" beachgoers, who, without them, couldn't manage to survive such a "rigorous" day at the shore. Deciphering the various goods and services offered by this sweaty, smiling clan is essential to a perfect day on the beach in Rio de Janeiro.

Halfway between the famous mosaic path and the water, along the stretches of sand in Copacabana, Ipanema, and Leblon, sit various open-walled tents, called *barracas* (ba-HA-kas). These tents anchor a family business that is based on renting chairs and umbrellas to beachgoers who are parked on their general plot of sand. An all-day chair costs 2 *reais* and an umbrella costs 3. The *barracas* also sell cold beer, water, soft drinks, and, our favorite, fresh *água de coco* (coconut water, a.k.a. coconut milk).

If you can manage to stand up or even sit up and raise your hand in the air, you will most certainly bring the attentive runners to your side for a quick order. You'll run up a tab that you will pay on the way out. It's good to keep in mind how many beers you had so you're not overcharged.

Maybe you're not interested in what the folks who "govern" your plot of sand have to offer. Maybe you'd prefer something more exotic, like a bag that opens up into a sarong, or a minichair on which to rest your head when sunbathing. For such items, you'll need to call on the men and women who roam the sands, from one end of the beach to the other, from dawn to dusk, calling out their wares and, hopefully, attracting your attention.

The most common roaming vendors sell ice cream, beer, soft drinks, *guaraná*, iced tea, *biscoito globo* (these are doughnut-shaped "cookies" that taste like very mildly flavored rice cakes, or basically, like *nothing*), and mate, which is a South American tea. The mate sellers lug around two cylinders of liquid on shoulder straps. One holds the mate tea, the other holds lemonade. When they approach, you can hear the ice

(continued on page 44)

thieves and ne'er-do-wells. It's best to walk along the beach avenue, Avenida Francisco, toward *Posto* 7 after dark.

The sand just beyond Rua Farme de Amoedo and the nearby kiosk is home to a large and attractive gay crowd. As always, the rainbow flag is the marker. This has swiftly become Rio's major gay destination, aside from the sand in front of Copacabana Palace. *Posto* 8 is where Ipanema's families gather. There are a number of playground-style swings, slides, and other amenities next to a kiosk that has been known to warm up milk! There's also a diaper-changing stand. *Posto* 9 is where the straight, young, and affluent gather. Here you will find some of the best-looking — and vain — men and women in the Western Hemisphere; they're the in-crowd (or so they think). *Posto* 10 is a gathering place for affluent families, older couples, and *voleibol* fanatics, who come to watch and learn from some of Brazil's most famous volleyball athletes. As in Copacabana, kiosks are numerous and serve almost anything, anytime.

Leblon

Just after the canal that separates Ipanema from Leblon, *Posto* 11 signals the beginning of Leblon Beach. This stretch of sand, which ends just after *Posto* 12, is home to Rio's most affluent families.

Not too many people gather near *Posto* 11, because most of the action is centered between *Postos* 8 and 10, but there is certainly spillover on weekends and in the summer. This area is most popular with young mothers and their families. It is not advisable to swim in front of *Posto* 11, because the canal there drains the *lagoa*, known to be polluted with runoff from *favelas*. Yuck!

Generally speaking, swimming around the canal just after it has rained or at high tide is not encouraged. Sewage runoff is always more prevalent after a shower, and although there are numerous lifeguards, you cannot trust them to see you just before a riptide sweeps you 200 — or more — yards to sea. Also, at high tide, surfers and body boarders abound in front of many sections along Ipanema and Leblon Beaches, especially in front of *Postos* 8, 9, 10, and 12. The beach area just next to Arpoador is also risky. To locals, this area is known as "*favela* break," because many *favela* kids come here to surf the large waves that break off the Arpoador rock point.

Like Ipanema Beach, Leblon is packed in the summer and on

(continued from page 42)

sloshing around inside. Ask for a *meia-meia* (half mate, half lemonade). They'll hand you a cup and open the spigot, first for the mate, then for the lemonade. The cost, like most of these items, is around 2 *reais*. The price is known to go up during the summer months of December to March.

Those selling more exotic foods, such as the *esfiha* — a closed sandwich made with spiced beef folded into flat Arab bread — or the natural sandwiches, will often charge more. The same is true for the vendors selling *açaí* and similar mixed juices. One of our favorite items is the *queijo coalho*, which is hot, salty, spiced cheese on a stick. It doesn't sound like a summertime beach treat, but it rocks! Prices for these unique treats range from 3 to 6 *reais*. If your Portuguese is spot-on and you look like a Brazilian, you might get the local rate, sometimes as much as 1 *real* cheaper. Another great way to get a discount is to always buy from the same vendor. Be friendly. Chat a little, if you can — ask about *futebol* or comment on the weather. These folks love a reason to stop walking and yelling.

The beach is also patrolled by wandering wannabe artists who will give you a well-designed tattoo that rubs off in a week or so (we hope!). Others will try to sell you kites, bikinis, clothes, handmade jewelry, sunblock, and even hammocks. Generally speaking, the more packed the beach, the more vendors you'll see weaving in and out of lazing sun soakers. Don't try to follow their path when flagging them down for a purchase — you will likely wind up stepping on someone's hand or hair.

Along the mosaic path that hugs the road, you can find shiatsu and other types of massage, finger-painted oil pieces, and handmade pipes and trinkets. Not to be overlooked is the "corn man," who cooks corn on the cob inside his little cart. There are also a multitude of pushcarts offering a wide array of appetizers, fresh coconut milk, and other drinks. Feel free to experiment with almost anything they offer — but we do advise that you avoid the shrimp. They're usually sold in groups of 15 to 20 and are skewered on a stick. They are lightly boiled in spiced water but finished off by sunlight. They may look enticing, but eating shrimp on the beach is a possible way to cut your day short due to stomach issues. After a sprint across the sand to your hotel, it's likely you'll be forced to stay indoors, next to a bathroom, for a day or two. Most people eat shrimp and are fine, but consider yourself warned!

weekends all year long. Though less known internationally and less packed with flesh, Leblon is very much like Ipanema—both beaches run into each other, separated only by the canal.

Barra da Tijuca

Located 10 miles/16 kilometers west of Ipanema, and just past the private slips where Lake Jacarepaguá spills into the Atlantic, the 5-mile/8-kilometer stretch of Barra da Tijuca (or just "Barra") begins. As with Leblon or Ipanema, Rio's upper class populates this long stretch of white sand. The only real difference is that the beach is a little farther from the noise of heavy traffic, and some of Rio's famous actors and *futebol* players often come here with an entourage of friends, family, and fans. On the weekends, it is possible to run into Romário (who has an apartment in the neighborhood and continues to celebrate his 1,000th career goal), Ronaldinho, or Roberto Carlos, when he's in town visiting from his adopted home in Spain. **Praia do Pepê**, toward the beginning of Barra, is especially known for regular star sighting. Leonardo DiCaprio, surf legend Kelly Slater, and former supermodel Elle McPherson have all been sighted here.

Expect Barra to be less crowded but more challenging to reach. Buses will take you out there, but you've got to pass by the infamous Rocinha *favela*, home to some 250,000 marginalized Brazilians. On very rare occasions, the tunnel connecting Barra da Tijuca to greater Rio could be closed by drug gangs, so the trip may get exciting from time to time! That being said, we do recommend that you visit Barra da Tijuca's pristine beach if you have a car and want to get away from the crowded shores in Ipanema, Leblon, or Copacabana. If that's not the case, keep it simple and stick to beaches closer to town.

Prainha

Worth mention, and certainly worth the effort to get there, the beach at Prainha just west of Barra da Tijuca offers fewer crowds, a beautiful setting, a small ecological park to explore, excellent surfing, and a cheap restaurant (called Mirante da Prainha) that serves fresh seafood and *feijão* ("black beans") for next to nothing. This beach is accessible only by car or taxi; no bus routes pass through the area. This is precisely why it's worth a visit. After a few days at Ipanema, the crowd can become insufferable, leaving one desirous of more privacy from staring eyes or simply a little more space. If you go to Prainha, make sure you get there early. By 3 p.m. the sun starts to duck behind the mountains — not a big deal in the summer, but a consideration in the winter months, when a lack of direct sunlight makes the beach a little too cold for comfort.

For surfers, Prainha is a must-see. With a group of four or five, a taxi ride is affordable, and most — if not all — *taxistas* know how to get there. It's approximately a 30-minute ride from Ipanema, and a day trip is well worth the time, effort, and expense. A round-trip taxi ride should not cost more than $25, and most taxi drivers will wait for you for free. After all, they're stoked to be there, too!

Useful Information When at the Beach

For just simple sunbathing on the beach, bring a pair of sunglasses, a bathing suit, a towel, and *little else*. It's easy to spot tourists with their huge beach bags. Do *not* bring them — you become a target for theft. Quick-witted thieves will steal everything they can, like dogs hampering for table scraps. If you sleep, use your bag as a pillow. The less you carry, the less attention you attract. So don't bring a big bag, flashy CD player, or a fat wallet to the beach. You'll keep it longer if it stays in the hotel safe.

A beach chair will not cost more than $2 to rent for the amount of time you're there. An umbrella is never more than $2 for the day. Beer on the beach is normally $2, and so are most drinks or food you will buy. Making eye contact with one of the many vendors walking by will, again, win you a couple minutes of professional, fast-talking Brazilian haggle. They will serve you at your seat.

Modesty does not exist on the sand. Part of the allure of sunbathing is that it gives Rio's youth the excuse to show off their bodies while surrounded by a feast of beauty. It's not uncommon to see a large cluster of bodies in a certain spot with large stretches of less populated sand. Men usually don't lie down on the sand, unless they're with a wife or a serious girlfriend. Sitting in a beach chair is accepted, but most *carioca* men simply stand, with feet shoulder-width apart and hands clasped behind their back, to *pegar sol*, or sunbathe.

Rio's beach culture extends to the city as well. It is quite normal to see half-naked men and women cruising the streets in search of some exotic juice, a paper, or a friend before heading just two or three city blocks to the beach. Bare-chested men order *suco* ("juice") from a corner juice bar in skimpy bathing suits and flip-flops. (We've seen some barefoot, with just a Speedo, and often wonder where they keep their cash.) So don't worry about leaving your hotel wearing only a bathing suit and flip-flops. It's de rigueur. Sleeveless shirts, tank tops, cleavage, biceps, and string bikinis are all normal and not alarming. In Rio it is practical, accepted, and even expected to wear as little clothing as possible during the heat of the day, especially if you plan to make a short trip to the beach along the way. Beachtime and urban wear and apparel is quite fashionable here.

⊛ Carnaval in Rio

Without question, *Carnaval* in Rio is the world's greatest and most famous annual party. Although Mardi Gras in New Orleans is probably a bigger drunk, the sheer depth and scope of Rio's celebration of the flesh boggles the mind (and will exhaust the body) and dwarfs the activities on the Louisiana bayou. There are hundreds of carnival celebrations dotting the Christian world, but this is the granddaddy of them all. It is so big, as a matter of fact, that it has become a spectator sport for most revelers and especially tourists. In Brazil, however, the *Carnavals* in Salvador and Olinda are as popular (and in some cases more popular with Brazilians) than the one in Rio.

Preparations for *Carnaval* begin almost as soon as the previous *Carnaval* ends. Officially, *Carnaval* starts on the Friday before Ash Wednesday and ends at midnight of Ash Wednesday. However, this being Brazil, the party is in reality much longer. In Rio, *Carnaval* is a three-pronged party push. It consists of the "big event" and the core element of the festivities, which (besides the human body) is the corps of samba schools (called *escolas*) — performing in the *Carnaval* parades. In any given year, there are 14 samba schools (they aren't actually real schools but are more like highly organized neighborhood associations) *fiercely* competing for top honors in the Grupo Especial, which is the elite division. There are many other schools in the Grupo de Accesso and youth schools, but the visitor will want to see the elite 14. The composition of the elite 14 changes yearly, so if a school doesn't cut it, it gets shamefully demoted to the Accesso level, while an Accesso school gets promoted to the big time. Obviously, no school wants to go down, so it's all or nothing come showtime.

Of course, *Carnaval* in Rio is much more than what goes down in the Sambódromo, the parade stadium. There are the *Carnaval* balls (*bailes*), a diverse melange of huge parties and probably the most active fun you can have as a tourist. There are also the street *bandas* and *blocos*, the street parties and impromptu processions that happen throughout the city and can pop up on a street corner without warning.

The Carnaval Parades

This is no two-hour show. For two nights (Sunday and Monday nights before Ash Wednesday) beginning at 7 p.m. (19:00) and lasting for about 11 hours (the sun is rising at the end), the samba schools parade through the **Sambódromo** (pronounced "sam-BO-drome-oo"), at a rate of seven schools per night. The Sambódromo is a 43,000 seat, 2,000-foot/600-meter-long stadium (more than six football fields long), located in Centro Rio. Built specifically for this event in 1984 and designed by Brazil's most famous architect, Oscar Niemeyer, the Sambódromo resembles a broad boulevard with permanent concrete grandstands and luxury boxes lining each side. It culminates in an archway that vaguely reminds us of the McDonald's golden arches gone cement. The Globo network has a neon perch across from section 9, and bobbing camera platforms are everywhere, for this event is televised nonstop throughout Brazil and via satellite all over the world. PA systems closely spaced down the Sambódromo blast each samba school's anthem (the *samba do enredo*) sung by the *puxador*, the school's emcee-singer, who is almost always male. The song is on a continuous loop and is drilled into the spectator's head whether one likes it or not.

Each samba school has 65–80 minutes to get through the stadium. Any less or more time means penalty points, which will effectively eliminate the school from the top prizes. Although this sounds like a lot of time, moving 3,000–6,000 costumed revelers at a precisely measured pace is no small task and is a coordinator's (*carnavalesco's*) nightmare. And costumed they are! We noticed that an extraordinary number of feathers are used—the world's exotic bird population must take a huge hit every year to costume the 50,000 or more dancers who participate. Indeed, from our vantage point in section 11, the spectacle of the bouncing, twirling throng slowly moving down the Sambódromo was an amazing sight we will never forget. We also noticed that it seems to take forever for the first section, called a wing—*alas*, in Portuguese—to reach us. Once the procession (*desfile*) passes the last of the judges (who are strategically spaced throughout the stadium), its pace picks up noticeably to the end of the stadium. If the school is behind pace (there are digital clocks everywhere ticking off the time spent, much like a soccer scoreboard), the whole procession speeds up as if kicked in the pants. Judges are wise to this, and they award points on how evenly paced the whole school is.

The structure of the samba school parade is basically as follows. Once a samba school has finished, the Sambódromo is swept and cleaned from end to end by workers who revel in the spotlight, often entertaining the crowd with their own sambas and antics. Then the Sambódromo emcee announces the next school, and the particular samba school's song begins (it's actually called the *samba*). The school's old folks (*commissão de frente*), who are the alumni—a samba honor guard, if you will—then enter the stadium. Each school has distinctive colors and flags, and if the school is big and popular, supporters will sweep through the Sambódromo distributing flags to wave—a true groovy souvy (we still have our Mangueira flag on display in our office). The *commissão de frente* sports the school's flags and displays the theme for the procession. Then comes the first wing (the *abre alas*) and the first of from five to eight of the most incredibly elaborate floats (*carros alegóricos*) we have ever seen, covered with topless women and men in very skimpy costumes, all dancing the samba in place. Following this is the *bateria*, the percussion corps made up of 200–400 drummers. Just after the Globo perch, the *bateria* pours into the Drummer's Niche (*recuo da bateria*—actually a bisecting street between sections 9 and 11 during non-*Carnaval* times) and power the procession through the stadium. We love percussion and relished sitting next to the *bateria* (walking hangovers, beware). Every school tries to recruit Brazilian celebrities (*destaques*) to ride on one of the floats, and the more popular the school, the bigger the celeb. Between the floats are the various *alas* of the school. Each *ala* has a totally different costume. We loved the *ala baiana*, Bahian women in the traditional hoop skirts (a nod to *Carnaval's* origins in Salvador), and the *passistas* (men and women of mixed race, usually on floats, who are traditionally the best dancers). Tucked into one of the *alas* is the *porta bandieras* and *mestre salas*, the official school-flag bearer and the dance master, both coveted and revered positions (sort of like being prom king and queen). The procession ends with the *velha guarda* ("old guard"). These are the most distinguished members of the school (usually the head of the school and his or her associates).

Judging criteria is complex, involving choice of theme (which is up to the school), theme song, energy, costumes, choreography, percussion balance, floats, design, discipline, logical flow of story, and props and decorations. Decisions are announced in the early afternoon on Ash Wednesday and are awaited like the birth of a first child. Programming in Rio is interrupted, and newspapers clamor to be the first to release the winning extra edition. As in figure skating, judging can seem unfair and biased. In the case of Rio's *Carnaval*, it often is! There is usually an outcry when what is universally considered the best school loses out to a more inferior performance. Hey, this is Brazil. There is always more than meets the eye.

The Parade of Champions reprises the top schools on the Saturday after the competition. However, part of the fun is not knowing who is going to win, being the first to see the specter of each school filling up the entire length of the stadium, and having the percussion of the *bateria* blasting away next to you as the entire school passes by.

Want to Join In?

Samba schools welcome a certain number of outsiders in the parade; they are a great source of hard currency and help to defray the cost for those members who can't afford the extravagant costumes. The cost for tourists runs anywhere from $150 to $500 (which is a lot more than members pay, but how often will you do this, and you are helping the school). The schools ask that participants arrive at least 14 days ahead of the event to rehearse and get fitted. We've heard that you can get there a week before and still participate, but it's up to the school. Since this is a cash cow, this program is well organized, with handlers fluent in English to walk the bewildered gringos through the steps.

Since we like winners, we suggest trying the Beija-Flor (www
.beija-flor.com.br), ⊛ Mangueira (www.mangueira.com.br), Imper-
atriz (www.imperatrizleopoldinense.com.br), and Viradouro (www
.unidosdoviradouro.com.br; this site is also in English) schools—in
that order. You can also check out the samba school league's Web site
(LIESA), at www.liesa.globo.com. Your hotel or tour operator can
make all the arrangements for you—recommended if you don't speak
Portuguese.

If You Just Want to Watch

You can buy tickets for one or both nights. The best seats in the best
sections are usually reserved by local tour companies, and at a premium cost. Unless you want to wait in line for tickets and take your
chances, we recommend just biting the bullet and shelling out the
bucks. Not only do you get the best seats, you also get extremely well-
organized, door-to-door service, with an ample number of English-
speaking guides. We were very impressed on how well-oiled the
system is. Another nice feature: Buses return you to your hotel every
hour, so if you just can't sit through another school, you can head
home on the next air-conditioned bus. Guides make sure that you
make it into the Sambódromo and to your seat, and they can help if
you need any assistance or have any questions. Often tickets are
included in the hotel's *Carnaval* package (since it is super-high season, most hotels do only packages for *Carnaval*, anyway). Be sure that
tickets to the nights you want (and the seats you want) are included,
and be sure to get vouchers for them when booking. For more information on *Carnaval* packages, contact Riotur at 55-21-2542-8080 or
visit its Web site at www.rio.rj.gov.br/riotur. You might also want to
check out www.rio-carnaval.net—a site we've found to be comprehensive and accurate with information and prices *Under no cir-
cumstances should you buy tickets from a scalper outside; they are
probably fakes.*

There are several different kinds of seating in the Sambódromo.
As with a sporting event in the U.S. and Canada, the luxury boxes,
called *camarotes*, are the most desirable and here offer the best viewing possibilities. These seat 12 people and are at the mezzanine level

(basically perched just above ground level to three stories high). They line the "runway" and cost (at current exchange rates) between $9,500 and $11,000 for boxes in sections 7, 9, and 11 for each night! That's between $790 and $925 a seat! Ouch! Then again, how many of you forked over $150–$500 recently to see the seemingly ageless Rolling Stones perform for two hours? If you have a party of 12, just think of the whale of a party in your very own *camarote*.

Although the *camarotes* are very grand, we didn't mind sitting in the bleachers (just like at our beloved Fenway Park). Called *arquibancada*, the elevation gives a great perspective, and you can watch other spectators while you're waiting for the parade to reach you. It's a game for us to guess where the people around us hail from. The *arquibancada* are above and behind the *camarotes*. Ticket prices are between $70 and $280 per seat a night for sections 7–11. Seats (they are really just concrete benches, but your tour operator will give you a souvenir cushion) in sections 9 and 11 are reserved, and in section 9 you will have an assigned seat. Note: Bring binoculars to zoom in on all the exposed flesh shakin' and bouncin' (and there is quite a bit!).

Then there are the street-level tables for four, called *cadeiras de pista*, which are very close to the action, and in front of them are the runway-side boxes, called *frisas*, which seat six to eight, have a small table, and are so wicked close to the parade that you can touch the revelers. Snobs that we pretend to be, we like to be slightly above the crowd, as it affords a better view. So we would not recommend the street-level seating. The *cadeiras de pista* and the *frisas* cost about $1,040–$3,500 per night per table or box, or about $170–$600 per seat a night.

The premier and most expensive spot at the Sambódromo is section 9, which is across from the Globo anchor perch. Obviously, the schools turn it on here. Next best is section 11, then section 7. We strongly suggest trying to get a spot in section 9. Hell, you've come all this way, so see it right! Don't bother with sections 6 and 13—they suck.

The Carnaval Balls

We like nothing more than a good party, and the *Carnaval* balls are right up our alley. The balls are a great way to meet both *cariocas* and citizens of the world. Just think of them as huge mixers where everyone is super friendly and willing. Costumes are not required, but it is *Carnaval*, so M.A.E. (Make An Effort).

The best events happen on the Friday, Saturday, and Tuesday before Ash Wednesday (Sunday and Monday nights are Parade Nights and the center of attention). Unlike tickets for the parade, these tickets are easy to get (often at the door) and are much cheaper, ranging from $25 to $60. Groups of friends can reserve, in advance, tables for four (around $200 to $500 — avoid tables bordering the dance floor), or a mezzanine box for 20 people (between $850 and $2,200). Places like the Teatro Scala in Leblon (296 Avenida Afrânio de Melo Franco, phone 21-2239-4448); the Help Disco (a hooker and thug magnet, located at 3432 Avenida Atlântica — you can't miss it, phone 21-2522-1296); and the gay club Le Boy in Copacabana (102 Rua Raul Pompéia, phone 21-2513-4993) have something going every night before Ash Wednesday. The renowned and gay X-Demente parties happen at Marina da Glória or Fundição Progresso (an old steel mill, Rua dos Arcos in Lapa, www.xdemente.com) on Saturday and Tuesday, and the gay *B.I.T.C.H.* party happens at the Clube Monte Líbano on Sunday in Leblon.

There are many balls and galas, but there are a few that are the most happening and the ones not to miss. On the Friday before Ash Wednesday, the soccer club Flamengo hosts the Red and Black Ball (*Baile Vermelho e Preto*) at Teatro Scala ($50) in Leblon. This is probably the most randy of the straight balls, famous for its barely clad and gorgeous women, and is televised on Brazilian TV. At the opposite end of the spectrum, the Copacabana Palace Great Ball (*Baile do Copa*) is held at the Copacabana Palace Hotel in Copacabana on the Saturday before Ash Wednesday. Attracting Rio's moneyed political and social elite as well as a variety of international celebs, stars, athletes, and models, this is a formal affair with men in black tie and masks and women in masks and gowns or elaborate costumes. Tickets run from $550 to $1,550 per person, depending on which room you elect as your hobnob base. Probably the most popular ball is the Gala Gay ($50) at the ornate Teatro Scala in Leblon on Shrove Tuesday. Expect to see the Brazilian equivalent of Joan and Melissa and their TV cameras on the red carpet at the theater's entry. This event is televised by several Brazilian networks. It is no longer a gay-only event, so guests of all persuasions mix and match here, surrounded by the Rio *Carnaval's* most outrageous costumes. Lots of transsexual drag queens illuminate the festivities and bare their beautiful and surgically enhanced breasts. Bare-chested, six-packed men mosh the dance floor as the temperature inside approaches the inferno. Don't miss this one. Most *Carnaval* balls have live bands with huge percussion sections; usually two bands alternate sets. With the exception of the Copacabana Palace, the music will be excruciatingly loud, so put some foam earplugs in your pocket just in case. Some advice: Less is more. Carry as little as possible, and use disposable cameras if you want to take pictures. Leave all valuables, jewels, Rolexes, and credit and ATM cards in the hotel safe. A photocopy of your passport and a driver's license are plenty for ID. Carry cash in a front pocket or in your socks. Buy tons of drink tickets when you arrive to avoid long lines later. (It's also a nice gesture to buy someone a drink.)

The balls often last until the morning comes. Temperatures and humidity inside reach steambath levels, so dress (or undress) accordingly. Be sure to drink lots of water to avoid dehydration. As always, be careful with illegal substances (they will be around), and use only *known* sources. Tourists are major targets for rip-off artists. Use utmost discretion if you do imbibe. Of course, we at Rum & Reggae don't condone this, but we're realists. Don't leave with anything not legal; police searches can be indiscriminate (and the bribe will cost you $100 or more). Why ruin another fabulous night?

As with any situation, knowledge is power. If you meet and befriend a *carioca*, ask him or her where the place to be is on a certain night. Chances are, he or she will be glad to show you around.

Street Bandas and Blocos

Although many people complain about the commercialization, cost, and spectator-only nature of Rio's *Carnaval* parades, some of the original spirit of *Carnaval* can still be found in the various street *bandas* and *blocos* (pronounced "BAHN-dush" and "BLOH-koosh") that happen all over the city. For the traveler, there are ample street festivities that happen in Zona Sul (Ipanema and Copacabana). All one needs to do is listen, then head for the sound.

A *banda* is basically a large organized neighborhood group—usually with a deafening PA system on a flatbed tractor-trailer—that gathers at a spot (either a bar or square). A *bloco* is a smaller, more spontaneous affair that can spring up anywhere, like a street corner or bar. Many of the beach bars (*barracas*) are the scene of numerous *blocos*. Both *bandas* and *blocos* involve music, percussion, drinking, and samba. As the crowd swells and swills, T-shirts with the *banda's* name are sold to raise money for the group—a great groovy souvy. After a couple of hours of what is called a concentration (*concentração*)—basically getting stewed—the *banda* goes mobile, following the truck and its music, samba-ing and bouncing, usually but not always along a planned route. Spectators are often swept up in the commotion, and cars stuck in the traffic mess have no choice but to wait it out. Feel free to join in at any time. We recommend following at the end of the crowd behind the truck, for easy access and exit strategies. There are even some *bandas*, like the **Concentra Mas Não Sai** ("Gather But Don't Leave"), that like only the concentration part. The *bandas* not to be missed are the **Banda de Ipanema**, a drag-queen extravaganza, concentrating at the Praça General Osório on the Saturday and Tuesday before Ash Wednesday; and the renowned **Banda da Carmen Miranda**, a drag-queen extravaganza deluxe, concentrating at the Praça Nossa Senhora da Paz, on the Sunday before Ash Wednesday. Another good *banda* is the **Simpatia é Quase Amor** ("Sympathy If Not Love") concentrating at the Praça General Osório on the Sunday before Ash Wednesday. In Copacabana, the **Banda da Sá Ferreira** is popular, concentrating at the corner of Avenida Atlântica and Rua Sá Ferreira, on the Saturday and Tuesday before Ash Wednesday.

Where to Stay

Rio has more hotel rooms than most Latin American cities—some very fancy, most standard fare. Year-round, many hotels remain fully booked, especially during New Year's and *Carnaval*. Don't expect to find a room quickly if you show up without reservations (which are strongly suggested). Fortunately, with a little planning, you'll find the perfect fit, from beachfront and luxurious to simple and budget-friendly, without too much trouble. As a general rule, hotels are not overly decorated, but they offer excellent service. Fancy décor can be found, but it comes with a price tag few are willing to stomach. Copacabana is home to more hotels per capita than any other

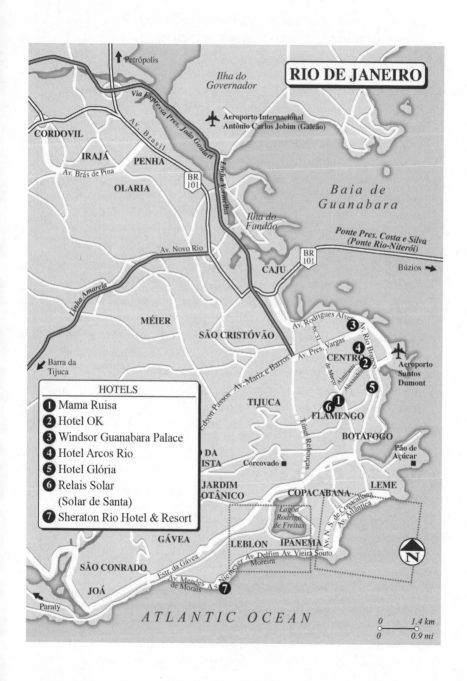

neighborhood in Rio, but you'll likely find the best value (and location) in Ipanema. The closer you are to the beach, the higher the price, with a few exceptions. Normally, moving two blocks in from the beachfront lowers the price without taking much shine off of comfort or style.

Centro, Lapa, and Santa Teresa

Mama Ruisa, 132 Rua Santa Cristina, Santa Teresa, Rio de Janeiro, RJ, Brazil. ℭ 55-21-2242-1281 ✎ 55-21-2210-0631, 💻 www.mamaruisa.com/english/index.asp, resa@mamaruisa.com

💲 **Very Pricey** and up (double or single occupancy) ⑪ **CP** deluxe airport service (100 reais) CC 7 rooms.

Once bought by Frenchman Jean Michel Ruis, this aristocrat's colonial home became a luxury B&B with an elegant and sophisticated French style. White walls, tall ceilings with stained glass, and the sunlight reflecting off the pool onto the surrounding palm trees all offer a unique sensation of purity. From the wrought-iron verandas you can start your morning with a dark coffee and view of Sugarloaf, Guanabara Bay, or the beaches of Zona Sul. Will you ever want to leave? While there are a number of comfortable well-furnished lounge areas for relaxing, the spacious living room may be too *designed* to do more than just stare. Luxury and a convenient location go hand in hand: You'll be only 15 minutes from Ipanema and Copacabana Beaches, 10 minutes from the historical center, 10 minutes from Lapa, and 20 minutes from the international airport. Beauty services include massages, pedicures, and, of course, manicures.

Hotel OK, 24 Rua Senador Dantas, Centro (Cinelândia), Rio de Janeiro, RJ, Brazil. ℭ 55-21-3479-4500, ✎ 55-21-3479-4600, 💻 www.hotelok.com.br

💲 **Pricey** and up ⑪ **BP** CC 150 rooms

The Cinelândia area has to be one of the most exciting locations for a downtown hotel. The Municipal Theatre, the Museum of Belas Artes, the Odeon cinema, and plenty of bars with outdoor seating are within two minutes of the hotel. We wonder about the name, though—who would call a hotel simply "OK"? Stepping into the reception area, we first noticed the expensive marble and seemingly antique furniture and fixtures —far from just OK. Opening its doors for the first time nearly 60 years ago, the hotel quickly became a well-known receptacle for the national political and social elite. The recent reforms have given a more modern edge to the shiny granite, chandeliers, and royal crests on the walls by adding a cyber café above the lobby and a plasma TV over the poolside bar (offering a view of Guanabara Bay, Corcovado, and the Cathedral—that church that looks like an industrial pyramid). Be careful with room selection here, for you might get a view of the back end of a dingy apartment building with somebody's drying laundry waving in the breeze.

This hotel is definitely not a place for children. The hallways lined with rooms wrap around an 18-story chasm that links the uppermost ceiling with the lobby. Between the landing and free fall is a 3½-foot protective wall. During the Pan-American games, the hotel filled up with families. Although no children went skydiving, the lobby often served as ground zero for dropped cell phones, forks and knives, towels, and anything else that fits in a small hand.

Hotel Arcos Rio, 117 Avenida Mem de Sá, Lapa, Rio de Janeiro, RJ, Brazil. ℭ 55-21-2224-3212, ✆ 55-21-2252-4732, 🖳 www.arcosriopalacehotel.com.br

💲 **Not So Cheap** and up 🍴 **CP** 🆑 130 rooms

Hotel Arcos Rio is the perfect launching pad (and crashing pad) for going out in Rio's rootsy Lapa district, Santa Teresa, and downtown. The rooms are quaint, not elegant, but inviting enough for a peaceful slumber—that is, if you're not in one of the rooms facing Mem de Sá, where the screeching brakes of every bus passing by seem loudest between 1 and 6 a.m. With limited Internet connection in the rooms (but four computers available), this hotel clearly aims for a different clientele than most other downtown locations do. Brazilian families and foreign tourists come and go, taking contracted tours and jumping on the *bondinho* ("tram" or "trolley") to Santa Teresa. When they return, they chuck their shoes and either sip a *caipirinha* on the terrace or pack into the tiny pool. Despite the small proportions of the pool, deck, and bar, the hotel keeps its chic edge, with well-finished wood contrasted with white marble, making for a polished yet relaxing décor.

Hotel Glória, 632 Rua do Russel, Glória, Rio de Janeiro, RJ, Brazil.

📞 55-21-2555-7272, 📠 55-21-2555-7282,

💻 www.hotelgloriario.com.br, hotel@hotelgloriario.com.br

💰 **Not So Cheap** and up 🍴 **CP** ©© 610 rooms

Located just a couple of miles from the Santos Dumont airport, the world-renowned Hotel Glória saw its heyday in the decades immediately following its 1920 inauguration. As an alternative to a spot in Zona Sul, Hotel Glória offers a centralized location in the Flamengo and Centro area. Renovations modernized the rooms while leaving a touch of class by way of old, heavy wooden bed frames with intricate carvings and posts, lampshades you might see in an ambassador's home, and wall decorations that remind you of what Rio used to look like. The furniture looks like pieces you'd expect to find in an antique store, yet less fragile. So you don't have to sit gently, but don't flop down, either! Of the two pools, the one with a design reminiscent of Oscar Niemeyer, the famous Brazilian architect, is interesting to look at, but the pool with the panoramic view and shaded seating area under a small batch of trees is the pick for a nice spot to read, write in a journal, or have a chat with a new friend. The wellness center boasts two saunas, a jogging track, a dance room, a meditation room, and massage rooms. Yoga and stretching classes are also offered. We almost laughed with surprise at the 2,100-square-foot Tony Regadas Gymnasium with low-impact floor and modern equipment in a naturally ventilated ambiance — totally unexpected in this blast-from-the-past hotel. In addition to the personal training offered, there are massage services that include a variety of styles: Esalen, Swedish, or Oriental. Expect excellent service from the proud staff. Be cautious when stepping out at night. The location, which years ago was magnificent, is now a little sketchy. So take a cab.

Windsor Guanabara Palace, 392 Avenida Presidente Vargas, Centro, Rio de Janeiro, RJ, Brazil. ℂ 55-21-2195-6000, ✆ 55-21-2516-1582, 🖳 www.windsorhoteis.com.br, crsp@windsorhoteis.com.br

💲 **Not So Cheap** and up ⑪ BP ℂℂ 531 rooms

- Where the honking and buzzing chaos of Rio Branco meets the mayhem of Avenida Presidente Vargas, you'll find the Brazilian businessman's refuge in Guanabara Palace. This place has got a business center that would make Kinko's jealous, and all the rooms are hardwired with broadband. The location is ideal for proximity to Rio's downtown attractions. The hotel itself offers a number of amenities, including a Jacuzzi and sauna area, a full pool, a decent weight room, and even an old-school piano bar. From the top-story pool you can slowly spin in a circle and take in Guanabara Bay, the Christ statue, and all of downtown. It's a view that few hotels in the city offer. The hallways resemble fancy Trump Tower corridors, blurring the line between vacation and the (elite) rat race, but you can't beat the location, especially if you're in Rio for a quick whirlwind of the tourist favorites and have little time for beach leisure.

  Our only real problem with this hotel is that it's full of businessmen in suits—probably the last thing we want to see on vacation. Energy companies often reserve all the rooms to take advantage of the 400-capacity conference rooms and restaurant seating area. But who knows, maybe you could score a job! Many, many conversations and deals have been had in this hotel over the simplicity of a Cuba Libre at the pool.

Relais Solar (Solar de Santa), 32 Ladeira do Meirelles, Santa Teresa, Rio de Janeiro, RJ, Brazil. ℂ 55-21-2221-2117 ✆ 55-21-2221-6679, 🖳 www.solardesanta.com, reservas@solardesanta.com.br

💲 **Cheap** and up 🍴 **CP** deluxe CC 5 rooms

Perched in the Atlantic rainforest on a hill in old colonial Rio, Relais Solar clearly parts with the city's older, traditionally styled hotels. As a restored colonial mansion fit for both casual travelers and debonair businessmen, the hotel's appeal knows no limit. Regional foods, an "honesty" bar with instructions on how to make a *caipirinha*, and regular wine, coffee, and regional food tasting will keep your palate on overdrive. An Internet room, a Mac G5 editing suite, and a fully functional multimedia conference room (adapted in the dining room) will keep you in the game at work, if necessary.

The rooms draw their influence from the trees outside the windows, with different bird and nature themes. Other amenities include organized tours, airport pickups, Wi-Fi, and the option to rent the entire house. Commenting on the furniture and art at the reception, we learned that it's locally made and, in fact, for sale. Simply can't part with the desk chair in your room? Buy it! You'll leave with an unforgettable experience and something new to add a Brazilian touch in your home. This hotel's only drawback is its distance from most of the city's attractions. But hey, that's why there are taxis, right?

Copacabana

⭐ **Copacabana Palace**, 1702 Avenida Atlântica, Copacabana, Rio de Janeiro, RJ, Brazil. ✆ 55-21-2548-7070, 📠 55-21-2235-7330, 🖥 www.copacabanapalace.com.br, reservas@copacabanapalace.com.br

💲 **Wicked Pricey** and up 🍴 **CP** CC 222 rooms

Opened in 1923, the Palace is Copacabana's most venerable hotel. It has attracted the rich and famous from all over the world for decades. Although it has lost some play due to some solid competition, the Palace is still a cornerstone landmark for luxury in Copacabana and is worth at least a visit. We have well-sourced information that the Palace remains the premier landing pad for international jet-setters in town for a show or sporting event. The Rolling Stones, Julia Roberts, and Sting

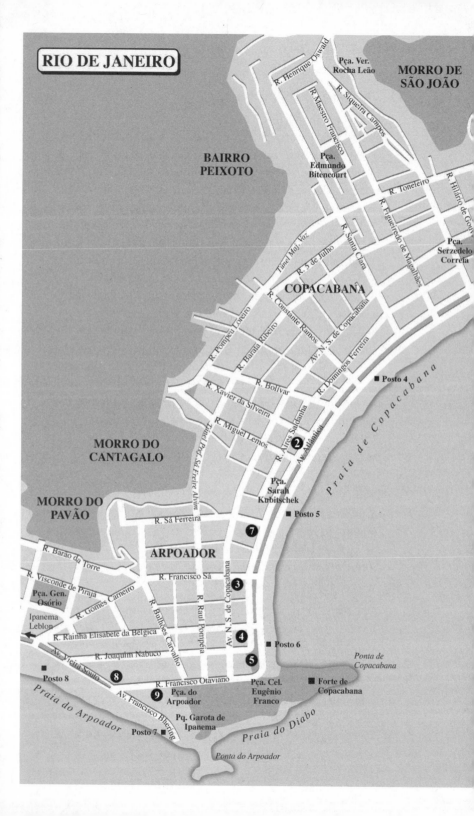

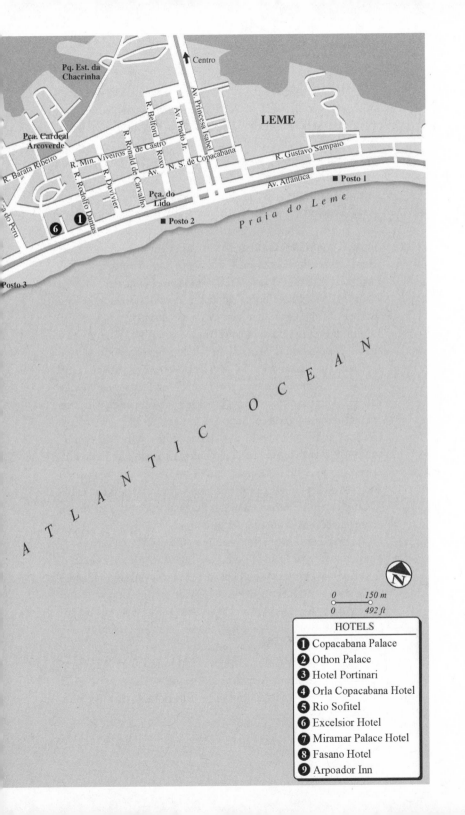

Pq. Est. da
Chacrinha

↑ Centro

R. Belford Roxo

Av. Prado Jr.

Av. Princesa Isabel

LEME

Pça. Cardeal
Arcoverde

R. Min. Viveiros

R. Ronald de Castro

R. Gustavo Sampaio

R. Barata Ribeiro

R. Rodolfo Dantas

R. Duvivier

Av. N. S. de Copacabana

Av. Atlântica

■ Posto 1

Pça. do
Lido

a do Peru

6 **1**

■ Posto 2

Praia do Leme

Posto 3

A T L A N T I C   O C E A N

N

| 0 | 150 m |
| 0 | 492 ft |

HOTELS

1 Copacabana Palace
2 Othon Palace
3 Hotel Portinari
4 Orla Copacabana Hotel
5 Rio Sofitel
6 Excelsior Hotel
7 Miramar Palace Hotel
8 Fasano Hotel
9 Arpoador Inn

have all had coffee at the poolside dining area. On the other side of the pool is one of Rio's finest restaurants, where you can't just walk in without a reservation. Oh, and long pants only. Walking into the lobby takes you decades into the past, when Frank Sinatra stayed here. The lighting fixtures alone are worth more than the taxicab, or even the luxury car (service included with the price of some rooms) that dropped you off.

The extremely spacious rooms are very elegant, a throwback to the first half of the 20th century. They seem aged but are well maintained; the furniture appears to be handmade; there are fresh flowers on the table or nightstand; and rugs designed with deep hues of red, blue, and orange decorate the beautiful wooden floors. Recent renovation has removed almost all of the inadequacies of past designs while maintaining the sharp lines, laced furniture coverings, and intricate wood designs that are still in style, simply because the Copacabana Palace says so! The front rooms are spectacular, as if you're visiting a museum of royal décor. Resplendent white satin curtains part to present a privileged view through windows that have seen decades of life come and go. You'll enjoy a range in room styles and amenities: classic suites with views, executive suites with a full business center, 1,100-square-foot penthouse suites with a 24-hour butler and a private pool. Each room comes with laundry service, 24-hour room service, cable TV, high-speed Internet (Wi-Fi in the business and pool areas), and 110 voltage, with adapter available.

As if all this were not enough, the Palace has recently opened a ✪ spa. Considered one of the most luxurious spas in the whole city, this "sophisticated urban sanctuary" takes up three floors and has a number of private treatment rooms and two couples' treatment rooms—a rarity in Rio. Special custom services are available. Ask for it, set the hour, and the hotel will arrange to bring in the right person if it doesn't offer the service in-house. A special spa menu was developed by Francesco Carli of the Cipriani restaurant. We guess that means good food. Of all the "palaces" Rio offers, this hotel is truly the only one worth the title.

Othon Palace, 3264 Avenida Atlântica, Copacabana, Rio de Janeiro, RJ, Brazil. ✆ 55-21-2106-1500; reservations: 55-21-2106-0200 , 💻 www.hoteis-othon.com.br, rio@othon.com.br

💼 **Wicked Pricey** and up 🍴 **CP** CC 602 rooms

The Othon Palace is the second tallest building along the beachfront in Copacabana. The view from the rooftop pool is spectacular. You can see all the way across to Ipanema, all of Copacabana, the hills behind, including Pão de Açúcar (Sugarloaf), and even a small slice of one of Copacabana's *favelas*. Each room in this enormous hotel has a slightly different décor. In some rooms, there is an interesting wall of yellow or brick-red tile, which is very unique when compared to the usual white walls elsewhere. Colors are bright blues, yellows, and reds, yet some rooms are classy, with a clean-cut black-and-white look. The nicest rooms offer amazing views because the walls are made of spotless glass, 2 inches thick. What a great place to have breakfast! The carpeted floors are plush and beg for bare feet. After a rough day on the beach, relax in your room with cable TV and 24-hour room service (including laundry services to keep your new Speedo dashing) or go up to the rooftop heated pool, weight room, sauna, and massage services, all opening up to ocean views. If you just can't stay away from the rat race that is your worklife, move up to a master suite equipped with full office services (fax, computer, printer, copier). Business vacations are made the easier with airport service and Wi-Fi in the common areas. The luxury in this hotel is noticeable, but it's not forced on you, like at the Caesar Palace. Its subtlety is refreshing and even enjoyable after just half an hour in the building.

Hotel Portinari, 17 Rua Francisco Sá, Copacabana, Rio de Janeiro, RJ, Brazil. ✆ 55-21-3222-8800, 📠 55-21-3813-1773 or 3813-1772, 💻 www.hotelportinari.com.br, reservas@hotelportinari.com.br

💼 **Very Pricey** and up 🍴 **EP** CC 66 rooms

The Portinari is arguably the most technologically advanced

hotel in Rio de Janeiro—a DVD player and high-speed Internet access are included in every room. Each floor has been decorated differently: a delicate classy look for the second floor, earth tones and wooden panels on the fourth floor, and simple elegance on the 12th floor. We're assuming that all the style is to make up for the limited room service (only until 11 p.m.) and the sorely missed pool and front view of the ocean. The other luxury amenities that have become standard in our recommended hotels are present, however—fitness center, laundry services, Jacuzzi, sauna, and business meeting rooms. The restaurant offers fine dining, and the bar and lounge downstairs complements a comfortable greeting area, complete with smooth sliding glass doors and a receptionist who speaks four languages. This hotel opened in September 2003, and it is still one of the newer kids on the block in Copacabana. Reservations are a must.

Orla Copacabana Hotel, 4122 Avenida Atlântica, Copacabana, Rio de Janeiro, RJ, Brazil. ℂ 55-21-2525-2425, 📠 55-21-2287-9134, 🖥 www.orlahotel.com.br, orla@orlahotel.com.br

💰 **Very Pricey** and up 🍴 CP 𝐂𝐂 115 rooms

The sleek, metallic exterior of this hotel looks like a thin spaceship squeezed between two buildings with the typical Copacabana architecture, circa 1970s. Inside, in the lobby, postmodern hues of whites and grays complement the black marble reception desk. The rooms are of the same flavor but with a little more daring design, with swirls of white on black. Padded headboards, as well as posh sofas and chairs, adorn some rooms. Internet, a safe, and cable television come with all rooms. The bathroom seems to be etched from one huge block of marble and is surprisingly big—ideal for double bathing. There is also a pool, sauna, and fitness center on the roof. After indulging in the restaurant's international cuisine, head up to the poolside bar for a killer view and one of the common selections of Brazil's exotic drinks.

Rio Sofitel, 4240 Avenida Atlântica, Copacabana, Rio de Janeiro, RJ, Brazil. ℂ 55-21-2525-1232, ✎ 55-21-2525-1200, 🖳 www.sofitel.com, sofitelrio@accorhotels.com.br

🛍 **Very Pricey and up** 🍴 **CP** ⓒⓒ 388 rooms

Definitely one of the most well-known hotels in Rio de Janeiro, the Rio Sofitel caters to traveling business executives, couples on honeymoons, VIPs, and anyone who wants to splurge a little while in Rio. Travel agents treat their top clients to Sofitel, and it is a frequently taken alternative to the Copacabana Palace. Situated on the corner between Copacabana and Ipanema, it is in an excellent location. For the dangerous mix of business and pleasure, Sofitel offers a Convention and Business Center, two pools, a gym, two saunas, a beauty salon, in-room Wi-Fi, massage services, a pool bar with a view of Sugarloaf, internationally recognized French cuisine in the restaurant, and 10 large posh rooms for business meetings (with seating for more than 2,000!). If that's too much action for you, seek refuge in your room; each has a private balcony, plasma cable TV, a safe, and 24-hour room service. The rooms are spacious with an extra touch of plush—the carpeting is thick, and you'll sink a couple of inches into any chair, sofa, or bed. The various room designs are all off-white with soft pastels. The TV is actually bigger than a microwave and not hung off the wall, spitting out wires, as in most Rio hotels. Translucent curtains complement thicker drapes that are held back by a thick weave of satin, but we prefer to keep the drapes open to take advantage of the great view. The circular pool on the roof is an excellent place to sun if you're tired of the constant haggling of Copacabana beach vendors on the sand. Bottom line: No doubt you'll get what you pay for in this well-managed hotel.

Excelsior Hotel, 1800 Avenida Atlântica, Copacabana, Rio de Janeiro, RJ, Brazil. ℂ 55-21-2545-6000, ✎ 55-21-2257-1850, 🖳 www.windsorhoteis.com, reservas.excelsior@windsorhoteis.com.br

🛍 **Not So Cheap and up** 🍴 **CP** ⓒⓒ 233 rooms

This hotel is home to perhaps more conventions than any other hotel in Copacabana—not exactly our thing. With a fully equipped convention center for business meetings, it comes with lots of suits, ties, convention ID tags, and loud foreigners complaining about this or that, embellishing tales of a late night in Ipanema, or engaged in heated discussions about business deals gone bad. The elevators are almost always full of such dull conversations. However, the hotel design is quite smart, the elevators are very fast, and the rooftop restaurant-pool combination with panoramic view is one of the nicest in town. The pool is bigger than you'd expect, and the waist-high guard railing is a nice break from other hotels that find it necessary to erect a 10-foot concrete wall to prevent falling, which may come in handy after staggering out of the weight room or sauna nearby. The master suite rooms are efficiently designed with the TV, dresser, and cabinets placed into the wall, not jutting out or hanging from the ceiling. The granite slab placed on top of the stained wooden drawers was a good idea. Floor-to-ceiling windows give the rooms an open-air feeling. The bathrooms are etched granite, and sliding glass doors keep the water from splashing out of the shower. If you can handle the swing and swagger of conventioneers, then have a go at the Excelsior. Oh, and don't be bothered by the group of locals hanging out around the entrance trying to sell trinkets. Just a wag or two of the index finger will keep them at bay.

Miramar Palace Hotel, 3668 Avenida Atlântica, Copacabana, Rio de Janeiro, RJ, Brazil. 🕾 55-21-2525-0303, 📠 55-21-2521-3294, 🖥 www.windsorhoteis.com, reservas.miramar@windsorhoteis.com.br

💲 **Not So Cheap** and up 🍴 **CP** 🆑 113 rooms

The best aspect of this hotel is the rooftop bar and the views of the beach and surroundings. On the backside by the sauna, during the day, you can see one of Copacabana's most well-known *favelas*, called Cantagalo, from a safe distance. Some of the rooms remind us of an elderly lady with a gaudy style who had the shakes while applying her brightly colored makeup. In contrast, the bathrooms are so white and clean they can sober you up in a moment, then remind you of a psychiatric ward in the next. Other rooms are more somber, as if they were the lady's dowdy husband, content to wear dark and drab browns, grays, and deep greens. The funny thing is that you'd never guess the rooms' lack of style from the clean, crisp presentation in the lobby. The rooms do have a modern touch, with cable TV, a safe, 24-hour room service, laundry service, and high-speed Internet. Due to its other services, such as a sauna, a fitness center, and an indoor pool, you might arrive at the conclusion that the decorator was just playing a practical joke. Perhaps this hotel should not be a first pick, but you should consider having at least one drink on the rooftop bar. The view it affords is worth twice the price of your drink.

Ipanema

⊛ **Fasano Hotel**, 80 Avenida Viera Souto, Ipanema, Rio de Janeiro, RJ, Brazil. ✆ 55-21-3202-4000, 📠 55-21-3202-4010, 🖥 www.fasano.com.br, rio@fasano.com.br

💲 **Wicked Pricey** and up 🍴 **CP** (CC) 81 rooms, 10 suites

In collaboration with famous designer Philippe Starck, the Fasano brand has finally arrived in Rio. As the newest hotel on the Ipanema block (and our favorite in this neighborhood), it brings a level of service, culinary practice, and style (what else would you expect from Monsieur Starck?) hard to come by in the beachfront city. From the outer façade and heavy but not overbearing security to the undulating drapes in the lobby and choice selections of tree-cut furniture, the Fasano Hotel has a unique rustic yet sophisticated look. The rooms come in shades of deeply stained wood and have plush couches and chairs that you might encounter in a Colorado mountain home, but it seems to fit into Rio's beachfront mood, even if a little on the dark side for this sunny town. The bright marble bathrooms have a modern, minimalist style, and the suites rival those of the Copacabana Palace, not necessarily in décor but in functionality and view. All rooms are complete with a plasma TV, Wi-Fi, a DVD and CD player, a private terrace, and a safe.

Motels in Rio de Janeiro

Motels in Rio are theme-packed privacy spots designed to be rented in hourly blocks and used specifically for you-know-what. They are not frowned upon. Rather, they are a necessity in a city where almost everyone has "the urge" but few have the space or place for privacy. Those in need include the university student who lives in a small apartment with five roommates, the married couple that still lives with mom, and the taxi driver we once met who maintains two wives, two separate families, and still manages to keep four other girlfriends on the side. (Hey, we're not sayin' we approve — we're just tellin' it like it is.) Whatever your reason for a motel in Rio, we recommend that you consider checking one out if you find yourself in a nice hotel that does not allow overnight guests (unless you sneak them in), or if you're in an adventurous mood and want to impress some *cariocas* with your knowledge of local private party spots with a view.

Motels normally charge by the hour, or in blocks of three, six, or eight hours. We know of one that charges up to 12 hours, but we didn't dare look at the price! Discretion is the motel's number one goal, so don't be surprised if the sheets are not silk and the paint is peeling. Most motels, however, will not disappoint. Widescreen televisions with a selection of entertainment, mirrors on the ceiling, champagne on ice, costumes, special chairs, shower ornaments, and, of course, a Jacuzzi, are all in the mix. If you get "lucky" at a club and decide to go for a motel, make sure you take only what you need, and make sure you don't pass out — you never know when your playmate could turn into a thief and leave you broke with a heavy bill to pay.

We recommend you check out **VIP**, at 418 Avenida Niemeyer in Leblon, just past the Sheraton hotel. Since the motel is in Leblon and not in the center of town, you're likely to be closer to your hotel if you chose one in Leblon or Ipanema. VIP is the nicest motel in Rio and has a number of rooms to choose from, including our favorite, the Sol, which weighs in at some $260 for an eight-hour block.

We hear, ahem, that the managers at VIP are very discreet and always welcome a party. Apart from its late-night motel scene, VIP is actually a great place to host a daytime party or get together with your travel

(continued on page 72)

The rooftop deck is what makes the Fasano possibly the best hotel in Rio. The deck is split in two, between a stained bamboo-covered eating area and the pool and sunning deck. Anchoring the eating area is a stainless steel bar where you can order yogurt smoothies or a sunset cocktail made with passion fruit. The cocktail is a perfect complement to one of Rio's best sunset spots. The menu is the most complete we've seen for a rooftop service, and the view from a bar stool is the best you'll find sitting at any bar in Ipanema. The front row seating, to the right of the bar and just behind the chest-high glass wall that rings the deck border, is an ideal spot to waste the day people-watching from just above a vibrating section of Ipanema sand. The deck's wading pool is like a huge white marble bowl with squared edges. It's not deep enough for diving, but the shallow section is perfect for lying on your back to soak in the sun and for taking a quick dunk to cool off. A decktop massage stand and exercise center complete Fasano's rooftop experience.

Rounding out the hotel's services is a spa, with a hammam (Turkish bath) and sauna, and beachfront service, much like Caesar Park, where comfortable chairs and umbrellas are placed in a location of your choice. A hotel employee stands by for drink orders, to replace a wet towel, or simply to watch your bag when you take a dip. Anchoring the Fasano brand is its restaurant, the Fasano Al Mare, where nationally famous chef Rogerio Fasano keeps a busy kitchen and a packed seating area. Reservations are required days in advance, and it is by far one of the best meals you'll come by in a hotel restaurant or any eating establishment in Rio. We're convinced that the Fasano has surpassed the Caesar Park as a hotel that represents the best that Rio has to offer in the luxury hotel class.

Caesar Park, 460 Avenida Vieira Souto, Ipanema, Rio de Janeiro, RJ, Brazil. ℂ 55-21-2525-2525, 📠 55-21-2521-6000, 🖥 www.caesarpark-rio.com, reservas.cprj@caesarpark.com.br
💲 **Very Pricey** and up 🍴 **CP** CC 186 rooms

(continued from page 70)

group or with a bunch of new friends. A number of very spacious suites, complete with sundecks, multiple showers, swimming pools, a grill, and a marvelous view make most of the VIP suites ideal for a festive gathering of eight or more. Check it out, but don't tell them we sent you. After all, they never knew we were there!

Bambina is another motel worthy of mention. Located at 65 Rua da Bambina in Botafogo, it's just a couple blocks from the Botafogo metro stop and offers a great value for the smaller yet quality rooms. Six-hour blocks rent for around $80 — a much better price than the top of the line VIP suites. Let's admit it, the Bambina is a great spot for that one-time encounter with someone you'll probably never see again. We recommend that you reserve the VIP only for a special friend or friends — people you'd like to encounter on your next trip to Rio.

The Caesar Park is a slightly pretentious yet classy and luxurious hotel. Located in the heart of Ipanema beach life, it offers everything you'd expect from a top-class hotel on the beach. The rooms are comfortable and distinctively designed. Many have an enclosed sunporch with floor-to-ceiling windows that provide excellent views. Black-and-white marble adorns the bathroom. The smart décor, based on deeply stained wood trim, complements the range of styles — from a modern crisp look, to soft relaxing earth tones.

Service on the sand is an option for guests who choose to hit Ipanema beach just across from the hotel, where you'll have the option to use the fabulously comfortable Caesar Park beach chairs and umbrellas. Beyond the breakfast area on the top floor is a relatively spacious sundeck with a small wading pool, perfect for a splash to cool off. The surrounding tables welcome hotel guests and tourists off the street for a meal with a view of the beach and the mountains. Just above the restaurant is a fully stocked fitness center, which, like the restaurant, has a fantastic view (quite a bonus for a fitness center). On the deck or anywhere else in the hotel, you will be treated like a king or queen, eat very, very well, but pay through the nose for even the slightest item.

Everest Rio Hotel, 1117 Rua Prudente de Morais, Ipanema, Rio de Janeiro, RJ, Brazil. ℭ 55-21-2525-2200, ✆ 55-21-2521-3198, 🖳 www.everest.com.br, everest@everest.com.br

💲 **Pricey** and up 🍴 **EP** ℂℂ 156 rooms

Although it doesn't provide the mountain of service or class you'd expect from the name, the Everest Rio Hotel does offer a complete package of comfort, good service, location, and options for food. This is the only hotel we found where you can have sushi in the lobby while waiting for your tour guide to arrive. All the rooms are of interesting, random designs. In one room the bed cover is a mesh of rainbow colors organized in vertical lines that run the length of the bed, which is backed up against a fake wooden headboard—all located under a framed print of a pointillist style from Europe's impressionist era. (Not recommended for a hangover!) Fortunately, cable TV and Internet access will keep you occupied as you nurse yourself back to health. Safes are standard in all rooms. The deluxe option offers a queen-size bed, and the executive option comes with a view of Ipanema Beach, a king-size bed, and a spacious living room area.

The rooftop restaurant is well decorated, with tables in both the sun and the shade. The pool is larger than most in this town and bordered by fake grass, which is nice for avoiding slipping, but we can't figure out why there is a concrete block covering a third of the sundeck. Otherwise, we were content with the Everest brand. It might not stand up to what the name implies, but a combination of good service and well-priced rooms might be hard to beat in Ipanema.

⭑ **Visconti Residence**, 1050 Rua Prudente de Morais, Ipanema, Rio de Janeiro, RJ, Brazil. ℭ 55-21-2111-8600, ✆ 55-21-2247-1099, 🖳 www.promenade.com.br/visconti/index.asp, visconti@terra.com.br

💲 **Pricey** and up 🍴 **BP** ℂℂ 48 rooms

We love this hotel; and we were told that guests who have previously stayed at Caesar Park don't ever go back after spending a night or two at the Visconti. Located just a block off the

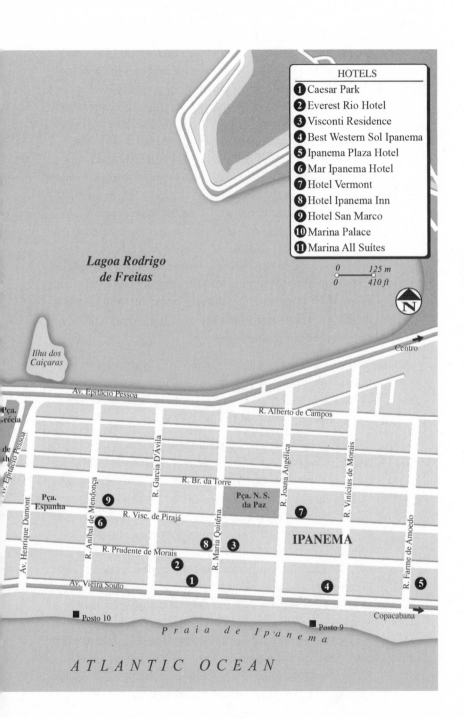

HOTELS

1. Caesar Park
2. Everest Rio Hotel
3. Visconti Residence
4. Best Western Sol Ipanema
5. Ipanema Plaza Hotel
6. Mar Ipanema Hotel
7. Hotel Vermont
8. Hotel Ipanema Inn
9. Hotel San Marco
10. Marina Palace
11. Marina All Suítes

Lagoa Rodrigo de Freitas

| 0 | 125 m |
| 0 | 410 ft |

N

Centro

Ilha dos Caiçaras

Av. Epitácio Pessoa

R. Alberto de Campos

Pça. récia

de ih

Av. Epitácio Pessoa

R. Garcia D'Ávila

R. Br. da Torre

R. Joana Angélica

R. Vinícius de Morais

Pça. Espanha

R. Aníbal de Mendonça

R. Visc. de Pirajá

Pça. N. S. da Paz

Av. Henrique Dumont

R. Prudente de Morais

R. Maria Quitéria

IPANEMA

R. Farme de Amoedo

Av. Vieira Souto

Posto 10

Posto 9

Copacabana

Praia de Ipanema

ATLANTIC OCEAN

beach, this hotel offers all the class and service, with only a little less luxury, and a very attractive and stylish staff. More than half the clients are in Rio on a business trip, so the hotel is very much oriented toward accommodating tailored suits, wing tips, and high heels. The rooms are decorated with seemingly expensive mahogany paneling and black leather couches and chairs—some of the most comfortable hotel furniture we've encountered. The apartments are very spacious, with a small balcony and a large-screen TV. Cable TV is now standard. Some rooms come with Internet access, and Wi-Fi is available in the lobby. A minikitchen is perhaps enough to pull together a quick breakfast, but little more. The subdued decoration is easy on the eyes and embodies relaxation, perfect after a long day of running around the center of town trying to get work done in a city made for play. Instead of a pool there's a Jacuzzi big enough for six to eight people, ideal for late-night negotiations!

Arpoador Inn, 177 Rua Francisco Otaviano, Ipanema, Rio de Janeiro, RJ, Brazil. ℭ 55-21-2523-0060, 55-21-2511-5094, 🖳 www.arpoadorinn.com.br, reservas@arpoadorinn.com.br

🧳 **Not So Cheap** and up 🍴 **CP** ℂℂ 50 rooms

Backed up to the beach, this traditional backpacker haven has attracted traveling crunchers from all over the world since 1974, but the hotel management has recently taken a more serious approach to attracting families and even business clients. Hence, daily rates have increased a bit. The rooms are still nothing special but cover all necessities. Cable TV is now standard, and you no longer have to ask the reception to turn on your a/c. The decoration is reminiscent of a Motel 6 or a Comfort Inn that you might find along a major highway in the United States—plain-Jane plaid designs on Herculon. There are private bathrooms with sliding glass doors on the shower, so at least it's a notch above those slimy and cheap shower curtains that stick to wet skin—a nice touch. We must admit that, for the location, you probably can't beat the price. You'll see what we mean if you walk out the back door, past the bright blue bar on the right, through the restaurant, and look upon the sands of Ipanema, just up from Arpoador rock. Book *well* in advance.

(★) **Best Western Sol Ipanema**, 320 Avenida Vieira Souto, Ipanema, Rio de Janeiro, RJ, Brazil. (✆) 55-21-2525-2020, (🖂) 55-21-2247-8484, (🖳) www.solipanema.com.br, hotel@solipanema.com.br

(💲) **Not So Cheap** and up (🍴) **BP** (CC) 90 rooms

The Sol Ipanema is one of the best-priced hotels in Rio de Janeiro — all other beachfront hotels are at least 20 percent more expensive. With lower pricing, however, comes less style, worn-out furniture, and less service than at other beachfront hotels. The hotel gave its reception area and lobby a recent overhaul, but in our opinion more is required because the place is getting on in years. For the price, the rooms are comfortable though somewhat cramped — sidestepping is necessary to pass between the bed and the chest of drawers. The walls are painfully white and could use some decorative art to break up the sterile effect. The beds are hard enough to give back support yet soft enough to allow for plenty of romper-room activity without significant bruising. The staff is very friendly, but don't expect anyone other than the reception staff to speak English. One of this hotel's best attributes is the rooftop sundeck and pool. What a view! Unfortunately, it's small, so we recommend that you get up there early to grab the one table or one of the four lounge chairs available.

(★) **Ipanema Plaza Hotel**, 34 Farme de Amoedo, Ipanema, Rio de Janeiro, RJ, Brazil. (✆) 55-21-3687-2000, (🖂) 55-21-3687-2001, (🖳) www.ipanemaplazahotel.com.br, reservas@ipanemaplazahotel.com.br

(💲) **Not So Cheap** and up (🍴) **CP** (CC) 140 rooms

This is our second favorite hotel in Ipanema. We were immediately drawn to the rooftop deck, where the poolside lounging is a perfect place to begin and end your day. The night lighting is especially relaxing. All rooms have an airy, open feel and are designed mostly with light colors and Rio's usual minimalist

style that, in the case of this hotel, was clearly put into practice in the details of the pillowcases and other bedding, bathroom decoration, color combination, and expensive furniture.
The recently added Ipanema Floor is especially interesting. We
recommend that you look into the Vista Mar Ipanema rooms,
complete with flat-screen TV, Wi-Fi, personalized room service (we're not sure about *how* personal that gets), and an ocean
view. The standard rooms come with the usual: cable TV, Internet, a safe, and room service. The suites have a DVD player
and a hydro-massage feature installed in the bathroom. The
hotel's Asian-fusion restaurant has recently expanded its
deck area for seating along both Prudente de Moraes and
Farme de Amoedo—perfect for watching some of Rio's
beautiful people as they walk by on their way to the sand. For
the gay crowd, this is *the* hotel for your Rio experience. The
staff is gay-friendly and is exceptionally plugged-in to the latest GLS (Gay, Lesbian, and *Simpatizantes*—"sympathizers" or
"friends") parties, both public and private.

Mar Ipanema Hotel, 539 Visconde de Pirajá, Ipanema, Rio de
Janeiro, RJ, Brazil. © 55-21-3875-9190, ✆ 55-21-2511-4038,
🖥 www.maripanema.com, maripanema@maripanema.com
💲 **Not So Cheap** and up 🍴 **EP** (CC) 77 rooms

The Mar Ipanema is located on the neighborhood's busiest
street, Visconde de Pirajá, right in the middle of everything.
Here you are two blocks from the beach and four from Lagoa,
an ideal location for easy access to anything in Leblon, Ipanema, or the Lagoa district. The rooms are tight but comfy, but
they are decorated with dull browns and whites that might
have been pulled off the set of *That '70s Show*. They could use
an upgrade. The bed is hard, and the management should
change the old curtains; a lack of sunlight in the rooms could
be the cause of a slight odor of mold. There is no view, so
you're paying for location, and it appears to us that this location is why the hotel does not offer any extra services. You'll
find only antennae and exhaust pipes on the roof—no deck,
to speak of.

Fortunately, a recent upgrade to the restaurant area has made this hotel a happenin' spot once again. The beer brewery chain Devassa has replaced the hotel's former restaurant. Now the lobby and restaurant area is one of the hippest spots in Ipanema for a late-afternoon or early-evening meeting for a beer or two after the beach. Rumors of Rio's rich and famous showing up to see what all the talk is about has spurred on an already vibrant evening crowd that, since Devassa's inauguration, has kept the brewery open late on most nights.

Hotel Vermont, 254 Visconde de Pirajá, Ipanema, Rio de Janeiro, RJ, Brazil. ℂ 55-21-3202-5500, ✆ 55-21-2267-7046, ▣ www.hotelvermont.com.br, reservas@hotelvermont.com.br

💲 **Cheap** and up ⑪ **CP** ⒞Ⓒ 84 rooms

A step up from the Hotel San Marco (listed below), the Vermont caters mostly to families traveling from Europe and the United States because it is in one of the safest parts of town. Yes, there are children, babies, and toddlers running around, banging into kneecaps everywhere. Although it is a family-focused atmosphere, the hotel is situated in what we consider to be the second best location (the best being the Ipanema Plaza) for Ipanema's gay-focused areas, which extend from Farme de Amoedo to the sand.

The childproof rooms come with all amenities, but the hues of brown and fake wood paneling reminded us that you get what you pay for. The beds are somewhat comfortable, even if a little soft and lumpy. We were pleasantly surprised to learn that the scratchy old sheets have finally been replaced with 180-count cotton sheets — not ideal, but a considerable upgrade. The rooms on the front end of the hotel are no longer as noisy as they used to be (although earplugs are still recommended), because the hotel has installed double-paned windows. You'll wake up earlier than you want to, but roll over and go back to sleep, because breakfast is served until midday. The hotel has supposedly installed broadband Internet in some rooms and claims Wi-Fi access in the lobby, but we couldn't get a signal. Cable television (yes, the unattractive kind that hangs off the wall), a minibar, a safe, and a/c are all now standard. The prices have gone up only slightly, so you're still getting what you paid for.

Hotel Ipanema Inn, 27 Rua Maria Quitéria, Ipanema, Rio de Janeiro, RJ, Brazil. 🕐 55-21-2523-6092, 🖂 55-21-2511-5094, 💻 www.riodejaneiroguide.com/hotel/ipanema_inn.htm, arpoador@unisys.com.br

💲 **Dirt Cheap** and up 🍴 **BP** ⓒⒸ 56 rooms

The Hotel Ipanema Inn is the cheapest hotel with such close proximity to the beach. Walk out the front door, turn right, and you're less than a block from Ipanema Beach. If you're on a budget, this place is excellent. Students and crunchers from all over the world claim this hotel as their home during their stay in Rio. The lobby offers Internet connection, and the restaurant sells only snacks; full meals should be found elsewhere (although the clientele is amazingly adept at running on snacks alone). The rooms are clean and simple with a dank brown décor; they are also small. The carpeted floor is yet another shade of brown, worn thin, and should be replaced. (We realize this is a budget deal, but c'mon!) The single beds are short and narrow, so we suggest you opt for a queen-size bed if you're wide or more than 6 feet tall. The rooms at the front of the hotel tend to be a little noisier than those in the back, but they have a decent view if you stick your head out the window. Bathrooms are all white tile, with a thin marble counter surrounding the small sink, and the shower has a sliding glass door. There's even a telephone by the toilet—in case of emergency.

Hotel San Marco, 524 Visconde de Pirajá, Ipanema, Rio de Janeiro, RJ, Brazil. 🕐 55-21-2540-5032, 🖂 55-21-2239-2654, 💻 www.sanmarcohotel.net, email@sanmarcohotel.net

💲 **Dirt Cheap** and up 🍴 **CP** ⓒⒸ 56 rooms

San Marco has been hosting young travelers since 1962. The rooms are simple, covering all the necessities. They even have a table and chairs, not a normal sight in Rio hotels. Don't expect satin and lace (we're guessing that the bedsheet thread count probably doesn't top 100), but you can't beat the price for such a good location. In some ways, we see the San Marco as basically a hostel with more comfort and privacy than you would normally expect in such a cheap place. Book well in advance to reserve a slot, and expect to see unshaven backpackers and smell body odor—à la Europe.

Leblon

Marina Palace, 630 Avenida Delfim Moreira, Praia do Leblon, Rio de Janeiro, RJ, Brazil. ℰ 55-21-2172-1001, 🖄 55-21-2172-1010, 🖳 www.hoteismarina.com.br, reservas@hotelmarina.com.br

🏷 **Very Pricey** and up 🍴 **EP** ⒸⒸ 150 rooms

The Palace is supposedly a highly polished counterpart to the Marina All Suites (listed below), but we're not convinced. Rooms for two or three guests are spacious and comfortable, with catchy designs and spectacular views, although there are no verandas. Beds, tables, and chairs all have a modern style but are still reminiscent of a Comfort Inn or a Motel 6, with old carpets and outdated orange formica tables. The paintings match the linens, and the windows offer a wide view of the beach—perhaps a saving grace. As at the All Suites, there is an infinity pool on the top floor, a sauna, and a training room. Many movie stars, including, most recently, Arnold Schwarzenegger (actually, is he still a movie star?), have stayed here for *Carnaval*. Despite some of its shortcomings, we'll accept that this hotel is a decent option for those looking for Leblon living and the quintessential Rio beach-life experience.

Marina All Suites, 696 Avenida Delfim Moreira, Praia do Leblon, Rio de Janeiro, RJ, Brazil. ℰ 55-21-2172-1100, 🖄 55-21-2172-1110, 🖳 www.hoteismarina.com.br, reservas@hotelmarina.com.br

🏷 **Not So Cheap** and up 🍴 **EP** ⒸⒸ 38 rooms

One of Rio's best hotels, the Marina All Suites offers 38 suites, 6 of which are designed by accomplished *carioca* architects. Each suite is a home away from home. A stereo and a large-screen TV occupy the living room, which doubles as a guest room or child's room. The kitchen covers all the basics, except for a stove. The master bedroom is luxurious and spacious, and the bed itself is larger than life—perhaps one of the biggest hotel beds in town. Despite this luxury, the décor is rather homely—hues of red, brown, and goldenrod are woven together in a plaid bed cover and on the wallpaper. Don't expect modern decorations, but there is excellent service. There is an infinity pool on the roof with a view of nearly all of Leblon and Ipanema Beach. A sauna and training room are just down the hall from the pool. The second-story restaurant has fine dining, also with an excellent view. Breakfast is served until 2 p.m., an important detail considering that most guests don't get home until the morning hours. Book well in advance.

Sheraton Rio Hotel & Resort, 121 Avenida Niemeyer, Leblon, Rio de Janeiro, RJ, Brazil. ℭ 55-21-2274-1122, 🖳 www.sheraton-rio.com.br, reservas.rio@sheraton.com

💼 **Not So Cheap** and up ⑪ **CP** Ⓒ 559 rooms

The Sheraton Hotel sits on the far edge of Leblon and appears to be located much closer to a local slum than it really is. Once you've entered the front breezeway, you'll forget that you were ever near a pocket of poverty. This megasize complex was recently voted the best hotel in the city by a regional business magazine—not bad, but we generally don't rely on business magazines for travel advice. Thus, it wouldn't surprise you that we find it to be a bit too corporate here. Also, we prefer to stay at a hotel that's located closer to the thick of the action on Ipanema or Leblon.

However, there is plenty to praise about the Sheraton. Anyone who visits this hotel can find almost everything right on the property. Beginning with the beach level, the hotel offers an in-house spa, a private beach with waterfront food-and-drink service, three heated pools (including a children's play pool), two lit tennis courts, beachside massage booths, a beach-side restaurant, and a poolside restaurant. The hotel's third restaurant, on the same level as the convention and meeting rooms, offers an entertaining Saturday brunch complete with live music and even more lively drinks. The rooms range from standard to presidential suite, but all come with a private balcony, 24-hour room service, some of the most comfortable beds in the business, and a kids program, especially designed to entertain the younger generation while the parents have a night out on the town.

For a prolonged stay in Rio de Janeiro, the Sheraton will work for families and business travelers who want everything in one spot and don't care about easy access to all the excitement that Rio has to offer. However, since the Sheraton is a bit removed from the heart of Rio's good times, we think couples would be happier in a more centrally located hotel.

Where to Eat

Any city as cosmopolitan as Rio offers a generous bounty of excellent eating spots. Suco bars will make you a natural juice drink and fast food. They are on nearly every corner and cater to the vast majority of cariocas, who always stop to have a juice sometime during the day. *Kilogramas* are restaurants that offer a buffet, and after you fill your plate, they weigh it and charge accordingly. *Churrascarias* are evening and weekend afternoon favorites because for one price they serve all the skewered meat you can eat, along with a generous buffet. Street vendors and *confeitarias* sell sweets and salty finger food called *salgados*. Of course, there are also the traditional sit-down dining experiences. In addition to our recommendations, there is a complete list of the best restaurants Rio de Janeiro has to offer in the *Restaurant Guide, Rio Show* published annually by the newspaper *O Globo*. It's Rio's version of Zagat's guide in the United States.

Centro and Lapa

$$$ **Bazzar Café**, 44 Avenida Rio Branco, Centro, 2253-1248
Originally home of the Institute of National Historic and

Artistic Heritage, Bazzar Café opened its doors in 2001 as a sexy eye-catcher on downtown's loudest street. Since then it has earned critical acclaim for its variety of contemporary cuisine, such as the *namorado* fish minicakes with plantain bananas and coconut and curry milk. The chefs must know something—they even made a gourmet hot dog sexy and popular. If you don't want to have lunch or dine, consider lounging on the patio with one of 10 different coffee-and-liqueur-based drinks, and watch the *cariocas* frenetically intertwining and bumping into one another on the main business strip in front. Open 10 a.m. to 8 p.m.; closed Saturday and Sunday.

$$ **Bistro do Paço**, 48 Praça Quinze, Centro, 2262-3613
Whereas the typical museum café serves overpriced dishes outstanding only for their mediocrity, Bistro do Paço has earned props as a stand-alone bistro with a sophisticated yet not overly ambitious menu. Although the Imperial Palace warrants its own block in your schedule, many frequent the bistro without even thinking twice about Don Pedro's declaration of independence made from the upstairs balcony (or the depressing decline of the palace, eventually becoming Rio's central post office). This all goes to say that, for some, the food is good enough to forget the history. Open 11:30 a.m. to 7:30 p.m., Monday through Friday, and noon to 7 p.m. on the weekend.

$$$ **Café Colombo**, 32 Rua Gonçalves Dias, Centro, 2232-2300
The doors of this historic café opened in 1894. It has offered good food, excellent service, and an impressive atmosphere ever since. Huge antique mirrors hang on all three walls of the main dining area and add to the larger-than-life antique decorations crowned by a stained-glass skylight. Sit on the second-story balcony to people-watch from above while eating lunch, drop in for a sweet-tooth snack, or simply stop by for a quick coffee and a look-see while rolling around the center of town. It's worth your time. Open weekdays and Saturday from 9 a.m. to 5 p.m. On Sunday, only the bottom half of the café is open, from 10 a.m. to 8 p.m.

$$$$ **Eça**, 128 Avenida Rio Branco, Centro, 2524-2401
Named after a Portuguese writer who was a great lover of wine
and fine foods, this restaurant excels in refinement, not only
for its award-winning dishes but also for its environment. Eça
is discreetly located like a pearl under one of the world-famous
H. Stern jewelry stores downtown. Although Belgium-born
chef Frédéric De Maeyer created a menu with modern recipes
and a French flair, Brazilian elements have increasingly added
an additional flavor to the mix. Polished mahogany tables contrast with elegant white curtains, and a wall displays well-
known phrases and passages from Eça's novels. It's an
environment that thrives on the rare harmony between cultural heritage and modern sophistication. Enjoy a delicious
meal, buy a diamond, and go to the nearest bookstore for an
Eça novel. Open only from noon to 4 p.m., Monday through
Friday.

$$ **Nova Capela**, 96 Avenida de Sá, Lapa, 2252-6228
During most of its 100 or more years of history, Nova Capela
has been the popular nightcap of the coolest *carioca* crowd
around—*sambistas*, intellectuals, rich *sophisticos*, two-cent
Lapa bohemians, and anyone else on the vanguard of *carioca*
culture. When you enter, take in a lungful of second-hand
smoke and instantly transport yourself into a Ruben Fonseca
passage. Black-and-white checkered floors balance an array of
pictures that highlight key cultural icons. If you're really in the
last chugs of your evening, order a Portuguese Porto wine or
a Brahma draft beer with a *bolinho de bacalhau*—a small, fried
ball of Portuguese codfish. Put a little pepper and olive oil on
your *bolinho*, sip your beer, and look into either the eyes of your
companion or those of the personalities on the wall. Open 11
a.m. to 5 a.m., all week.

Santa Teresa

$$$$ **Aprazível**, 62 Rua Aprazível, Santa Teresa, 3852-4935
When Chef Ana Castilho opened her house for a community
event in the mid-1990s, she had no idea that her hilltop home
would eventually become one of the best Brazilian cuisine

establishments in town. With nighttime views of sparkling Guanabara Bay and the downtown buildings, and with outdoor dining tables interspersed among Atlantic rainforest trees, her home became a romantic and charming favorite among Santa Teresa and *carioca* socialites. There's something uniquely magical about dining here. Dishes such as pumpkin cream soup with prawns, tart apple and cream, and the entree *peixe tropical* (grilled fish in an orange sauce, coconut rice, and baked bananas) are flavorful and refined. Dining in candlelight, you're bound to fall in love with someone. This is a must-see and do, even if you're not interested in Santa Teresa. Taxi is the only way in and out, and drivers often get lost, so take the restaurant's number with you in case the driver needs to get directions. About 15 minutes before you're ready to ask for the check, ask for a cab. That way, when you're making your way out, the taxi will already be waiting. Open Thursday to Saturday from noon to 1 a.m. and Sunday from noon to 11:30 p.m.

$$$ **Espírito Santa**, 264 Rua Almirante Alexandrino, Largo dos Guimarães, Santa Teresa, 2508-7095
Two years ago, the stylish Espírito Santa ("Spirit of Santa [Teresa]") opened and exposed locals to Amazonian dishes that even *cariocas* found exotic. With their Portuguese roots, *cariocas* love fish. But what about piranha soup? And what about tacacá — a *mandioca* root, shrimp, and leafy jambu soup, so indigenous that it tingles your mouth? For the true Santa Teresa experience, take the *bondinho* ("tram" or "trolley") and jump right off at the restaurant's entrance. And don't forget the balcony out back. Try a passion fruit *caipirinha* and bask in the view of the famous old Rio houses in the valley. Open Monday to Wednesday from 11:30 a.m. to 6 p.m., Thursday to Saturday from 11:30 a.m. to midnight, and Sunday from 11:30 a.m. to 7 p.m.

$$ **Sobrenatural**, 432 Rua Almirante Alexandrino, Santa Teresa, 2224-1003
Popularity is a double-edged sword. Sobrenatural is a hotbed for lovers of samba, *caipirinhas*, and seafood. The *moqueca* (seafood stew with fish of your choice) comes with coconut

milk, palm oil, shrimp sauce (your call), and rice. It's a meal like none you've ever experienced—rich in flavor, history, and cultural context that's completely Brazilian. The popularity of this dish keeps locals coming back all the time. The spacious seating area gets tight as the night goes on, and energetic Brazilians turn this part of the restaurant into an ad-hoc dance club. Loud talking, singing, and guffawing ensue. It's a magnet that stands the test of time. Open Sunday to Thursday from 11:30 a.m. to 11 p.m., and until 1 a.m. on the weekend.

Copacabana

$$ **Amir**, 55 Rua Ronald de Carvalho, Loja C, Copacabana, 2275-5596
Rio's Arabian or Middle Eastern food options are practically nonexistent. So when we found a gem like Amir, one that has won Best Arabian Food Restaurant in Rio for the last four years, we went early and stayed late. Deep red walls complement doorways and walls adorned with the intricately detailed wooden arcs. We loved the strong scent of spices and herbs that greeted us upon entry, and we were equally happy to find that the couples' servings were enough for three or maybe four people—what a great deal. Until *O Globo* puts out another soap opera with an Arabian theme to spark *carioca* interest, it might be awhile before Amir has any serious competition. Expect all the usual Arabian fare for a decent price. Open Monday from 6 p.m. to midnight, and all other days from noon to midnight.

$$ **Armazém da Carioca**, 31 Avenida Nossa Senhora de Copacabana, Loja B, Copacabana, 2275-4049
Yet another stylish refuge in the seediness of Copacabana's street urchin catwalk, this restaurant pays homage to the upbeat renaissance spirit of the 1950s, with maple wood chairs covered in satin and art deco–inspired lamps. This modernist edge spits in the eye of the local *botecos* ("taverns") stuck on the heavy Brazilian staple diet. Here you've actually got options. (Celebrate, vegetarians! No more Margarita pizzas for lunch and dinner every day!) You'll find light entrée options such as

grilled eggplant marinated in a fine herb sauce, and for the traditional meat lovers, the juicy barbecued hamburger, with enough gusto to raise an eyebrow or two at the carnivore-only establishments everywhere else. Go on Monday because you'll get an added twist — the Levianas, an all-female band, will be up at the mike. Open 5 p.m. to 3 a.m., Monday through Saturday; closed Sunday.

$$ **Café do Forte**, 1 Praça Coronel Eugenio Franco, Copacabana, 2521-1032

Colombo operates a café out of a small corner of the Copacabana Fort, a working military base in Rio. Passing through the front gates of Fort Copacabana, visitors must purchase a R$2 pass to enter the tourist area, off to the left and past the honor guard. The café itself offers excellent seating with views overlooking a nearby stretch of Copacabana Beach. There are few places in the city where one can sit in the shade with a view of Rio's famous skyline while listening to the waves and dining on such well-prepared salads, sandwiches, and finger foods. This café is ideal for a lazy lunch during the week, when there is a greater chance for a smooth entry. On weekends and holidays this spot fills quickly, so expect a longer wait for one of the coveted seaside tables. After your meal, take a moment to walk deeper into the fort and up the steps onto the cannon rampart. The view is spectacular.

$ **Cervantes**, 335 Avenida Prado Junior, Loja B, Copacabana, 2275-6147

Fifty years ago, the owners of Cervantes had no clue that their sandwich stint to gain a few extra bucks at their food mart would evolve into the best sandwich joint (voted for years on end) in Zona Sul. Real perfection only came later, when the more recent Spanish owners turned the original experiment into a labor of love. Walk in, and perhaps the first thing you will notice is how many times you trip over the legs of different chairs. Yes, the place is hoppin', and every inch serves the eager eater in some way. Paper sheets sloppily adorn the tabletops, but for good reason — *chopp* ("draft beer") flows and overflows.

Hopefully you won't be too trashed to treasure the unique soft and crispy bread on your sandwich (although we doubt that you'll overlook the zing of the pineapple, the house trademark). Mind you, this is no lame luncheonette's *sanduiche natural* that you would find on any corner—this is a sandwich lover's pleasure dome. Peruse the odd circus on the beachside after midnight, and then, even if you're still alone, drop by Cervantes before hitting the sack. Open noon to 4 a.m., Monday through Thursday, noon to 6 p.m. on Friday and Saturday, and noon to 3 p.m. on Sunday.

$$$$ **Lê Pré Catelan**, 4240 Avenida Atlântica (level E in Hotel Sofitel), Copacabana, 2525-1160

After a radical facelift, Lê Pré Catelan dropped its art nouveau design for a much more contemporary vibe. With a bill teetering at $1 million, the interior design was flooded by linear shapes, an emphasis on contrast with white and black coloring, and elegant lamps with various colors and tones, all of which opens up to a spectacular view of the sea off Copacabana Beach. Fine French cuisine is still the word, but with some twists in recipes and presentations. Yet another award winner on our list, the restaurant is hard to pass. Check out the insanely popular R$140 deal (appetizer, main dish, and dessert), which is ordered by 80 percent of the diners. It's stylish, romantic, and serves delicious food—this place is a dater's paradise. Open 7 p.m. to midnight, all week.

$ **O Caranguejo**, 771 Rua Barata Ribeiro (corner of Xavier da Silveira), Copacabana, 2235-1249

Copacabana is best known for its wacky mixture of residents and visitors and for a sense of informality (or, better said, *vagabundagem!*). These traits often lead some to think that any food establishment not set within ebony walls will give you a night of lovin' with your local commode. Don't be fooled! At first glance, O Caranguejo seems as busy and grimy as a bus station bar, with a jumbling of Brazilians from all walks of life. Get past the faded-out chalk daily specials announcements and the weathered wood-post barrier separating the diners from the sidewalk, and you'll see that there's nothing to fear. In fact, these *empada* (a stuffed meat pastry) lovers spill out onto the sidewalk and stand at the bar with mouths watering for the next round. The shrimp *empada* is the local favorite and just melts in your mouth. Oh, don't bite too hard, though, because the small olive inside is far from pitless. No point in cutting your *empada* marathon after the first bite. The beer will flow, the orders will zip, and you'll leave without feeling guilty because it's cheap as hell. Inside you'll find many seafood dishes that are also loved by the locals. Open Tuesday through Sunday, 8 a.m. to 2 a.m. (start and end your day here!)

$$$ **Siri Mole**, 50 Rua Francisco Otaviano, Copacabana, 2267-0894
Serving a rich dose of award-winning Bahian cuisine, Siri Mole is a home away from home for Brazilian Northeasterners. You might find, however, that overdosing on the menu is quick and easy. Acarajé and the various spicy *moquecas* will keep your belly burning. If you're going to try Bahian dishes, do it safely in a restaurant known for quality; avoid the sidewalk-based rotund ladies wrapped in white sheets and frying God-knows-what in two-month-old cooking oil and calling it "Acarajé *auténtico*." These food experiments are best for biology students hungry for bacteria farms. Enjoy Bahian culinary culture from those who really know what they're doing. Open noon to midnight, Tuesday to Sunday, and 7 p.m. to midnight on Monday.

Ipanema

$ **Armazém do Café**, 77 Rua Maria Quitéria, Ipanema, 2522-5039
This chain of several cafés between the city's center and Barra da Tijuca is perhaps the only café chain in Rio where you can get any coffee drink you want. Voted the best espresso in 2007, the coffee here continues to be our favorite in the city for an afternoon *cafezinho* ("little cup of coffee"). The small tables and chairs are not too comfortable, so don't expect to hang out too long in the tightly arranged seating area. Some of the cafés are so small that there are no tables or chairs—bar-side sipping

Beachfront Kiosks

In the last two years, a whole new breed of upscale kiosks has sprouted, providing a musical chairs alternative along the beach to the larger restaurant one-stop shops on the city side of Avenida Atlântica. Its reputable cuisine ranges from regional to international. You can make your way down the undulating sidewalk design (shown on the cover of this book) for a fast drink or a sit-down dining experience. Perhaps the most exciting delicacy to devour is the eye candy strutting along in the glowing dim of the sunset! We suggest either starting or ending your walk with **Cachaçaria Manga Rosa** near Rua Figueiredo Magalhães. Sip or slurp one or many of the award-winning *cachaças* (R$5 to R$12) from Minas Gerais, and then gracefully pick up and move on to dine, snack, or full-on booze it up—Brahma beer now has its own well-deserved kiosk! If you plan to party afterward, you might want to start here and then make your way in the direction of Help or some of the other Copacabana nightspots. There is also a variety of seafood and Bahian dishes from **Vivenda do Camarão** (shrimp, shrimp, and more shrimp, R$14), **Bar and Champainheria Copacabana** (succulent fish plates with fun names like "Ele é Carioca," meaning "He's a Carioca" R$22), and the popular **Siri Mole** (crab cakes and *moqueca*, R$30 and above). If you're into grease and fatty foods (great for a hangover killer), go to the **TGI Friday's** kiosk in Leme and get a burger and then on to Bob's (the Brazilian equivalent of McDonald's) for a chocolate shake.

only. Even if you're not a café *affectionante* and don't like French café–style seating, you still might want to stop by to check out the broad sweets selection. All cafés are open daily from 9 a.m. to 6 p.m. Cash is preferred, but credit cards are accepted. See www.armazemdocafe.com.br for other locations.

$$ **Barril 1800**, 110 Avenida Vieira Souto, Ipanema, 2523-0085
This major tourist hangout overlooks Ipanema Beach, just down from the Arpoador rock, serves ice cold beer, and has a decent menu. It attracts beachgoers in the afternoon who are interested in a *salgado* ("snack") or *chopp*. Drop by if you're in the area; otherwise, it's not that important—just a regular

restaurant with a nice view of the beach. Barril will accept credit cards, but with a stingy attitude. It's open from 10:30 a.m.
until 1:30 a.m.

$$$ **Bazzar**, 538 Rua Barão da Torre, Ipanema, 3202-2884
Located in a quiet residential area, this romantic restaurant is
perfect for a quiet evening dinner away from Ipanema's usu-
al fray. The minimalist yet comfortable design is well lit with
unobtrusive low-level lighting, adding to the romantic atmos-
phere. No smoking is allowed inside, so many would-be smok-
ers often choose the front deck seating. The high ceiling in the
front dining area complements the floor-to-ceiling window,
giving the area an open, airy feel. We liked the black marble
bar. The lower ceiling toward the back, next to an interior gar-
den, is perhaps the most romantic setting, unless you'd pre-
fer a candlelit table on the deck. Try the corn crème and goat
cheese soup or the lamb with Indian curry dish. The wine
selection is worth mentioning, and so are the desserts. We
found the service above par for Rio. Open all week from mid-
day to 1 a.m.

$$ ⊛ **Brasileirinho**, 1 Rua Jangadeiros, Ipanema, 2513-5184
Owned by a *mineiro* (someone from the state of Minas
Gerais), this restaurant specializes in food from that state and
the typical Brazilian *feijoada*—a complete, multicourse meal
of beans cooked with meat, alongside or on top of rice with
greens, and a shot of *cachaça*, for two, four, or six people. Situated right on the Praça General Osório and next to the Irish
Pub, this spot is an ideal complement to a Sunday afternoon
at Ipanema's Feira Hippie. Have a solid meal before you slide
next door to have a Guinness on tap. Our Mineiro friend opens
at midday and closes at midnight. He prefers cash but will take
any major credit card for a table of three or more guests.

$$ **Confeitaria Ipanema**, 325 Avenida Visconde de Pirajá,
Ipanema, 2522-6900
This popular quick-stop, everything shop caters to *cariocas* on
their way to and from work, the beach, a party, or simply on
the go. Purchase your juice, *salgado* ("snack"), or coffee at one

of the many cashiers, then take your receipt to the counter and make your order. On the weekends, this place is especially busy and full of scantly clad Brazilians taking a moment from beach time to refuel on carbos, sugar, caffeine, or starch. A recent face-lift did little more than add some gaudy decoration and replace the old and cracked trash cans that double as stand-up table tops. It's open daily from 7 a.m. to 9 p.m. No credit cards.

$$$$$ ⊛ **Fasano Al Mare** (in the Fasano Hotel), 80 Avenida Viera Souto, Ipanema, 3202-4000

If your bank account resembles that of a certain well-known Brazilian supermodel, this restaurant, inside the trendy Fasano Hotel, should make your must-dine list. If, like the rest of us, you've got a little less green than "The Body," it's still worthy of a (very) special occasion. The hottest reservation in town is brought to us by award-winning chef and restaurateur Regerio Fasano, who appointed an executive chef from a Michelin-starred restaurant in Italy to run the kitchen, which turns out Mediterrean-inspired seafood dishes highlighting local Brazilian fish and Italian branzino (a European sea bass with a white firm flake). Don't miss the lemon risotto with rock lobster or the whitefish tartare with saffron and tomato—two dishes sure to wow you.

Much like the hotel, the restaurant is done in a minimalist style: Warm, cherry Brazilian wood floors and tables are accented with beige and white linens. Service has been spotty but seems to be improving. Be sure to arrive early (or stick around after dinner) and check out the adjoining Londra bar, which has a trendy and glamorous vibe along with live music nightly. The high-priced cocktails are worth the price of admission for some serious people-watching. Open for breakfast, lunch, and dinner.

$$$ ⊛ **Felice Café**, 30 Rua Gomes Carneiro, Ipanema, 2522-7749

The Felice Café likes to think of itself as a bar and ice cream shop, but we prefer to think of it as one of our favorite restaurants in Ipanema. Simply put, you have everything you need for breakfast, lunch, and dinner, as well as excellent ice cream, cold beer, mixed drinks, and even Wi-Fi, all in one hip spot that plays decent ambient lounge music (and has great service). A surprisingly complete menu offers a number of salad choices rivaled only by Gula Gula, located on the other side of Ipanema. The fish and pasta dishes are tough to beat, and a choice of items from the grill, complete with two side dishes and a choice of sauce, makes for easy mixing and matching to form your own creation. Located just a block from the beachfront, this restaurant couldn't be in a better spot. The restaurant caters to bikini- and Speedo-clad beachgoers, a vibrant GLS (Gay, Lesbian, and Simpatizantes) crowd, and young couples looking for a spot to have a nice meal. Open Monday to Thursday from noon to 1 a.m., Friday from noon to 3 a.m., Saturday from 10 a.m. to 3 a.m., and Sunday from 10 a.m. to 1 a.m.

$$ ⊛ **Frontera**, 128 Avenida Visconde de Pirajá, Ipanema, 3289-2350

This is probably the nicest *kilograma* in Ipanema and one of the few places that offers Wi-Fi—it's quite common for tourists and *cariocas* alike to stop off for a coffee and some "surfing." As the name suggests, this restaurant offers a rotating number of dishes from Greece, France, Spain, and the Middle East. The Dutch chef, Mark Kwaks, keeps an interesting rotation of international dishes not likely found elsewhere in Rio. Sushi and a *churrasco* are in place, as well as the normal fare of juices, beer, and soft drinks. Frontera tends to get very crowded during the lunch hour and after beach hours in the summer. Tips are not included. Open Monday through Saturday from 11 a.m. to midnight, and until 11 p.m. on Sunday.

$$$ **Garota de Ipanema**, 49 Rua Vinicius de Moraes, Ipanema, 2523-3787

This restaurant attracts tourists (and locals trying to sell anything from a piece of gum to zipper bags and a little samba) like no other. The name alone should convince you why. The words to the song that made Ipanema famous, "The Girl from

Ipanema" (*Garota de Ipanema*), were written in a prior incarnation of this establishment by Vinicius de Moraes himself. (Note: Antônio Carlos Jobim composed the tune.) The food is excellent but perhaps a little overpriced. You should try the *picanha na chapa*—two rows of sliced, raw beef steaming on a hot plate. It's an indoor barbecue! Sit away from the streetside tables to avoid beggars and panhandlers Rio-style. Open 11 a.m. to 2 a.m. It accepts credit cards, but some of the older waiters will request that you tip them in cash.

$$ ⊛ **Gula Gula,** 57 Henrique Dumont, Ipanema, 2259-3084
With locations in Centro, Leblon, Barra, and Gávea, among other places, this spot, just a block off Ipanema Beach, is one of our top choices for a casual lunch break or a romantic dinner. The split-level space is a refurbished house from a time when Ipanema was mostly farmland and rural family houses. A number of atmospheres—a bright and energized front room, a wood-paneled and romantic back room seating area, and an outdoor garden spot (with a number of larger tables for small parties)—offer a range of dining experiences. The broad-ranging menu specializes in salads (14 different choices), quiches, and options off the grill. Go for the *frango ao pesto* (mixture of chicken, fusilli, and pesto) or the *batata frita* (mixture of chicken, carrots, peas, corn, and crispy fries). If you have room after filling up at Gula ("gluttony"), the *torta mousse de chocolate com sorvete* (hot chocoate mousse with ice cream) is *deliciosa*. Service can sometimes be slack, but if you take a chill pill, it's definitely worth it. Open weekdays until midnight, and until 1 a.m. on Saturday and Sunday.

$$ **Itahy**, Rua Barão de Torre, Ipanema, 2247-3356
This charming little pizzeria has open-air dining on one of Ipanema's most frequented street corners. It offers a broad menu, excellent service, and a decent *chopp*. Historical pictures of Rio adorn the walls, and, as in most bars and restaurants in Rio, you can order a bottle of liquor and drink as much as you want at the table. The bottle is marked with graduated measurements to indicate your consumption and, hence, the

price. For some reason, Itahy is a top choice for hard-liquor drinkers. Order cheesy rice, a steak, pizza, or your own personal tableside grill. The food is always good, and the price is right. Cash is preferred, but credit cards are accepted with a disgruntled "hrumph."

$$ **Kilograma**, 644 Avenida Visconde de Pirajá, Ipanema, 2512-8220
As the name itself might suggest, Kilograma is one of the ultimates in *kilograma*-style restaurants, combining a sushi bar, *churrascaria*, and an impressive buffet to offer one-stop shopping for any type of meal you can pull together. A long list of mixed drinks, *sucos* ("juices"), beer, wine, and liqueur and an ample dessert bar pull together a full dining experience that you will not easily find elsewhere. *Kilograma* restaurants in both Ipanema and Copacabana serve regulars and local families one, two, and sometimes three nights (or days) a week. It's open daily from 11 a.m. to 11 p.m.

$$ **Mistura Fina**, 769 Rua Rainha Elizabeth, Ipanema, 2523-1703
Having left its old location in Lagoa, and now in a new, more spacious house overlooking the beach just down the road from General Osório Park, Mistura Fina continues its age-old tradition of blending a restaurant with a piano bar and space for live music. Scheduled performers keep it alive with evening shows that range from jazz and bossa nova to old school singers who reminisce about the days of Tom Jobim. The laid-back atmosphere is one of the city's best spots in which to enjoy Rio's slower rhythms while sipping on your favorite whiskey. This place attracts an older crowd, but the music is timeless. Open daily from 6 p.m. until the last person leaves. It has live shows every Friday and Saturday. Cash is preferred; only American Express is accepted.

$$ **New Natural**, 173 Rua Barão da Torre, Ipanema, 2287-0301
We continue to love this *kilograma* restaurant, which for years has been a favorite of vegetarian *cariocas*. It's located off the main drag and attracts a local crowd of regulars with a robust lunch crowd. The excellent food is light and prepared

Rio's Fruit and Natural Juices

Brazil is world renowned for wild, random fruit; some you've seen at your local market, others you've never heard of. Since Rio de Janeiro is perhaps one of the top cities in the world for experimenting with fruit and fruit juices, you're in a great position to try new flavors that you won't find elsewhere. From corner juice bars to a wide range of natural juice offerings at many restaurants, there are a number of places that give you the option to zing your palate. You just have to know how to ask.

For a vitamin C boost, try *acerola* with orange juice. Acerola is a small red berry about the size of a cherry that has 20 times the amount of vitamin C per berry than your average Florida orange. For less acid and to put more "smooth" in your smoothie, try acerola with strawberries. Another mixture we like, with orange juice, is pineapple — **abacaxi** (aba-ka-SHE). Peppermint with pineapple is another common juice among *cariocas*.

Cajú, the fruit that grows with the cashew nut, has a very sharp taste and smell. It is rich in vitamins A, B, and C. Alone, the juice can be slightly thick and pulpy on the tongue, which leaves a residue on your teeth, so we like to mix it with orange juice or mango juice. Mango also goes well with mint leaves, creating a creamy, slightly green drink that definitely looks worse than it tastes. On a "colder" day (like, say, 80°F), many *cariocas* ask for *abacate* ("avocado") with milk, which automatically comes blended with a little sugar. It might sound like yuck, but if you like avocados and if you like milk, this hearty "meal in a glass" is a great morning blast alongside your *cafezinho* ("little cup of coffee").

Another fruit that should be blended with sugar is *açaí*; otherwise it tastes like dirt. Açaí is an Amazon fruit that is rich in calories, proteins, fiber, vitamin E, and minerals. Açaí is often mixed with *guaraná*, a small red fruit normally seen in powder or liquefied form that is considered a natural energy boost. You might have seen this power-shot option in your local smoothie bar. An *açaí* shake should be eaten with a spoon and is excellent when blended with kiwi or banana.

Other fruits worth checking out include *pitanga, amora, jabuticaba, carambola,* and *fruta do conde*. The *pitanga* looks like a swollen cherry with acne. It's rich in vitamin C, calcium, phosphorous, and iron, and it's great to stop diarrhea. This is a tough fruit to find. Some people mix it with strawberries or kiwi to cut the somewhat sour

(*continued on page 98*)

(continued from page 97)

taste. The *amora* is the Brazilian version of a raspberry. It is often mixed with strawberries when prepared in "red berry" drinks. The *jabuticaba* is like a grape but sweeter, with a thicker skin and more seeds — we like to freeze them before eating. The juice is hard to find, but when you do, try mixing it with passion fruit, known in Brazil as *maracujá*. The *carambola* is Brazilian star fruit, but it is much, much bigger than what folks in the States are used to seeing. We like to mix *carambola* with orange juice or papaya and then add sugar for a sweet, thick drink. Finally, the *fruta do conde* is an ugly green thing with sweet white fruit that you suck off the seeds. It is impossible to eat this fruit without getting messy, but it's worth a try!

The best places to see these fruits and try them for free are at the rolling street markets in Ipanema. On Monday, you'll find the market along the length of Avenida Henrique Dumont, between Visconde de Pirajá and Vieira Souto. On Tuesday the market sets up in Praça General Osório, and on Friday, the market rings the outer rung of Praça Nossa Senhora da Paz and is probably the best one to visit because it attracts more fruit stands than the other three.

with health-conscious attention. A health-food store adjoining the dining area sells otherwise hard-to-find health-food products, teas, herbs, and spices. Open from 10 a.m. to 8 p.m. daily.

$$$$ **Porcão**, 298 Rua Barão Torre, Ipanema, 2522-0999
This is a top-of-the line *churrascaria* and part of a well-run chain. For about $30 you get all the food you can eat plus royal treatment from a host of waiters, attendees, hosts, and men carrying a variety of choice meat cuts on a sword. A simple *tá bom* ("OK") gets you a slice of meat. Use the provided prongs to take the meat off the sword as it's cut. Expect the service to be excellent, even if the servers are constantly in your face. Eating out at a *churrascaria* is a quintessential Brazilian experience. Porcão simply happens to be the most famous. The Ipanema establishment is frequented by Brazil's most beloved *futebol*, music, and movie stars. It opens at midday and closes at 1:30 a.m., seven days a week.

\$\$\$ **Satyricon**, 192 Barao da Torre, Ipanema, 2521-0627

Given this restaurant's close location to a hotel that caters specifically to Brazilian businessmen, we were pleasantly surprised to see that the service and food was not at the mediocre level we're accustomed to finding in some restaurants that are actually located in hotels. Even Madonna once dined here. The Mediterranean cuisine is served by bow-tied waiters who have clearly been trained by a detail-oriented perfectionist. The seafood dishes are prepared with fish caught daily and are some of the best we've had in Rio. The pastas, especially the gnocchi, are worth a repeat visit. The extensive wine list is backed up by a glass-walled wine cellar located in the middle of the dining area. Sometimes you can watch your waiter enter the cellar, select your wine, and, once you give the OK, pour it into a decanter for some airing before it's served. The tables are well spaced, lending themselves to intimate moments or sensitive business discussions. For more privacy, ask for a table in the private dining room, where for an additional service charge you have complete isolation, except for a pair of waiters who remain just out of earshot for up-to-the-second service; just lift an eyebrow. Open daily from noon to 1 a.m.

Jardim Botânico

\$\$ **Bráz**, 129 Rua Maria Angélica, Jardim Botanico, 2535-0687

This is perhaps the best spot in the city for pizza. Oven-baked pizzas made with fresh ingredients are the pride of this often packed, old-school establishment. The owner is preoccupied with two things: perfect pizzas and a packed house. Don't expect to find a table easily during peak dining hours at lunch and dinner. The close seating might also unnerve those who are not accustomed to French-style seating. The overly aggressive waitstaff might put some people off, too. Be sure to make your food order with your drinks, otherwise you might be forgotten. We recommend that you try the refreshing Basílica, with arugula pesto, cherry tomatoes, and mozzarella, or the Margherita—a well-known combination of mozzarella with basil. Open daily from 6:30 p.m. to 12:30 a.m., and until 1:30 a.m. on Friday and Saturday.

$$ **Capricciosa**, 37 Rua Maria Angélica, Jardim Botânico, 2523-3394
This restaurant has a location in Ipanema, but the Jardim Botânico spot is well known for its wine list. If you're into wine and want a good selection, this is your place. If not, don't worry about it. Drop by here for dinner after an afternoon in the Lagoa district circumnavigating the lagoon, walking in the gardens, or cruising the trails in Parque da Tijuca. Wine is served weekdays from 6 p.m. until 1 a.m. On Friday and Saturday it's served until 2 a.m. On Sunday it's available from 5 p.m. until 1 a.m.

$$$ **Quadrifoligo**, 19 Rua JJ Seabra, Jardim Botanico, 2294-1433
Owned and run by a São Paulo native—an adopted *carioca* and a daughter of Italian immigrants—this decidedly Italian restaurant has created dishes that in short time became citywide classics that have been repeated in other Italian restaurants in Ipanema, Leblon, and the Centro. But there are some dishes you won't find elsewhere in the city—or in the country, for that matter. Check out the ravioli stuffed with pears, gorgonzola cheese, and acorn sauce, or the grilled *cavaquinha* (small Brazilian lobster) served with tomato, heart of palm, a touch of ginger, and freshly steamed legumes. For dessert try the homemade cinnamon ice cream topped with strawberry slivers or the white chocolate mousse topped with passion fruit sauce. It's tough to beat! The small seating area promises personalized service but fills quickly. Arrive early for a guaranteed seat. Open daily from noon to 3:30 p.m. and from 7:30 p.m. until midnight. Lunch is served until 5 p.m., and dinner is served until 1 a.m. on Saturday and Sunday.

Lagoa

$ **Café del Lago**, Orla da Lagoa, Parque dos Patins kiosk 8, Lagoa, 2239-9005
Situated right on the lagoon with a close-up shot of the Christ statue, this little café spot treats you to some spectacular

scenery, especially in the evening. The pasta is decent, and so is the rest of the food, considering the low prices. However, it's the view that makes this spot worthwhile. The café is open from midday until midnight. No credit cards.

$$$ **66 Bistrô**, 66 Avenida Alexandre Ferreira, Lagoa, 2266-0838

Long leather couches, flowing curtains, and low lighting create a laid-back atmosphere that exudes confidence in the food served here. Run by a fourth-generation chef, this family-owned restaurant serves plates reminiscent of a French bistro, but with a specific Brazilian flare. Some of the most requested dishes include escargot, steak tartar, and the daily catch served with the chef's white sauce and basmati rice. A complete wine list complements an aggressive menu — aggressive according to Gabriel o Pensador, that is, a famous Brazilian rap artist who eats here when he's in town. Star spotting is a regular occurrence here, but you're more likely to find a great meal in a part of town you might otherwise not have a chance to visit. Open Tuesday to Sunday from midday to 4 p.m. and Saturday and Sunday from 7:30 p.m. to 12:30 a.m.; lunch until 6 p.m.; closed Monday.

$$$ **Yasuto Tanaka**, 1210 Epitacio Pessoa, Lagoa, 2522-9006

Named for the city's most celebrated sushi chef, this Japanese restaurant offers more than excellent food. Views of the lagoon and the Christ statue in the distance can be had from most tables, and the service is excellent. Shrimp tempura is worth an order. For the risk taker in you, try the Tanaka Combination — an eclectic selection created by the man himself. For sashimi lovers, this is your place. The sophisticated look and feel of this restaurant can be felt from the moment a bow-tied gentleman opens the door at the stretched awning covering the entrance stairway and the interior. For a well-heeled night of Japanese cuisine, splendid views, and pampered treatment, Tanaka's restaurant is at the top of the list. Tanaka keeps a long list of Japanese-imported saki. Even the Brazilian saki might be made by the Japanese, too — after all, Brazil has the largest

Japanese population outside Japan. Open daily from 6 p.m. to 12:30 a.m. and on Friday and Saturday from midday.

Leblon

$ **Bibi Sucos,** 591 Avenida Ataulfo de Paiva, Leblon, 2259-4298
Yet another juice bar. It is just as cheap as any other, but you might enjoy the Leblon surroundings better than many of the ragged Copacabana sidewalk *suco* bars. Expect it to be always full, and don't wait to make eye contact to put in your order. Pushing and shouting, not polite patience, will get you a drink here. After 3 p.m. this place is packed with dozens of teenage Leblon locals who are getting a snack before heading home for an afternoon nap after a long day at the beach. Hours are from 8 a.m. until 2 a.m. No credit cards.

$ **Café do Alto,** 71 Rua Alberto Rangel, Alto Leblon, 2512-0096
As the name suggests, this little spot is high up. Take a cab into the farthest reaches of Alto Leblon for what we consider an ideal morning breakfast experience straight out of Rio's northeastern, or *nordestino,* culture. Tapioca, a flourlike substance that when cooked congeals into a crepelike pancake, is the base for this small restaurant's array of dishes. A breakfast buffet complements the tapioca offering, along with a row of fruit juices and sparking water, complete with a choice of mint leaves or rosemary. The café is located inside a small social club, Club Campestre, so expect a family atmosphere. Since the café is located in a private club, you won't be able to enjoy the poolside seating on the other side of the café's walls, but you can enjoy the view. Come with a book or your travel journal. It's a perfect reading break from Rio's heat. The northeastern owner and his staff will be the last to tell you to go! Open Tuesday to Sunday from 9 a.m. to 8 p.m.

$$$ **Ech Café,** 78 Rua Dias Ferreira, Leblon, 2512-5651
With an interior design inspired by the jazz roots of New Orleans's yesteryears, this restaurant gives off a distinctly

Cuban feel; the waiters are dressed in Cuban garb, complete with a wide-brimmed hat. Ech Café is one of the few dining establishments in Rio that has a humidor and a selection of Cuban and Dominican cigars that are delivered to your table along with a clipper and a match. One of the city's best *mojitos* complements a wide array of dishes borrowed from New Orleans cajun cuisine, a choice of French selections, and some of Rio's own local favorites. Live jazz is sometimes available, but it's never that great. Don't expect to escape the heady smoke, either. Come here to smoke a cigar and have some whiskey and a heavy meal, or don't come at all. Open daily from 11 a.m. to 1:30 a.m.

$$ **Fratelli**, 983 Avenida General San Martin, Leblon, 2259-6699
Another *kilograma*, but with Italian flare. The buffet here is excellent but leaves little room to maneuver around the crowd of self-important Leblon locals who are here to enjoy the food as much as to see and be seen for lunch. Expect a yuppie crowd, mid-30s and up. It has good pizza. Fratelli is open weekdays from 6 p.m. until 1 a.m. and on Saturday and Sunday from midday to 1 a.m.

$$$ **Garcia e Rodrigues**, 1251 Avenida Ataulfo de Paiva, Leblon, 3206-4100
This chic joint is a gathering spot for many of the rich and famous who live in Leblon. Seated at the circular table in the back corner of the second story, we've often spied some of Rio's hottest soap opera stars holding court with friends and family at a late breakfast. We happen to enjoy this place for the incredible selection of wine, the strong coffee, and the fact that it serves breakfast all day — perfect for sleeping in. The selection of meats and cheeses, along with bread and other picnic favorites, is not to be overlooked. We've also noticed a number of quiches not found anywhere else. The menu is nothing special, but what makes this a great spot is not so much the food as what's behind the display window and who's sitting upstairs. Open daily from 8 a.m. to 12:30 a.m. and on Friday and Saturday until 1 a.m.

$$$ ⊛ **Nam Thai**, 95 Rua Rainha Guilhermina, Leblon, 2259-
2962
Like Amir in Copacabana, Nam Thai is the city's premier spot
for Thai food. It might not be your first pick for lunch or din-
ner, since there is no traditional Brazilian fare served, but Thai
lovers can't go too far without scratching that itch. The Bra-
zilian chef makes several trips a year to Thailand to find inspi-
ration for new dishes. It's why the menu is constantly
changing yet anchored with staples such as Pad Thai and the
usual choices of red, yellow, and green curry with beef,
chicken, or pork along with that special Thai rice. The menu
conveniently notes which dishes are mild, hot, and scorching.
The décor is interesting, but nothing special aside from the
waterfall design to the left as you walk in. Spacing is com-
fortable enough to have private moments, and the waitstaff is
solid. Open from midday to 4 p.m. and from 7 p.m. to mid-
night, Tuesday to Friday, Monday for dinner only, Saturday
from noon to 1 a.m., and Sunday from noon to 11 p.m.

$$$ **Salitre**, 857 Rua General San Martin, Leblon, 3205-6977
Salitre is by far our favorite wine store in Rio. We're pleased
to report that this award-winning wine selection comes
complete with a full-time restaurant—serving all day, from a
splendid breakfast to an evening dining experience—that
rivals some of Rio's best restaurants. The deck is the restaurant's choice spot, but make sure you select your wine
before heading upstairs. If you're not sure what you want, ask
the waiters. They're surprisingly knowledgeable about ideal
wine combinations for various seafood and meat dishes on the
menu. If they're stumped, the manager will be sure to know.
Don't miss out on the basement wine cellar, the storage place
for some of the rarest wines we've found in Brazil. Open daily from 8 a.m. to midnight, Monday from 6 p.m., and Saturday and Sunday until 1 a.m.

$$ **Wraps**, 290 Avenida Afrânio de Melo Franco (Leblon
Shopping Mall, top-floor food court across from Bibi
Sucos), Leblon, 3138-8369

We stumbled upon this health-nut restaurant when looking for a decent meal at the Leblon Shopping Mall and were quickly impressed and pleasantly surprised by what this little restaurant chain has to offer. Its salads and wraps are super fresh and are available with a wide range of organic ingredients. We are smoothie lovers and thought that Wraps had some of the best smoothie combos in all of Rio (go for the Capri). Also, there's a nice view of the Christ statue from just about any table in the place. Open Sunday to Thursday from noon until 11 p.m. and Friday and Saturday from noon to 1 a.m.

Prainha

$ **Mirante da Prainha**, 689 Avenida Estado de Guanabara, Prainha, 9964-1220
Located at the far end of Prainha Beach, this is truly a no-shirt, no-shoes joint. Walk in and have a seat; someone will be with you, well, not so shortly. The time it takes to order and receive your food is worth the wait, however. It's so good and so cheap that it will make you laugh. The view of Prainha is spectacular, with the high-rises of Barra da Tijuca in the distance. Open from 11 a.m. until early evening, depending on the surf, food stock, and that morning's catch. No credit cards.

Going Out

When the *cariocas* decide to fully embrace *lazer* ("leisure"), they present you, me, or any other foreign visitor with a party, and these people know what the word *party* means. After all, *Carnaval* is Rio, or Rio is *Carnaval*—take your pick. The music, dance, dress, and drink together create a synergy of movement that captures everyone, even the rhythmically challenged.

A wonderful nighttime experience is available seven days a week in eight different areas of town: Centro, Lapa, and Santa Teresa downtown; Copacabana, Gávea, Ipanema, Lagoa, and Leblon in Zona Sul; and—sometimes—Barra da Tijuca in Zona Oeste. Ipanema and Leblon are generally the hottest of the bunch, but Centro has been coming on strong in the last few years. You will often find that in one night you can hit a street party to get your drink on, go clubbing and dance for hours, and then chill out in the early morning hours with a glass of beer and some pizza.

Cariocas stretch the evening into morning nearly every time they go out, and they are known to tackle the night an average of four to five times a week. Think you can hang? Napping in the mid-afternoon will probably work its way into your routine. Whatever you do, wherever you go, make at least one night last until morning. Be sure to witness Ipanema Beach at sunrise. It is one of the most beautiful moments to be had in Rio de Janeiro (even after an all-night bender).

All of the pubs, clubs, and spots listed here can be reached by taxi by simply telling your driver the name of where you want to go. Don't expect to pay more than $10 to go from Leblon to Barra da Tijuca, or $12 to go from Leblon to downtown. Most fares will average in the $4–$6 range—all very affordable, especially if you go out with a few friends or a date. Do not take the bus after dark. On the way home, don't consider *anything* but a cab. Doing otherwise is simply not safe and is an excellent use of poor judgment.

Most clubs and bars in Rio operate on a drink-now, pay-later system. Upon entering almost any bar or club, you will be handed a small sheet of paper that looks something like a score sheet from some standardized test in your past. On it the bartender or waiter will mark your consumption of food and drink. At the end of your stay, you pay at the *caixa* ("cashier") and give the scorecard to the doorman, who allows you to leave only if the card is stamped. Nicer establishments simply use a credit-card-size *cartão*, which is scanned each time you order something. Do not—repeat, do not—lose your scorecard or *cartão*; doing so automatically wins you a $50 bill, and sometimes more, depending on the establishment. Straight clubs expect you to dress nicely (jeans are fine)—flip-flops and a tank top get you in only if you're female. Gay clubs are more relaxed.

Many nighttime destinations simply take cash only, because foreign credit cards don't always take well in Rio. Consider bringing a handful of cash when you go out. Stash some in your sock or bra, some in two or more pockets, and some down your pants or skirt to mitigate the risk of pickpocket thievery. *Avoid a wallet or keeping bulky objects in your pockets. Bring identification;* many clubs will ask for it. Handbags should be kept well within reach while inside, and definitely on your shoulder while walking around. As a general rule, if you plan to go out in Zona Sul, consider bringing up to $85. It will ensure a fun evening, perhaps breakfast, and a cab ride home, no matter where you end up in the morning. If you plan to head to Lapa or to any street party, you will not need as much. Clubs will charge from $10 to $50 and more, depending on how much you drink. A big night in Rio might take you over $70, which is pretty cheap, considering you're on vacation!

Every week, the daily newspapers of Rio publish a guide to restaurants, movies, live music, expositions, and pretty much all the information you need to stay busy checking out Rio's nightlife. We recommend that you purchase an *O Globo* or a *Journal do Brasil*, on Friday, for their detailed guides (unfortunately, they're in Portuguese). Check www.samba-choro.com.br for a listing of the latest in live music in Rio and other cities.

If you're not sure where you want to go or what you want to do, there are a number of hot spots in the Zona Sul area where people gather around a high concentration of bars and late-night restaurants. In Ipanema, you're most likely to find the largest GLS (Gay, Lesbian and Simpatizantes, meaning "sympathizers" or "friends") crowd on weeknights and especially on weekends along Farme de Amoedo between Visconde de Pirajá and Prudente de Moraes. The same crowd frequents an area just beyond the car dealership on Teixeira de Melo, between Prudente de Moraes and Vieira Souto. For a more straight crowd, look into the Farme de Amoedo stretch between Barão da Torre and Visconde de Pirajá. The scene that stretches along Barão da Torre between Joana Angélica and Maria Quitéria attracts the children of Rio's *novo rico*, and the gathering that usually occurs after 2 a.m. on Maria Quitéria near the corner with Prudente de Moraes attracts more of a bohemian crowd that often pushes the party to a nearby kiosk on the beach. Finally, a younger crowd tends to converge on Paul Redfern, between Visconde de Pirajá and just across Prudente de Moraes.

In Leblon, the highest concentration of people normally occurs on General San Martin between Aristides Espinola and Jerônimo Monteiro. A new club on San Martin, just before Aristides Espinola, also gathers a crowd along with its venerable neighbor, GuapoLoco. Leblon's late-night scene is undoubtedly gathered around the Pizzaria Guanabara on the corner of Avenida Ataulfo de Paiva and Aristides

Espinola. Expect the crowd here to vibrate well into the dawn hours.
There are three distinct nighttime experiences in Rio de Janeiro: chilling out, the street party, and the dance hall (or clubbing). Apart from these three primary colors of Rio nightlife, you will always find special blends of color and experience, or a fiery mix of luck, booze, and fate that leads you to a plush room complete with a heart-shaped bed, mirrors on the ceiling, a bubbly hot tub, and champagne on ice (a.k.a. Rio's unique motel experience).

Centro and Lapa

Arcos do Lapa, Rio's best street party, in the middle of Lapa
Perhaps the only nighttime street-party action in the center of town is the area concentrated around the city's ancient aqueduct and its arches. Around and under the aqueduct, constructed in 1732, *cariocas* from all cast and color swirl about yelling, laughing, and enjoying the night. Tubes of *cachaça*, mixed with honey, sour apples, or grapes can be purchased for 50 cents from numerous street vendors. Be careful—each tube is loaded with the equivalent of two shots of this potent sugarcane rum, but the mixture is such that we could barely taste the *cachaça*. *Caipirinhas* and beer are also readily available for $1–$2. In addition to selling booze, street vendors hawk wares from handcrafts to cheesy trinkets. Making eye contact with any of them almost guarantees a couple minutes of Brazilian-style haggle in your face.

Various clubs and bars punctuate the two rows of ancient buildings that define the boundaries of the Lapa street party. Some of the bars and clubs on the street side require invitations to enter; many are insider-type joints. Others, located off the street between the two rows of buildings, are rustic, with doors open wide, music blaring, and only a concrete floor to offer. But that's enough to entertain the dozens of *cariocas* who pack in to dance, kiss, and sweat. At the very end of the off-street cul-de-sac, ancient steps leading to Santa Teresa offer refuge for pairs seeking a little more privacy. If it's late night, don't be surprised to see explicit material *ao vivo* there. Please exercise caution at these events.

⊛ **Carioca da Gema**, 79 Rua Mem de Sá, Lapa, 2221-0043

Despite its location in the Lapa, where mostly college kids hang out, Carioca da Gema attracts mature couples from the Zona Sul who want to get their drink on and do some serious dancing, yet in a casual environment. The rising stars of Rio's samba scene play here on a regular basis. It's not uncommon to pay to see a lesser-known artist and wind up listening to a much more famous *sambista* who has stopped in after her show to give the younger artist a boost. By 10 p.m., tables and chairs are removed, and nearly the whole crowd is up and dancing. If you want to just check out the scene and people-watch, climb the shorter set of stairs in the main hall. If you manage to land a table on this midlevel *barzinho* ("little bar"), you'll get drinks faster as well as an excellent view of the stage and dancing public. See www.barcariocadagema.com.br for show information, prices, and more.

Central Cultural Carioca, 37 Rua do Teatro, Centro, 2252-6468

Located next to the famous Candélaria Catholic Church by the Praça Tiradentes, this *carioca* favorite is little known among tourists. But don't think you can arrive after 10 p.m. and walk right in. Due to its popularity and small size, the limited capacity denies entry to late arrivals until some of those inside have left, which is rare until after early morning. Once you're handed the bar-tab sheet and allowed in, the pulsating music instantly hits you in the chest. A short walk up the narrow flight of stairs reveals one of the most rootsy samba bars still in existence in Rio. It is obviously a very old building, and the bowed floorboards denote decades of visitors. By 10 p.m. most of the chairs and tables are pushed to the side or center, allowing ample room for dancing. A small stage at the end of the narrow building balances the small bar next to the steps. Get a drink and wade through the onlookers to move to the music, or push your way to one side to take it all in. Rio's most popular samba artists drop in to collaborate with their friends, or they book a night or two in a row simply because they love the acoustics and the small, cozy feeling of the place. This bar is a must-see cultural experience, especially if you like samba.

More information on shows and prices can be found at www.centroculturalcarioca.com.br/home.php.

Cine Lapa, 23 Avenida Mem de Sá, Lapa, 2539-0216 or 2509-5166
Right in front of the Arcos you'll find a number of old buildings with all sorts of late night fun going on. Cine Lapa lies among them, its interior decorated with sheets covering cement walls, where the music bounces, mixed from rock to contemporary new wave, depending on the night. Prepare yourself for a sea of bodies after midnight—and a mix, at that, from Brazilian hippies to goth hounds, all bouncing or trancing out at the films that are projected on the walls. Afterwards, follow the flow into the heart of Lapa, buy a can of Skol, and eat some curious super burger with the rest of the urchins. This is Lapa at its dearest. For more info, visit www.matrizonline.com.br.

Club Democráticos, 91 Rua do Riachuelo, Lapa, 2252-4611
Founded in 1867, this is perhaps the oldest samba music hall still in existence in Rio de Janeiro. The old building's interior atmosphere speaks volumes of the samba that has been played, and listened to, within this small space. Despite the quality of samba artists the club regularly attracts, a limited sound system leaves you wishing the management would spend a little more money on the speakers. Nevertheless, the cozy atmosphere and purity of the samba fans will deliver you a memorable experience of the soul of *carioca*, and Brazilian, music.

Club Six, 38 Rua das Marrecas, Centro, 2512-3230
One of Rio's hottest clubs, Club Six is true to its name, offering *six* different dancing environments, all housed within an old industrial building. Steel stairs and doors, hanging chains, and thick, almost plastic curtains in deep reds and blues complement low-level lighting and rivet-filled walls painted black. Rio's in-crowd comes here to experience electronic, ambient, lounge, hip-hop, rock 'n' roll, and popular dance music all in one place, in one night. Expect heavy security (which is a good thing because the crowds here have been

a bit "too edgy" of late — there are rumors of drugs being sold in the bathrooms). Arrive on Friday or Saturday after midnight, and you might want to bring sunglasses, 'cause most don't walk out until after dawn. Visit www.clubsix.com.br for more info on nightly music and admission prices.

Estrela da Lapa, 69 Avenida Mem de Sá, Lapa, 2507-6686

Estrela da Lapa ("Star of Lapa") rose from the ashes of a large colonial building erected in 1898. The reconstruction sought to merge historical patrimony with the modern, maintaining the eclectic art nouveau influence of its origins. The (con)fusion of styles applies to the music as well. Keep your eye on the music lineups! Despite the identity problem, some say it's typically *carioca* to have a million different styles of music in one place — samba, *chorinho*, *electronica*, rock, and pop. Good thing there's Devassa *chopp* (simply the best nationally produced tap beer in Rio) to gloss over any rough transitions in music genres. Dance, drink, dance. (You might want to dress hot.) For more info, go to www.estreladalapa.com.br

Fundição Progresso, 24–50 Rua dos Arcos, Lapa, 2220-5070

An impressive concrete music hall, situated right next to the aqueduct, hosts a wide variety of live music and electronic dance parties, including the monthly gay X-Demente parties. Inside the building there is a stage with stadium seating and an area in front for dancing. On a lower level, a dance floor allows still others to enjoy DJ-spun electronic music, while a small restaurant located off to one side on the main floor attends to those with late-night munchies. Shows range from samba to *forró*, reggae, and rock, and prices range from $5 to $10 depending on the band. Visit any show on Friday or Saturday and you will see *cariocas* partying full tilt. For more information on live events and prices, visit www.fundicao.org.

Rio Scenarium, 20 Rua do Lavradio, Lapa, 3147-9005

Past the Aqueduct and the music hall, about two blocks down the road, a well-known samba bar awaits your visit. This three-level samba joint is punctuated with chairs and tables and decorated with all kinds of strange trinkets, art, sculptures, and other antique-looking pieces. The food here is great and not too expensive. As usual, you will be given a bar-tab sheet on which to mark your consumption. Don't lose it! On the first floor, there is a small stage and dancing area. The second floor offers a balcony that looks down on the stage and dancing area. The top floor offers a much more relaxed, chill-out zone, with a separate bar and decent service. Tuesday night is hoppin'. For more info, visit www.rioscenarium.com.br.

Trapiche Gamboa, 155 Sacadura Cabral, Centro, 2516-0868
Often voted the best live music in the city, this old-school samba bar attracts roots samba artists from around the country, as well as those *carioca sambistas* that will never be discovered because they don't really want to be. Only at places like Trapiche will you discover them and a samba that few other tourists will ever hear. Live shows occur every night from Tuesday to Saturday, and there is one surprise Sunday a month. Friday and Saturday nights are the busiest. Don't be surprised to see older couples here — they're actually the generation that animates the party! Did you know there's a couples version of the samba? Go to Trapiche to check it out. Arrive and leave only via taxi. Check www.trapichegamboa.com.br for shows, prices, and schedules.

Santa Teresa

One of the few neighborhoods in Rio with a view, Santa Teresa sits on top of a small hill right next to Lapa. The nightlife here is focused on Bar do Juarez, one of the rootsiest little samba bars in town.

Bar do Juarez, 98 Estrada Joaquim Mamede, Santa Teresa, 2257-0063
Juarez hosts the coolest samba street party and chill-out scene in town every Friday night, starting at 11 p.m. The views of the northern side of town are breathtaking. Sip on a cold, cheap beer while listening to Rio's top samba performers grace this dive with their Brazilian soul. Some people claim that you can sometimes hear automatic gunfire coming from the shanty town down the hill, but that has fortunately never been us. It's

the closest you'll get to a *favela* at 3 a.m.—fortunately there's no access to Santa Teresa from the *favela*, located a few hundred yards down the mountain from the bar. Take a cab to wind your way up to the top, get out when you can't go any farther, and walk toward the music. The samba is simply incredible.

Casarão Hermê, 193 Rua Hermenegildo de Barros, Santa Teresa, 2253-2358

Casarão Hermê is known as a cultural and art center housed in a two-story home built in 1853. Once reformed by local architect Alfred Brito, it came to life as a hoppin' bar and dance club on Friday and Saturday nights. On Sunday it changes hats and offers free salsa and bolero dance lessons. Mind the program! This is yet another *carioca* establishment that frenetically changes personalities each night. You'll find a cool fusion of food (look for the well-known Clube do Sushi on some Thursdays), plastic arts, live music, theatrical presentations, and other interactive artistic activities. You're guaranteed to meet an eclectic mix of young and old residents of Santa Teresa and beyond. Don't miss the view from the veranda! For more info, visit www.casaraoherme.com.br.

Copacabana

Unless you're here to rock out at a beach concert or to celebrate Reveillon (one of the world's greatest New Year's Eve parties—see below), Copacabana offers little by way of evening activities. Also, it can be unsafe, especially near the tunnel that separates Copacabana from Ipanema at Rua Migel Lemos, where bandits hang out, waiting for a score.

Bunker, 94 Rua Raul Pompéia, Copacabana, 2247-8724

Despite recent changes in management, Bunker continues being the best-known dance club (without hooker feeding grounds) in Copacabana. Marrying techno, electro, drum 'n' bass, hip-hop, '80s rock-goth, funk, and, occasional metal, Bunker's appeal attracts hordes of folks from different strokes. Although the owners purport to fit up to 800 bootyshakers, we can't imagine it swelling beyond 500 without getting a face full of your neighbor's Axe body spray. Yes, it gets packed. But there are plenty of lights, smoke, poles, and sexy corners to squirm into and onto, and there are always curious exchanges in such a space busting with pheromones. Caution: If you get licked, don't expect it to be for free. Visit www .bunkerclub.com.br for more info.

Help, 3432 Avenida Atlântica, Copacabana, 2522-1296

This late-night club, opened in the mid-1980s, is open seven days a week and is a gathering place for single foreign men. Nearly all of Copacabana's alleged 5,000-plus prostitutes spend at least two nights a week here working the floor, looking for a score. If you're truly into checking out the outer rim of Rio's nightlife, enter Help, but with some caution — pickpockets abound, and the drinks are often watered down — the bartenders know a drunk foreigner when they see one. It's best to keep an eye on them when they pour your drink, and say something if your drink is weak. The street scene in front of Help is relatively safe all night long, provided you don't mind being repeatedly accosted by trolling prostitutes, transvestites, or the random homeless person asking for a drink or food. In the early morning hours, this scene wanes some, but it often continues relatively strong until about 7 or 8 a.m. The heat of the morning sun finally drives the night away, and Help once again becomes quiet and listless — that is, until the next time the clock strikes midnight.

Mariuzinn, 435 Avenida Nossa Senhora de Copacabana, Copacabana, 2545-7672 or 7813-1122

If you want a break from the international techno-rock circuit of clubs, consider Mariuzinn, where salsa is the name of the game. With less space for guiding your partner, there are no excuses! Even if you don't know how to dance, you'll quickly learn how to hold a piercing gaze. Dress comfortably, but don't be afraid to wear your clothes tighter. The soft glow of lamplights on the redwood interior kindles an energy heightened only by the pulsating music.

New Year's Eve in Rio (Reveillon)

I magine that you're dressed in white, armed with a chilled bottle of champagne, a bundle of flowers, and a list of people to kiss. Now imagine you're in the middle of millions of people dressed in white, hundreds of thousands of bottles and flowers, and surrounded by free kisses. Just add fireworks and Copacabana Beach, and you're in Rio de Janeiro for New Year's Eve.

You don't need to purchase expensive tickets (well, apart from the flight), nor do you need to worry about long lines or party crashing at the friend of your friend of your friend's place. New Year's Eve in Rio de Janeiro (referred to as Reveillon, pronounced *hev-ay-YAWN*) requires little more than wearing white and being willing to put up with people everywhere. It's a people-watcher's heaven. Even the naughty are dressed in angelic white!

The concentration for New Year's spills over onto Avenida Atlântica in Copacabana. We advise that you start heading toward the sand at least 30 minutes before midnight. The closer you get, the more you'll have to shove a little if you want to actually make it to the water's edge. The flower throwers will be in your way. In Rio, there is a New Year's tradition to throw a flower in the ocean as an offer to Iemanjá, the goddess of the ocean, according to Afro-Brazilian religious beliefs. In exchange for the flower, she is supposed to bring you success and happiness in the new year.

O nce you're situated, you won't have to wait long until someone nearby begins shouting the countdown. There's no official ball, as in New York, just a general feeling that the end of the year is nigh. When the year is over, according to your watch, pop the cork, grab a kiss, and enjoy the show.

The five- to seven-minute fireworks display off the waters of Copacabana is one of the best we've seen anywhere. Other shows occur across the country, but Rio's is the best by far. The rockets are launched from barges out on the water, making for an effect of lights in the sky and a reflection on the ocean's surface. (They used to be launched from the beach, which, though quite dramatic, had an obvious set of safety concerns that went along with it.) Sometimes it rains, which never seems to affect people's spirits, but it's no good for the fireworks. If you get a clear night, it will be a night to remember.

(continued on page 116)

(continued from page 115)

Time to welcome in the new year. Grab your date or a new friend and start making your way from Copacabana to Ipanema. Every year, the city brings in a famous DJ or some band, but usually it's both. We've seen the Black Eyed Peas and DJ Tiësto on the same night! Including that one incredible night, we've never had a problem with the music. It's loud, it pulses, and best of all, everyone around is dancing. You'll have no choice but to let it go.

Set up at *Posto* 8 and *Posto* 9, where separate stages face the water or the sand and make for a perfect atmosphere for dancing on the beach until the morning hours. Again, you don't need to pay for more than what you drink and eat. We recommend that you stay away from the mystery meat on a stick. If you're not into beer, then try the tubes of *cachaça*, which are sold for one *real*, or try the minitubes, which are sold for about 10 cents apiece. The *cachaça* in these tubes is color-coded according to the mixture: grape juice, orange juice, honey, or lemon.

We like to purchase a few tubes for personal consumption as well as a handful of the little sample-size tubes to share with new friends. Be careful! There's more *cachaça* in those long tubes than you might think. It's well disguised! Dressed in all white, you'll be sure to stand out if you drink too much and wear it on your shirt. Of course, should that happen, the good news is that nobody cares, and the ocean is only steps away.

2A2: Couple's Club, 885 F Rua Figueiredo de Magalhães, Copacabana, no telephone

2A2 holds a unique position as the "only" swingers club in Rio, but we're sure you can find a more grungy and lawless version in the red-light district of the city. Its claim to fame is that it serves just the couples who are bold and free-spirited enough to enter its space, those looking for something else in their day-to-day relationship. The first floor is deceptively innocent, with various styles of live and DJ music (most often sexy electronic and techno, but with the typical *carioca* everything-in-between mix), an upscale sound system, and a chic modern leather seating area. Upstairs, however, the fun begins, albeit with strict abiding to the mutual-consent rule and a specific set of behavior guidelines listed on the entryway (and also accessible on its Web site). Anything or nothing can happen—you decide. We'll leave you with perhaps the most important tip: Don't take a partner who tends to get jealous. And don't fall victim to the fantasy that the second floor is a land of naked Rodrigo Santoros and Gisele Bundchens. Paradise's limitation: The not-so-hotties tend to lose their inhibitions faster than the hotties. Masquerades, stripteases, and other theme nights add to the potion. For more info, see www.2a2.com.br.

Gávea

Squeezed between the Botanical Gardens and the Jockey Club, this small neighborhood is Rio's college-kid zone. The city's premier private university generates sustained levels of young *cariocas*, who all spend a solid amount of time partying in Gávea.

Baixa Gávea, Praça Santos Dumont, Gávea
Get in a cab and tell the *taxista* that you want to go to Praça Santos Dumont in Gávea. The string of streetside bars and restaurants here is known as Baixa Gávea, another of Rio's great street parties. If you arrive after 9 o'clock on almost any night, the street will be littered with beautiful university-age *cariocas* mixing it up, with a solid representation from both the 20-something and over-30 crowds. Next to Lapa, Baixa Gávea delivers as a street party, without the touch of sketch. The people-watching is top-notch and easy on the eyes. Beer is very cheap. You're bound to run into someone you know, think you know, just met the other day, or kissed last night.

Zero Zero, 240 Avenida Padre Leonel Franca, Gávea, 2540-8041
Built into the side of a planetarium, this popular destination serves a wide community in Rio's nightlife, from straight to gay and young to middle-age. The outside patio is perfect for chilling and talking to new acquaintances. Just inside, the plush environment splashed in white soothes the senses, but don't bump into the glass door as you make your way into the dance room! We have seen plenty of sore noses! The actual clubbing area is lined with a bar on the left side and a table on

the right, again adorned with opaque glass, succulent lighting and plush white pleather folds and buttons. A space cadet–style bathroom is worth a visit even if it does make you dizzy to walk in there. The dance floor, though small, offers plenty of room for the rotation of enthusiasts who dance hard, take a break, and come back for more. Every weekend brings in a full house, and guest DJs often keep the party cranking into the wee hours of the morning. On Sunday, the GLS party attracts a colorful, festive crowd. Arrive before midnight to ensure a spot inside, and expect to pay a cover charge of at least $5.

Ipanema

In Ipanema you will find the bulk of nightlife that Rio has to offer for all tourists. There are too many bars to mention, but the ones we've listed here are definitely worth a visit (or two).

⊛ **Baronetti**, 354 Rua Barão de Torre, Ipanema, 2522-1460
When the upper-crust youth from Barra and Leblon come to party with their Ipanema buddies, this is usually the meeting spot. A wide array of Rio's younger soap opera stars often run into their ex-this and ex-thats at Baronetti, making the morning tabloids. Two doors down from Cristal, on the northern side of Praça Nossa Senhora da Paz, this dance club is a Friday, Saturday, and Sunday night favorite, and it's known for good music, ranging from hip-hop and house to electronic. Most of the floor on the first level is open for dancing, but the area at the rear is VIP only (and very expensive). Upstairs is a small sushi bar and a seating area, both for VIPs only. If you must know, prices range from $500 for a couch along the edge of the dance floor, some $800 for a table in the back on the first floor, and up to $2,000 for a table upstairs. Ridiculous, right? Arrive before 11 p.m., bring some form of ID, and dress up to ensure entry. By midnight, the crowd that has gathered in the street waiting to enter attracts a wide array of street vendors. By early morning (and as late as 4 a.m.), the street scene in front of this hip little joint is just as happenin' as the bump 'n' grind inside. Look for our friend who operates a hot dog and cold beer stand from the back of a smallish Volkswagen

bus from midnight until dawn. Men drop $35 to get in on most nights, but women pay half that. There is a $10 consumption minimum.

Cristal, 334A Rua Barão de Torre, Ipanema, 2247-8220

A popular destination for the midnight to 4 a.m. stretch, Cristal is the former Nova. Under new management and a reformed look, Cristal is now made for dancing and attracts a college crowd that's happy to spend mom and dad's hard-earned money on libation or to steal a kiss from a new acquaintance. The saying that women in Rio expect to be kissed within 15 minutes of meeting you is often proven here. Let the time pass, and you'll find that your new dance partner is swinging her hips with some other guy across the floor! Two levels are nearly completely devoid of tables and chairs. Those in place are for paying customers only, purchased for $100 or more. The first-story dance floor is close-quarters only, and it often packs in some sort of live music, from a hip-hop and samba fusion to Brazilian indie rock. The second floor is the DJ's domain, and the tight dance floor overlooks the Praça de Nossa Senhora da Paz, with a view of the Catholic Church of the same name. Second-floor music is mostly the hip-hop that you've already heard, or else house or electronic. No one stops dancing from midnight to 4 a.m., so expect to shake your groove thang. Get there early, before 11:30 p.m., and you're guaranteed to get inside. Arrive after 1 a.m., and you'll be waiting in line. A mere $15 gets you in the door, but you will be charged a minimum of $20 on the way out. So make sure you spend that extra five bucks on buying a round, or on your own consumption, before leaving. Tuesday night is just as happenin' as Friday, only less packed — more room for dancing. Pay on the third floor on your way out to save some time, or just dance until the lights come on!

Emporio, 37 Rua Maria Quitéria, Ipanema, 2523-3040

Ipanema's version of a dive, this college hangout and quasi–street party is a favorite among the hip and artsy 20-somethings in Ipanema and Leblon. Expect to hear loud rock music on a budget sound system. The party often spills out onto the street, where taxis hang out, college buddies spawn great ideas for future scams, and Rio's affluent youth generally hang out to celebrate life and show off the latest styles in clothes and shoes. Don't dress up too much, however, or you might be the target of those bohemian types always on the lookout to tease the bourgeoisie. This place will essentially take off at any point in the evening, from 10 p.m. until 4 a.m. There usually is no line to get in, but the time it takes you to get a drink is based on your persistence. The small bar in the back to the right can handle only so much demand. Many who go to Lapa for a live show come back to the Emporio to trade stories and tell tales of the evening. This is Ipanema's street party scene on any night of the week, and certainly an ideal spot to grab the night's last drink. (For safety, we advise visiting this rowdy late-night hangout only if you're with a group of Brazilian friends.)

The Irish Pub, 14A Rua Jangadeiros, Praça General Osório, Ipanema, 2513-3044

The spacious arrangement of this small bar is a nice break from feeling like a sardine, pressed against people on all four sides. This well-heeled joint is relaxing, offers good service, keeps cold Heineken on tap, and attracts a wide range of *cariocas* and tourists alike. Don't come here expecting to hook up. Come with a date, with a couple of friends for a good conversation, or to practice your Portuguese. Don't worry, you won't need to shout.

Lord Jim Pub, 63 Rua Paul Redfern, Ipanema, 2259-3047

This three-story British pub is much like its counterpart, Shenanigans, located on the other side of Ipanema. It serves British food and drink and caters to a large ex-pat crowd as well as Brazilians from both Ipanema and Leblon. Unlike at Shenanigans, there's a stage here for live music, which often attracts rock 'n' roll groups and a feisty crowd to go with it. Stop by here on your way to Leblon, or, if you're into a packed, raging crowd on Sunday night, then by all means make Lord Jim a priority!

Shenanigans, 112 Avenida Visconde de Pirajá, Ipanema, 2267-5860
This Irish pub attracts mostly tourists, ex-patriots looking for a taste of home, and *carioca* men and women who want to practice their English or hook up with a foreigner. The Guinness and Newcastle served on tap, a wide-screen television that shows sports other than soccer, and a regulation-size pool table all offer a change of pace from the Brazilian culture that saturates almost every other bar in Rio. Tuesday night is good for cheap tacos, served in abundance and at a discount. Come here before 9 p.m. to get a table, and try to get over to the balcony overlooking the Praça General Osório, especially if you don't smoke cigarettes. Unfortunately, the doormen pack them in at this bar, which creates a situation of organized chaos, pressed flesh, and undoubtedly spilled drinks on your arm, shirt, or shoes. The long wait to pay and leave sometimes creates an anticlimactic experience.

Sindicato do Choppe, 85 Rua Farme de Amoedo, Ipanema, 2523-1745
This easygoing early-evening hangout hosts a wide array of *cariocas* and is a great place to chill out, meet with friends, or get ready for the evening. *Chopp* ("draft beer," often spelled *"choppe"*) connoisseurs will tell you that this place has one of the best draft beers in town. A table is usually easy to find all night long, but don't expect to seat four if there is a *partido do futebol* displayed on the various televisions hung from the ceiling. One of our favorite pastimes is to order a meter of beer, which is a column of beer with a center beam of pure ice, and see how fast we can finish it. The food is decent, but we'd stay away from anything more than finger food. There's not much accounting for what goes on in that kitchen.

Tô Nem Aí, 57 Farme de Amoedo, Ipanema, 2247-8403
Named after the frequently used Brazilian term for "I don't really give a shit," this bar is perhaps best known for its front-deck seating and wine on tap, which we've found to be surprisingly cold and refreshing. The flat-screen televisions add to some of the entertainment value here, but we come back for the people-watching—indoor and out, the airy feeling of this

bar attracts tourists, locals, and the GLS crowd alike. Run by an Italian manager, the food is decent, even if the service is substandard.

Vinicius Piano Bar, 39 Rua Vinicius de Moraes, Ipanema, 2523-4757
    This two-story piano and jazz bar is located right across the street from where Vinicius de Moraes wrote some of the first words to his internationally famous song, *Garota de Ipanema* ("The Girl from Ipanema"). Blues and jazz artists regularly play here, attracting a crowd from college-age kids to older, more refined Brazilians. Arrive early to get a good table, and expect to pay at least $8 to get into any live show.

Lagoa (including Humaitá and Jardim Botânico)

This beautiful lagoon is surrounded by an excellent footpath. Circled around the lagoon are small, distinct neighborhoods, tourist attractions, and row upon row of bars and clubs too numerous to mention. However, in the northeast corner of Lagoa lies the Humaitá neighborhood. Humaitá offers two attractions. Once all the stores at Cobal (Humaitá's public market) close, the restaurants attract mostly Brazilians from the Lagoa district for wining and dining. In addition, the **Ballroom**, one of Rio's many venues for live music, is here. It's like a big jazz bar with the usual tables and chairs, a generous stage, and plenty of room in front to dance. Finally, in the quiet Jardim Botânico neighborhood, one will find the Carolina Café — the bar most worthy of mention.

Carolina Café, 10 Rua J.J. Seabra, Jardim Botânico, 2540-0705
    Considered by Rio's culture magazine, *Veja*, as the place to see and be seen in the Botanical Garden district, the Carolina Café is most dear to our hearts for its wide selection of imported beer. It's safe to say that if you're missing your favorite brew, you can stop by or call the Carolina, for they might have it on tap or in a bottle. Aside from the beer, a large selection of sandwiches will keep you flipping through the menu for a while. The food is of suitable quality for bar fare, but its claim of serving the best burger in the city is vastly overblown — at least, most Americans will be sorely disappointed in its quality. Stop

by for a mellow evening, a date, a chat with an old friend, or just to get reacquainted with a long-lost love of fine international brew.

⊛ Leblon

Brazilians like to go out in Leblon because there are very few foreigners who "invade" this district. Nevertheless, this is the hottest neighborhood, by far, for a Rio nightlife experience.

⊛ **Academia da Cachaça**, 28 Rua Conde Bernadotte, Leblon, 2529-2680

Squeezed into a sanitary strip mall at the back side of Leblon, Academia de Cachaça is well known for one thing: the almighty *caipirinha*. Here you can choose from a wide array of *cachaça* from almost anywhere in Brazil, or simply vodka, to add to your *caipirinha*, with a choice of kiwi, tangerine, lemon, lime, strawberries, *maracujá* ("passion fruit"), or some other exotic fruit in season. Many types of *cariocas* stop by the Academia on their way to a club in Leblon or Gávea. If you're a *cachaça* fan, definitely make a stop at this place. Even if you're not into *caipirinha*, you'll be surprised at the smoothness of drinking the *cachaça* straight, taken traditionally in a small shot glass. But be careful; like fine tequila, fine *cachaça* starts a fire in your gut that won't soon diminish!

⊛ **Bracarense**, 85B Rua José Linhares, Leblon, 2294-3549

Many locals come to this bar to enjoy what folks consider the best *chopp* in town, and the establishment proudly shows off framed award certificates for service, food, and — of course — *chopp*. Stop by here around 9 p.m. to try the beer and finger food, to people-watch, and to make your plans for the evening. The crowd peaks around 11, and the bar closes soon after, at midnight. Try a plate of *carne seca* ("dried meat") if you're hungry; it's fantastic.

⊛ **Devassa**, 1241 Rua General San Martin, Leblon, 2540-6087

Also known for its excellent *chopp*, this stylish open-air bar attracts many of Leblon's professional 20-somethings looking to relax after work or in the early evening. Start your evening in Leblon, here, and walk half a block to Melt (listed below) for a solid night of good beer and music surrounded by Rio's most polished *cariocas*. This bar is perhaps best known around town because it is also a brewery. In many other bars, clubs, and pubs you will find Devassa in bottle or on tap. So if you like the creamy smooth taste, definitely go to the source. You can find a blond, a brunette, or a redheaded lager any time of the night.

GuapoLoco, 48 Rua Rainha Guilhermina, Leblon, 2259-6031
The Mexican restaurant stops serving dinner plates around 10 p.m. and becomes a full-time club with an extensive bar. Guapo-Loco attracts a 3 to 1 girl-to-guy ratio, and many of them are Rio's college kids, who come here to kick off the evening with a few drinks with friends or to pick up a date for the night. Just $15 gets you in the door, and you have two hours to consume as much as you can (beer, margaritas, water, and finger food), from 11 p.m. to 1 a.m. Arrival after 10 p.m. wins you a slot in the line that stretches down the block, and unless you're in the front or know the right people, you can forget about getting in after 11 p.m. Come early or go somewhere else.

⊛ The House Bar, 1011 Rua General San Martin, Leblon, 2249-2161
Located around the corner from GuapoLoco, this snappy hangout is reminiscent of Melt (listed below), only it's much cooler. Formerly known as Bom Bar, this bar attracts a younger crowd. As at GuapoLoco, the girl-to-guy ratio is normally 3 to 1. The music is generally better, there is more room for dancing upstairs, roaming bartenders make it easy to stay on the dance floor (even if you want a drink), and there are fewer tourists. By midnight, the dance floor is packed. Take a break and head downstairs, where the cool air is refreshing and open tables offer corners for making out with a new friend, chatting, or simply taking a break from dancing in heels while you sample from the sushi menu. Come before 10 p.m. to be sure you get in. Expect to pay a $15 consumption minimum. Thursday and Friday nights are often the busiest.

Jobi, 1166 Avenida Ataulfo de Paiva, Leblon, 2274-0547

Since 1956 this very popular small bar has been known for excellent food, great service, and good draft beer. On weeknights this place is packed from early evening to 3 or 4 a.m. On Thursday, Friday, and Saturday, the bar stays open until the last customer has left. Jobi is a small historic establishment with a good reputation. Don't be discouraged by the line.

⊛ **Melt**, 47 Rua Rita Ludolf, Leblon, 2249-9309

Some of the most beautiful men and women in Rio come to Melt to see and be seen. The first floor is a chill-out atmosphere, offering plenty of space to sit and hang out with friends and acquaintances you met on the beach earlier in the day. The bar, stretching from one end of the right wall to the other, offers any drink you can imagine, an abundance of stools, and a great height advantage for surveying the crowd's beauty. Upstairs is for dancing only and has a bar to tend to your thirst, but be careful descending the stairs! Many drunk men and women have taken the long plunge. Melt often hires DJs who know what they're doing. Also, *electrosamba* bands—a mix of house-style beats with samba rhythm—play live music two nights a week, most often on Saturday and Wednesday. Expect to pay at least a $7 cover, give up a phone number (your hotel number will do) and your name, and be handed a black credit-card-size *cartão*. Hand it to the bartender each time you ask for a drink, and, at the end of the night, pay at the small window located on the bottom floor in the back corner, next to the entrance to the bathroom. Come before 9 p.m. to get a table and before 10 p.m. to avoid the long line that often forms on Tuesday, Wednesday, Friday, and Saturday.

Pizzaria Guanabara, 1228 Avenida Ataulfo de Paiva, Leblon, 2294-0797

This streetside pizza joint spills out onto the sidewalk with tables and chairs full of Brazilians from 9 p.m. until 6 a.m. seven nights a week. *Chopp* is served along with a full menu of food, all night long. Come here to meet friends and get a beer before heading out. Make it a stop on the way to Ipanema, or just flow into the place in the early morning to grab one last *chopp* and some grub before heading home to play or pass out. However you want it, Pizzaria Guanabara delivers. It is almost always full, and some claim it's easier to park a car in downtown Rio than it is to get a table at the Pizzaria. People-watching makes it worth the wait.

Barra da Tijuca

This neighborhood is about as far out as you want to go to find a good time, unless you have a car, a self-sustaining party crowd, and an out-of-the-way destination in mind. Considering that there are many other, better options in Ipanema, Leblon, and the areas around Lagoa, not even those who live in Barra da Tijuca prefer to go out there. However, there is a **Shenanigans**, a **GuapoLoco**, and a **Devassa** in Barra da Tijuca. They are pretty much the same as their counterparts in Ipanema and Leblon, so there is no sense in visiting unless you're under duress. A **Hard Rock Cafe**, complete with everything annoying about that place, is perhaps the coolest bar in Barra da Tijuca that will allow you in without waiting in line. There are many fun bars in Barra da Tijuca, but none are really worth the trip from Ipanema or Leblon, where there are better spots and you're close to other neighborhoods, like Lagoa or Baixa Gávea. Nevertheless, if you're up for the cab fare, then by all means go.

Nuth Lounge, 999 Avenida Armando Lombardi, Barra da Tijuca, 3153-8595

Pronounced "nooch," this is a well-established club that is absolutely bumpin' most nights, especially Sunday. Don't expect to get in unless you can walk, talk, and gawk like a Brazilian; otherwise you'll see why this insider's club is so darn hard to get into! Even if you're on the invitee list, you're not guaranteed entry. If you're a guy willing to stand in line for up to two hours, make sure there's a 3 to 1 girl-to-guy ratio in that line; otherwise forget it—the bouncers tend to let in three girls for every one guy. Arrive well before 10:30 p.m. to improve your chances of getting by bouncers notorious for discriminating against tourists.

Going Out—Gay, Lesbian, and Simpatizantes (GLS)

Rio is home to literally dozens of nightclubs, bars, and saunas that cater to gay men and women and their friends, called *simpatizantes* down here. Many of these spots are so off the beaten track that tourists never make it far enough from the mainstream clubs to explore the depths of gay nightlife that Rio has to offer. Rest assured, however, that some hours spent on Ipanema Beach halfway between *Posto* 8 and *Posto* 9, or on Copacabana Beach in front of the Copacabana Palace, will most likely win you a new friend or two for hookups or whatever. Here we offer a list of some of the popular options, as well as the lesser known yet most fun locales that are sure to entertain you for hours on end, all night, or the length of a drink or two.

To get the up-to-the-minute info on Rio's gay and lesbian happenings, check out www.riogayguide.com.

⊛ **Bar Bofetada**, 87 Rua Farme de Amoedo, Ipanema, 2227-6992
This small bar is the best-known gay meet-and-greet after-beach spot in Ipanema. For its size, this bar attracts one of the largest gay crowds in Rio. Eye candy abounds. During *Carnaval*, this same street turns into a gay-only area, attracting an international crowd. The annual Gay Pride Parade, which happens every year in July, will surely pass by Bofetada. Organizers expect at least 1 million participants each year. In the afternoon, on hot days, a large crowd of gay men simply hangs out in *sungas* (basically, "Speedos") drinking a cold *chopp* while waiting for luck, or a hot guy, to come their way. At night, a local DJ usually sets up his equipment right in front of the bar and plays electro and samba from 11 p.m. until the sun rises. The bar is open from midday until the morning, seven days a week.

Clube Monte Líbano, 701 Borges de Medeiros, Leblon, 2512-8833
Rio's second largest *festa de gay* ("gay party") happens once a month. Referred to as "Barbies In Total Control Here" or simply *B.I.T.C.H.* parties, they are run and organized by Rio's "Barbies," gay men who are absolutely ripped, and some of the most well-built men in Rio. Techno, electronic, club, and drum

and bass music swells the crowd into rhythmic dance and movement. These monthly parties cost $12 to enter, and they happen in different places monthly, but Clube Monte Líbano seems to be the popular spot at the moment. Check out www.bitch.com.br for updates on these fabulous parties.

Dama de Ferro, 288 Rua Vinícius de Moraes, Ipanema, 2247-2330
The Lady of Iron welcomes you with an entrance made of metal and a decoration theme that is a throwback to the world depicted in the early 1980s sci-fi movie *Blade Runner.* Two environments are offered: art studio and a dance hall with proper club surroundings. The studio features plastic art made by Rio locals Verônica Lima and Richard Gallo, whose good taste and free-form style help to balance the club's otherwise angular environs. The floor on the bottom level presents an interesting design that uses various shapes of sperm, and from the bathroom on the first floor, one can look up and see dancing feet above, making for rather provocative, eye-catching moments. DJs spin electro, rock, samba-funk, and the latest hip-hop from a table that's made from an old red bathtub. The club is open from Thursday to Saturday, midnight to 10 a.m. Just $6 gets you in, but the art will cost a bit more!

Expresso Carioca, 76 Rua Farme de Amoedo, Loja A, Ipanema, 2523-3787
Locals often stop by the Expresso, which is known as a swinging singles joint, at the beginning of the night to meet up with friends or meet someone new. This GLS-friendly establishment maintains a rotation of interesting, if a little strange, decoration. For the price, the usual fare of drinks, from Sex on the Beach to Piña Colada, can't be beat. The scene often spills out of the open front doors onto the sidewalk seating area, where on normal weekends a small street party sometimes forms between 10 p.m. and midnight. During *Carnaval,* this small bar becomes a center of activity for the GLS parties that spontaneously occur along the length of Farme de Amoedo.

Fosfobox, 143 Rua Siqueira Campos, Loja 22A, Copacabana, 2548-7498

Set about a block behind the Siqueira Campos metro stop, Fosfobox is easily recognizable by its nearly perpetual nightly crowd after 10 p.m. The routine is simple: Arrive at 10, buy a few bottles of Skol from the neighboring bar, chat with the leather-booted 20-somethings, exchange glances, and get in line. Don't venture too far out from the entrance—angry upstairs neighbors have been known to dump water and God-knows-what-else onto the bubbly victims below. Inside is a crowded three-floored club and lounge bar (so you're sure to see the hottie you checked out in line), with plenty of convenient make-out corners and couches. Music ranges from funk to new wave to techno. A strong GLS vibe keeps this club hopping into the (late) early hours, but the pounding music may deafen you. Don't miss the '80s theme parties!

Galeria Café, 31 Rua Teixeira de Melo, Ipanema, 2523-8250

This club opens at 2 p.m. from Wednesday to Sunday to cater to the beach crowd that wanders over from *Posto* 8 (really *Posto* "8.5") for a drink, to look at art, or to check out the eclectic decoration that features well-dressed dummies and interesting shapes formed from strands of aluminum foil. The fun starts at around 11 p.m. and keeps pumping until the last client has left. Local DJs who play a mix of *electrosamba*, funk, rock, and house keep the place bumping on Wednesday and Thursday nights. Every Friday the club hosts a dance party that attracts a diverse crowd from all over town. The DJs return for more on Saturday and Sunday. From the artwork and funky designs to the beautiful *cariocas*, this club is a feast for the eyes and easy on the wallet. Admission is $7; very reasonably priced cocktails await you inside.

⊛ **La Girl**, 102 Rua Raul Pompeia, Copacabana, 2247-8342

It comes as no surprise that this is the sister club of Le Boy. However, it's a far cry from the rowdiness of its *uber*-popular, gym-bunny neighbor and presents a much more intimate setting. It has a comfortable bar and a small but fun dance floor, where the women come to hear either live music or DJs six nights a week. For more info, visit www.lagirl.com.br.

⊛ **Le Boy,** 102 Rua Raul Pompeia, Copacabana, 2513-4993
From Tuesday to Sunday, the most popular gay club in Rio is thumping. Once it was a theatre, and the renovations left a large open space that holds nearly 1,000 of the hottest bods from the neighborhood and beyond. Expect a 20-minute drag show almost every night, with especially high energy on Friday night. Although Rio's adoration for the GLS clubs has kept the club market booming, Le Boy has stuck around by catering more to the boys and their boys. Maybe start early in the evening at Le Boy's upstairs fitness center and bathhouse, and then continue to the dance floor. Be safe when leaving this club after hours—there have been some reports of muggings in the area, so hop in a cab right outside the club. For more information, visit www.leboy.com.br.

Nova Leblon, 522 Rua Barão da Torre, Ipanema, 2247-9169
This sauna caters to gay Brazilian men taking a break from rigors of the business day as well as travelers from Brazil and abroad. Discretion and cleanliness are top priority. Massages cost $10, apart from the $12 price to enter. Novo Leblon offers both dry heat and vapor saunas. A bar area caters to individuals who are interested in having a drink before stepping into a private video room or having a haircut, manicure, or pedicure. This is the best gay sauna we found in Rio. It's a great place to meet people or simply relax after a long night of dancing and cavorting in the throws of Rio's sensual and sultry ways. The sauna is open from Monday to Friday, midday to 6 a.m.

X-Demente parties, different venues throughout Rio (see www.xdemente.com)
These *festas de gays* ("gay parties") are the largest in Brazil and known worldwide. Located in the famous Fundação Progresso in Rio's Lapa district and in Marina da Glória, among other places, these huge parties can have up to 5,000-plus, mostly very buff gay guys, from all over Brazil and the world. They're all here to party, dance, and have fun. Resident DJs— and many world-renowned guest DJs—spin the latest tribal, house, and so on. The *festas* start at 11 p.m. and go well into the

morning. Buying tickets ahead of time will save you $7 off the door price of $17. These parties happen on an irregular basis, so visit the Web site for info on the next party.

Zero Zero, 240 Avenida Padre Leonel Franca, Gávea, 2540-8041
This popular weekend spot attracts an enthusiastic crowd for its gay party on Sunday. On other nights, it caters to a mixed crowd that enjoys chilling on the outside patio or heading to the plush interior, where a small dance floor awaits.

Nearby Destination: Niterói

A beautiful 20-minute ferry ride across Rio's Guanabara Bay takes you to Niterói. As you approach Niterói, one of the first things you'll notice is the curious structure that appears: Shaped like a flying saucer ensconced in stone, or perhaps the upper portion of the USS *Enterprise*, is the **Museu de Arte Contemporânea** (Museum of Contemporary Art). Designed by renowned architect Oscar Niemeyer, the museum houses some of the coolest, yet somehow weird, art in the greater Rio area. Outside the museum, from the observatory deck, spectacular views of Rio's great tourist attractions — the Cristo Redentor (Christ the Redeemer) statue and Pão de Açúcar (Sugarloaf Mountain) — can be seen. The museum is open from Tuesday to Sunday, 10 a.m. to 6 p.m. Admission is free. Apart from the unusual art collection, Niterói has a bunch of little-known beaches, nooks, and crannies along the coast where you can escape from Rio's fleshy beach experience and find a great view. Our favorite beaches are **Praia de Itacoatiara**, known to attract a surfing group and a younger crowd, and **Praia de Camboinhas**, where beachfront kiosk restaurants will serve you that morning's catch on a table in the sand.

If you're in Niterói for the evening, you can check out the **Bar Saideira** (139 Rua Traves de Macedo, 2714-2042) or the **Convés Bar** (137 Rua Coronel Tamarindo, 3026-6321). One of the restaurants worth visiting is **Restaurante a Mineira** (353 Avenida Quintino Bocaiúva, 2714-3676), which boasts more than 50 dishes to choose from and has one of the best servings of Mineira food (food from Minas Gerais) available in the state of Rio de Janeiro.

Ferries to Niterói leave the docks in Rio at the end of Praça XV every 20 minutes from 6 a.m. to 5 p.m. Ferries leave every 10 to 12 minutes between 5 and 7 p.m., every 15 minutes from 7 to 8 p.m., every 20 minutes from 8 to 10 p.m., every 30 minutes from 10 p.m. to midnight, and every hour from midnight to 6 a.m. Note that there are various ferry options, each of a different speed, so some ferries can do the trip in about 10 minutes (but why rush this scenic voyage?). Since the city agreed to subsidize the ferry system a few years ago, tickets cost only about $1 each way. A cab will take you to the museum or the surrounding beaches of Niterói for about $15.

Stuff to See and Do

You can cover many of Rio's most appealing daytime tourist attractions and beaches in less than a week. It's the nightlife that will take you months to fully explore. This is a party town like no other. Work schedules are adjusted in the morning hours, naps are taken in the afternoon, and all serious work ceases at sundown, when the town really comes to life. Yet there is something to be said for daytime activities. Although they are not necessarily into the steppin' out routine that many of Rio's visitors assume upon arrival, the locals manage to balance a healthy nightlife with an equally healthy daytime routine. Whether it's for a run along the beach, surfing, launching off Gávea Rock in a hang glider, or simply a stroll through the park, *cariocas* manage to get out during the day. If you want to do the same, we've listed some suggestions for you to consider.

Biblioteca Nacional

Founded in 1910, the National Library houses more than nine million titles, including Bibles as old as the printing press, some of Brazil's oldest published journals, and a plethora of Brazil's historical documents. The library, located at 219 Avenida Rio Branco, is open weekdays from 9 a.m. to 8 p.m. and on Saturday from 9 a.m. to 3 p.m. Guided tours begin at 11 a.m., 1 p.m., and 3 p.m., and admission is free.

Catedral Metropolitana

Located not far from the Praça Cinelândia, in the heart of Rio's financial district, is the most oddly shaped place of worship in the Western Hemisphere. Designed by Edgar de Oliveira Fonseca and shaped like a cone, it is 246 feet/75 meters tall and 348 feet/106 meters in diameter at its base. If you're in the area, stop by the Catedral, at 245 Avenida República do Chile, for a quick visit. It just might be worth your while, but make sure you stay away at night. The base of this cone is crawling with all sorts of unsavory characters, and they're more interested in mugging you than offering a prayer.

Centro Cultural Banco do Brasil

Formerly the headquarters of one of Brazil's largest banks, this modern museum holds two theatres, four show rooms, a cinema and video room, a library with more than 100,000 titles, and an amazing bookstore. This museum focuses on cultural displays of Brazil's past and present. One of the most visited expositions is an arrangement of Brazilian history vis-à-vis the various monetary devices used by the country, from sugarcane and gold to the modern day *real*. Visit www .bb.com.br/cultura for updated information on schedules, shows, expositions, and pricing.

Cinelândia

The area of town known as Cinelândia is formally titled Praça Floriano and offers the most comprehensive one-stop cultural experience you can have in Rio. The plaza itself is a swirl of life and energy. Have a seat and get an eyeful of every type of Rio citizen, from homeless to the rarely seen *carioca* wearing a tie. The plaza is surrounded by three of Rio's most antiquated attractions: the Teatro Municipal, the Biblioteca National, and the Museu Nacional de Belas Artes (detailed below).

Corcovado and the Cristo Redentor (Christ the Redeemer) Statue

The city's best vista is from the enormous statue, Cristo Redentor (Christ the Redeemer), at the top of Corcovado (2,309 feet/704 meters). Recently voted as one of the New Seven Wonders of the World, the statue can be seen from nearly any spot in Rio. Conversely, from the foot of the statue, you can see nearly the whole city. The view is truly spectacular. Pose here to join the throngs of tourists taking pictures to prove to their friends back home that they were actually in Rio de Janeiro. You'll be glad you did.

The train that takes most visitors to the top of Corcovado is older than the statue of Jesus you're going to visit. Inaugurated in October 1884, the train was used to haul the disassembled pieces of the statue to the top of the hill. At the time, it was run by steam and was an engineering feat. Leaving from Cosme Velho Station, the train takes you for nearly 2.5 miles/4 kilometers through tropical rainforest and offers spectacular views of Rio's Zona Norte. Trains depart from the station every half hour from 8:30 a.m. to 6:30 p.m. A ticket costs $14. Kids under 6 years old get a free ride; kids 6 to 12 are charged only $6. It's best to take a bus to Botafogo, then hop in a cab and ask the driver to take you to the *trem do Corcovado*. There is also a road that leads up the back side of Corcovado and ends in a parking lot just beneath and behind the statue. Most *taxistas* will take you to the top and back down for a reasonable price — $15 or so in the low season and $25 or more in the Brazilian summer months, around Christmas and *Carnaval*.

Fairs and Street Markets

On any corner, at any time in Ipanema or Copacabana, you can find yourself in the middle of a spontaneous street market. Whether walking to your hotel along Visconde de Pirajá, or Vieira de Souto in Ipanema, or on Nossa Senhora da Paz in Copacabana, you're bound to pass a makeshift stand of cardboard boxes or simply a blanket with an assemblage of random trinkets for sale. These illegal vendors are part of the random and sometimes interactive street experience that awaits anyone willing to spend more than a day in Rio. We think they're certainly worth a look, but if you want a more serious, and legal, fair experience, you'll have to travel to specific spots at the right time.

Feira Hippie (The Hippie Fair)

The most famous fair among Rio's tourists is the Hippie Fair in Ipanema. Every Sunday, rain or shine, vendors gather at Praça General Osório and spend all day Sunday, from around 8 a.m. until 8 p.m., hanging out, waiting for someone to show enough interest to stop, look, and maybe purchase. There are certainly a number of stands that sell Rio tourist trinkets, like Christ statue key chains and "I Love Rio" shirts, but what's more interesting are the serious vendors who target the local neighborhood community with their handmade wooden furniture from southern Brazil, or the hand-carved and deeply stained wooden African sculptures and face masks. Some of the most comfortable beanbag chairs, called "poofies," are always on sale, and so are hanging chairs that might fit perfectly in that one corner of your apartment that you can't manage to fill. You will find incredible buys on rugs, hammocks, and leather goods, too.

At the four corners of the park, Bahiana food stands maintain steady sales of spicy Bahian food prepared by Salvador women who are wrapped in white, complete with the custom white head wrap you might have seen in the movie *Women on Top*. Like most of the other vendors in the park, the Bahians are relaxed and not in a hurry to give you service. They're in for the long haul and know that moving fast invites little more than a sweaty brow. The business-only vendors tend to be the men selling semiprecious stones. With their digital scales and cheap ties, they seem a little out of place, but no one really cares. The only other hard worker we've seen here is the guy dressed in the Brazilian national soccer team uniform. He usually has a whistle in his mouth as he balances numerous round objects on his foot before kicking them in the air to catch on the back of his neck. We always like to watch when he's playing with an egg.

Our favorite spot in this gathering of artisan talent is right in the middle. On the inside of the corrugated steel fence that borders the park you'll find any number of racks used to hang freshly painted canvases, complete with all the themes you might expect inspired artists in Ipanema to paint: the ocean and beach, natural foliage, and, of course, *favelas*. More than a place to sell their wares, the middle of Praça General Osório on Sundays is a place for the neighborhood's artists to gather, hang out, and show one another their latest paintings. If they sell something, fine; if not, that's also fine. Either way, the low-key atmosphere is one of interesting and sometimes beautiful art, without any of the pretension you might find elsewhere. To hit this fair, grab any cab on Sunday and tell the driver you're headed to Praça General Osório.

FEIRA NORDESTINA (NORTHEASTERNER FAIR)

Just past the center of town, in Sao Cristovão, sits a relatively new construction that looks more like a mini soccer stadium than a fairgrounds for the exclusive use of the city's northeasterner communities. Within Rio, a "northeasterner" is anyone from Brazil's northern states, starting with Bahia and then moving up the coast from there. Northeasterners include people from Pernambuco, Alagoas, and Paraiba, among others. Due to Brazil's economic expansions and contractions over the decades and through the 20th century, waves of urbanization brought thousands of northeasterners to Rio in search of work and a better life. They left their lands behind but brought their culture along.

This fair is a celebration of that culture, and we do mean celebration. From around midday on Saturday to midday on Sunday, the city's northeasterner community gathers in this central location to sell some arts and crafts, do a little cooking, and maybe make a little money. However, the primary attraction is not the money made by selling trinkets—it's the party.

Cold beer and *cachaça* flows. Food is everywhere—just walk a few steps in any direction. You won't find the refined artists or semiprecious-stone vendors you saw in Ipanema. You will find a wide selection of arts and crafts, trinkets, and many items you might come across elsewhere, but you shouldn't come to this fair with Christmas shopping in mind. You come to party.

People here are in a mood to hang out, get drunk, dance, and forget about the hard life they live elsewhere in Rio. If you don't plan on visiting Brazil's northeastern reaches, then this fair is a must-see. It's an extremely dense drop of Brazil's northeastern culture, all in an area about the size of a soccer field. Brazil's African roots—African-based religions, dance, and spirit—are everywhere: in the music, in the eyes of everyone you meet, and at the bottom of every cup of whatever you might be courageous enough to drink. It's hard to avoid spontaneous *capoeira* (a combination of Brazilian dance and martial arts that is popular in the Northeast), shouting, jokes, eruptive laughter, bloodshot eyes, and the undissolved remnants of whatever you just drank. Cajú juice mixed with *cachaça* is a favorite of ours.

This is just the daytime pace. If you want to have a peek without getting dirty, come and go before dark. Once the sun sets, the area around the fair becomes less desirable. Wandering around for a taxi is not a good idea, but as long as you stay inside the ministadium, you're OK. Well, at least you're safe from the danger of Rio's dark underbelly.

If you choose to stay, be prepared to weather an all-night party like none other you've experienced. We admit, some weekends are a bust, but if the mood is right—and you'll feel it—then the party is going to roll, or *bombar*, as they say in Rio. Live music is the preferred method, and random dancing will break out in pockets around you as vendors store their wares for the night. They have now forgotten about making money and have slipped into a distinctly northeasterner state of *lazer*, which is much more energetic, more sensual, and more interactive than the *cariocas'* well-known version. We've watched as young men from the north grab an unknown female to begin dancing a *lambada*, which is something a bit sexier than salsa. Within minutes they're kissing. Men playing dice around a cardboard table are dressed in tank tops, flip-flops, and frayed shorts. They're shouting, slapping the dice, smacking each other on the back, and telling jokes between pouring beer. During the week they're construction workers, but here, on the weekend, they're among friends and in their own element. It's a beautiful site. Laughs are for free, and smiles remain constant.

You'll hear *axé*, *forró*, and maybe some samba, but it's the drums (and maybe the food and drink, too) that keep us coming back.

So consider yourself warned: If you hit this fair in the evening, stay the night and bring enough money to keep yourself lubed until morning. We recommend that you travel with a couple of friends, because nobody will believe your stories of the night you spent at Rio's Northeasterner Fair unless you've got eyewitnesses.

THE "OTHER" FAIR

We call the small artisan fair held every night between the two lanes of Avenida Atlântica in Copacabana the "other" fair because when we ask people at the Hippie Fair where we might find a particular artist or a wider selection of T-shirts, we're told to try the "other" fair.

Held nightly, the "other" fair stretches for about a block in either direction in front of the Help disco. Moving up the beach, toward *Posto* 4, you're most likely to find art. If you head in the opposite direction, you'll find more clothes—such as cool T-shirts that you won't find at the mall, or sarongs (*kangas*) like the ones they sell on Ipanema Beach (but here they're only half the price).

The vendors at this fair, much like the artists at the Hippie Fair, are in a relaxed mode. They're at the fair to see one another more so than they are to make money. No one here is a capitalist. So don't get upset if you're not getting the attention you think you deserve even if you're prepared to buy half their wares. It's likely that you'll encounter vendors here who put just as much value in a good joke or a can of very cold beer. The real benefit of this fair is that it's daily. You don't have to wait until Sunday to get those last-minute gifts you want to take home to your mom or your little brother. If it can wait, we recommend that you hit the Hippie Fair first. Hit this fair if you're in immediate need of that cool and random shirt so you can tell all your inquiring friends back home, "I got it in Rio."

Fishing and Boat Trips

Atlantic Ocean fishing off the coast of Rio offers a great opportunity to hook a marlin as well as other fish you probably won't catch in the Northern Hemisphere. The prices are not cheap, but they're deeply discounted compared to what you might pay in Costa Rica or off the coast of Florida. If you're not into sport fishing, how about a seven-day, six-night sea cruise? Sailing lessons are also available. For fishing options, check out www.estacaodapesca.com.br and click on the banner at the bottom for prices and updated phone numbers. For other boating options, check out the highly recommended Marlin Yacht outfit (www.marlinyacht.com.br).

Golf

Brazil might not be known for its golf, but for those looking for a change of pace, consider playing a round at Rio's ⍟ **Gávea Golf and Country Club** (3322-4141). Known as one of Brazil's (and the world's) greatest courses, Gávea possesses moderately challenging terrain. It is a par 68, 6,800-yard course with spectacular views—holes 15 to 18 pass through the mountainous forest, and holes 10 to 14 run along the beach. The course is semiprivate, but many hotels have an arrangement with Gávea that allows their guests to play there. A round costs about $105.

Hang Gliding and Paragliding off Pedra da Gávea

Rio is one of the few tropical cities where you can leap off a rock at least 3,300 feet/1,000 meters high and land on the sand without getting hurt. The view during your circling flight down is better than anything you've seen from the Christ statue or even in a helicopter. If you've got the guts, take on what is arguably Rio's second most fantastic daytime experience (we happen to think skydiving beats using a glider, but that's us.) Diapers are not included! Sky Center Rio (www.skycenter.com.br) comes highly recommended by many of our

hotel manager friends. Rio Hang Gliding (www.riohanggliding
.com) and Just Fly (www.justfly.com.br) are two other well-known
guide companies. The price for a flight with transfer is usually around
$120 a person.

⊛ Helicopter Ride

For a stunning view with perhaps a little less of an adrenaline boost
than hurtling off the aforementioned Pedra da Gávea, you should consider hiring a helicopter. There are three preset routes that most visitors choose. Route 1 circles past the Christ statue and Sugarloaf with
a quick sprint past the Lagoon and Ipanema. It costs $75 a head and
lasts about five minutes. Route 2 sweeps past Sugarloaf but skips the
Christ statue, running along Ipanema and Leblon Beaches with a
sweep over Gávea and the lagoon. It also costs about $75 a head and
lasts five minutes. Route 3 incorporates both routes 1 and 2, lasts closer to 10 minutes, and costs about $115 a head. Finally, you can rent the
helicopter for up to an hour and just tell the pilot where you want to
go! You're gonna pay, though (about $415 a head). Ask to arrange a trip
through your hotel, or contact Helisight (www.helisight.com.br;
2511-2124 or 2542-7895)), which has helipads in Lagoa, Urca, or Dona
Marta. Lagoa is probably your easiest option—the pad is right next to
Café Lagoa.

Jardim Botânico

Rio de Janeiro is privileged to have such a well-preserved garden,
Jardim Botânico, from its historical past. Dom João VI founded the
park in 1808 but kept it to himself and his family for many years. It
was not open to the public until his son, Dom Pedro I, took over and
opened the great steel gate in 1822. One hundred years later, the garden was declared a UNESCO biosphere reserve.

There are flowers from Asia, trees from the Africa, Chinese bam-
boo, and the likes of plants and trees we've never seen anywhere else.
The orchid greenhouse is a wonder of smells and beautiful flowers,
and some of the bromeliads truly look alien. If you're into plants, take
some time to stroll through this massive garden, which is home to
hundreds of types of flora. It's open from 8 a.m. to 5 p.m. and costs
$3.50 to enter.

Lagoa

The beautiful lagoon, officially named Lagoa Rodrigo de Freitas (but just referred to as Lagoa), situated just inland from Ipanema at the foot of Corcovado, has a track that circumnavigates its waters. Rent a bike or walk to make a clockwise trip around the lagoon, another natural beauty that *cariocas* have come to love. Along the way, you're sure to pass a number of kiosks serving nearly everything from a simple coconut milk drink to sushi.

Maracanã Stadium

Some of the best *futebol* Brazil has to offer happens every Sunday at the cathedral to Brazilian *futebol*, Maracanã Stadium. It was built in 1950 for the World Cup, when nearly 200,000 fans piled into the 155,000-seat stadium (yeah, you do the math—"plenty" of comfy standing room!) to watch Brazil lose to Uruguay. Recent construction on this behemoth has reduced its seating capacity to just over 103,000 seats, which we figure should keep the crowds to under a million for a big match. (Ok, we exaggerate, but you get the picture). Come here on Sunday afternoon to watch Brazilians go crazy for their favorite team. Games between city rivals Flamengo and Fluminense (known as Fla-Flu) are particularly lively. Be prepared for a frenzied crowd, and consider leaving quickly after the game, for tourists are often targets for upset fans. For safety, it would be best to go with Brazilian friends or with a tour company.

Museu Nacional de Belas Artes

Located right across the street from the Teatro Municipal and the Biblioteca Nacional, this is a must-see for art lovers. Founded in 1937, the museum is housed in Brazil's former National School of Belas Artes. The museum, located at 199 Avenida Rio Branco, is open Wednesday to Friday from 10 a.m. to 6 p.m. and Saturday and Sunday from 2 to 6 p.m. Admission is free.

Pão de Açúcar (Sugarloaf Mountain)

The dome-shaped rock of Pão de Açúcar is one of Rio's most recognized symbols. The trip by tram to the 1,299-foot/396-meter summit affords a view like one you've never seen. If it's a windy day, you just might get a shot of adrenaline as the tram sways in the wind while you climb to the dome. Get up there just before sunset and stay after dark to enjoy the *second* best view (the view from Corcovado, of course, being the best) of the city. In the summertime, the small stage on top of Urca Hill (the first stop) offers live music on the weekends, beginning just after sunset. The tram costs $12, departs every 30 minutes, and operates from 8 a.m. to 10 p.m.

Parque Nacional da Tijuca

Cariocas claim the Parque Nacional da Tijuca (or just Parque da Tijuca, for short) is the largest national park within city borders in the world. They might be right. Once you step into Tijuca Park, you're stepping out of Rio. The numerous trails offer excellent views of the city and coastline from a decent elevation, and you won't hear horns, squeaky brakes, or buses zooming by. It's quite a relaxing experience, especially after a number of days bustling around the crowded streets of Ipanema and Copacabana.

Praça Quinze de Novembro

Located downtown, just inland from the public docks, this is where the Portuguese royal family spent time when it lived in Rio. The odd-looking structure set off to one side toward the end of the plaza is Rio's first and free drinking fountain. Long defunct and bereft of water, it stands as a monument to times when the city's leaders were more thoughtful of the poor. From the fountain, toward the docks where ferries will shuttle you to Niterói, is Rio's most skittish yet persistent street fair. It's commonly referred to as the thieves' fair, not because you'll get robbed if you go, but because most everything you see is "hot." A nearby museum, on the western side of the plaza, sells some of the best books and historical prints to be found. The cathedral across the street to the north was used exclusively by the royal family, and through the arc to the east you will find some of the best tourist-free bars and restaurants that Rio has to offer. This area is particularly lively on Thursday evening.

Samba Schools and Samba Clubs

We're not talkin' about those goofy samba shows for people on bus tours. Rio's rich tradition surrounding *Carnaval* is rooted solely in the city's variety of samba schools, each more than decades old and run by dedicated, if a bit sketchy, businesspeople who live and breathe samba. These schools are the source of new samba songs that are used every year at *Carnaval* and are the sponsoring group for all the floats and costumes you normally see during the *Carnaval* parade. Unfortunately, nearly all the samba schools are located in difficult-to-reach neighborhoods that are in unsafe areas of the city. We recommend that you visit only the schools listed here for a live samba school performance: **Salgueiro** (104 Rua Silva Teles, Tijuca, 2288-3065), with public shows every Saturday at 10 p.m., or **São Clemente** (3102 Avenida Presidente Vargas, Centro, 2223-0641) with public shows every Saturday at 10 p.m. Make sure you go with a local, or an arranged tour. See www.rio-carnival.net for more information on samba schools, including history, colors, and samba songs by year.

Scuba Diving

Rio state does not offer the world's greatest diving. In fact, it doesn't even have the country's best diving (you'd probably want to head to Fernando de Noronha for that). However, there are a couple nearby locations that should suffice should you have the desire. For more information, see the chapters on Búzios and Ilha Grande.

Surfing

Brazil doesn't rank in the world's top surfing destinations, but with thousands of miles of coast, it's hard not to find a decent wave. Be warned: Brazilian surfers are aggressive and in some cases territorial. Don't be surprised if you get blocked off a wave or if a local drops in on you. If you can arrange it, go surfing with a local. Around Rio, the best surf spots are in front of *Posto* 8 and *Posto* 10 in Ipanema, between *Posto* 11 and *Posto* 12 in Leblon, and at the point breaks near Arpoador Rock in Ipanema or at the opposite end in Leblon. The beach breaks are constantly changing, but they remain fairly consistent with decent but small and fast, mostly left-breaking waves. For larger, rolling waves, check out the breaks at Recreio and Prainha. All the information you'll possibly need is at www.waves.com.br, or you can simply hop on the surf bus for a tour of the areas best surf spots (www.surfbus.com.br). Finally, if you need gear or simply some local surf flavor, check out Galeria River, just up the road from the Copacabana Fort on Rua Francisco Otaviano.

Teatro Municipal

Rio's Municipal Theatre, located at the northern end of Cinelândia, opened in 1910 complete with a unique design inspired by the Paris Opera. Initially, the theatre was an exhibition hall for statues and artwork from Europe, but soon a stage was built to accommodate the increasing number of French and Italian musicians, symphonies, dance troupes, and acting academies that were seeking a place to perform while visiting Rio de Janeiro. The same tradition holds today: Many of the performing arts from around the world dare not stop through Rio without a run at the Municipal Theatre. Adding to the international mix is a broad range of Brazilian locals who consider Rio's Municipal Theatre to be a major stepping-stone to making it on the international scene. To this day, nearly 100 years after the doors opened, the Municipal Theatre remains a magical venue for live music, opera, and ballet. Check www.theatromunicipal.rj.gov.br for program schedules and ticket pricing.

Uruguania

Located just blocks away from the Catedral Metropolitana, and just off the Uruguania metro stop, hundreds of street vendors form an impromptu market to net business from the swirl of humanity that filters through here. Find nearly anything you need, want, or shouldn't buy but will. Prepare to bargain if the prices are not clearly displayed, and keep an eye on your goods. This spot attracts quick hands and fleeing feet. Along Rua Buenos Aires, you'll find a number of items you never knew existed and some you wish you never saw. Keep walking and you'll stumble headlong into Rio's little known and even smaller Chinatown. It's fun to surface in the middle of blustering humanity; give it a shot.

Don't Miss

Açaí shake

Visit the nearest juice bar and order this high-powered Amazonian fruit smoothie (pronounced "ás-a-YEE"). It's like having a meal in a cup and is one of the most exotic fruits in Brazil.

Arpoador Rock

Located at the far end of Ipanema Beach (near Copacabana). The view overlooking Ipanema, Dois Irmãos, and the other coastal mountains at sunset is priceless. This is perhaps the best place in town to sit and watch the waves break against the rocks as you ponder life (or just try to remember what you did last night).

Bar Juarez

A most rootsy samba–street party experience at the top of Santa Teresa on Friday. Don't get there too early or you might miss the party! *Cariocas* start late and finish early (as in a.m.).

The Best of Gay Rio

Gay Pride week, New Year's Eve, and *Carnaval*.

Café Colombo

Take a coffee or have lunch in this spectacular and historic restaurant located in downtown Rio. It's a working piece of art.

Corcovado and the Cristo Redentor (Christ the Redeemer) statue

A photo of the iconic Christ statue at the top of Corcovado will win you respect and approval at home (but don't forget to snap off a few photos of the best view in town—the one looking *down* from the Christ statue as opposed to up at it).

Feira Hippie

Rio's famous Hippie Fair will give you a taste, in under an hour, of what the rest of Brazil has to offer. We like to first walk clockwise around the inner ring, then counterclockwise around the outer ring, and then cut through the artists in the middle as we head toward Brasileirinho.

Ipanema Beach

By day this place is packed with beauty. A sunrise experience here is a common rite of passage for those all-night revelers who manage to make it that far, and, yes, the kiosks are still open and will serve you whatever you'd like.

Lapa street party

Dive headfirst into the craziest swirl of Brazilian madness that Rio has to offer.

Maracanã

Visit this immense *futebol* stadium for a Sunday afternoon *futebol* match to understand why Brazilians really do dominate the world when it comes to *futebol*, their national sport.

Pão de Açúcar (Sugarloaf)

Not only is the view spectacular, but if you time it right, sunset on the top is a priceless photo op. Some of us also remember 007 and the *Jaws* character battling it out atop Pão de Açúcar's tram in the movie *Moonraker*.

Prainha Beach

This beautiful little beach just west of Barra da Tijuca is worth the trip if you want a change of pace from Ipanema, Leblon, and Copa.

Sambódromo

During *Carnaval*, the Sambódromo fills up with cheering spectators and row after row of costumed samba dancers. Grab a seat in the stands and hold on! As with everywhere else in Rio during *Carnaval*, things tend to get rambunctious. Sections 9 and 11 are the best spots.

Búzios

TOURISTO SCALE

🔔 🔔 🔔 🔔 🔔 🔔 🔔 🔔 (8)

WE LIKE TO THINK OF BÚZIOS (ALSO KNOWN AS ARMAÇÃO dos Búzios) as Rio's answer to Cape Cod's Nantucket. This once-upon-a-time lazy beach town has been groomed for greatness in tourism for nearly five decades, and, like Nantucket, it has beaches, charm, and nightlife and is a hot spot for the in crowd. Over the years, a constant flow of international celebrities, pioneered by Brigitte Bardot, Brazilian social heavyweights, and a robust Argentine ex-pat crowd has brought investment, style, and support for a solid tourism sector. It also rivals any place in the country for tourists from Europe and the United States. (Búzios is one of the few places in Brazil where English is widely spoken.)

The most famous part of town is **Rua das Pedras**. It's a seaside road made of ill-fitting stones that serves as a glitz strip for folks to go shopping, eat out, and party in the street. On Brazilian summer nights, this road is usually loaded with a "parade" of tourists. The center of town, Praça Santos Dumont, is just one block inland. Around the plaza and down Rua Manuel Turíbio de Farias, which runs parallel to Rua das Pedras, there is more of the same, with restaurants, boutiques, and bars that have attracted tourists for years.

Along the Orla Bardot, a one-way street that extends from Rua das Pedras north toward Armação and Ossos Beaches, you will find a slew of nice restaurants and bars, each with its own slice of ocean view. The historical remnants of Búzios — the fishing village — are focused around Praça dos Ossos and the northernmost end of Armação. This part of town is not nearly as fabulous as the center, but it has more soul. It is a mellow alternative to the pomp and circumstance that tends to overwhelm along Rua das Pedras. The *pousadas* ("inns") here are simple, family owned, and surprisingly comfortable. The owners

Búzios: Key Facts

Location	109 miles/176 kilometers east of Rio de Janeiro
	15 miles/24 kilometers northeast of Cabo Frio
	370 miles/ 596 kilometers northeast of São Paulo
Population	Around 20,000 (no one has bothered counting for a while)
Area Code	22
Beer to Drink	*Chopp*
Rum to Drink	*Cachaça*
Music to Hear	Whatever is live
Tourism	The town tourist office is located at Praça Santos Dumont and is open from 9 a.m. to 9 p.m. Check out www.buziosonline.com.br, or www.buziosturismo.com.br for more info.

will stay up all night sharing stories and telling you about Búzios, Brazil, Argentina, and their view of the world, if you let them.

Yes, Búzios has glamour, but travelers come to this 5-mile/8-kilometer-long peninsula for its 11 diverse but attractive beaches. Punctuated around the peninsula, various beaches attract different crowds. At some, you'll encounter elite families and their friends, mixed in with a few locals. At others, you'll find surfers and/or nudists. The center of town, and the main tourist dock, is right on **Praia do Canto**. **Praia Armação** looks upon the fishing harbor. **Praia dos Ossos** is a protected, backyard beach for the small houses built along the water.

Farther from the center of town and down the peninsula, numerous neighborhoods display their own appeal. They are full of wealthy Brazilians with beach homes in Búzios and, apart from numerous *pousadas*, contain little more than cheesy tourist trinket shops, a handful of restaurants, and the same stores one would find in any small town—hardware, pharmacy, barber, and so on. However, the neighborhoods of Ferradura, Manguinhos, and Geribá each have long white-sand beaches that overflow with tourists in the summer. Many other great beaches, such as João Fernandes, Brava, Olho de Boi, Azeda, João Fernandinho, Ferradura, Geribá, and Tartaruga, are discussed in the Focus section.

Finally, you will not leave Búzios without running into someone from Argentina. Most of them are tourists, just like you, but the ex-pat Argentines who have been living in Búzios for 15 to 20 years are a rare breed indeed. If you find yourself in conversation with one, don't be too hasty about leaving. They are a rich resource of region-al history, an alternative point of view to Brazil, and, more often than not, generous and sincere.

The Briefest History

Armação de Búzios, along with Cabo Frio and Arraial do Cabo to the south, was settled in the 17th century, much to the chagrin of the local Indians who were already there (isn't that always the case?). Nu-merous coves, inlets, and small bays attracted trader and pirate ships that sought shelter from Atlantic storms. After the Portuguese built a fort at Cabo Frio to protect their claim, Búzios eventually evolved into a sleepy fishing village wrapped around present-day Ossos Beach.

The village export, whale oil, was shipped to Rio de Janeiro to light the capital's street lamps for decades. Fishing and killing whales kept the village in business until tourism settled in. (How grateful those whales must be to us tourists!) Búzios remained an unknown para-dise until a young actress from the United States, Brigitte Bardot, dis-covered the beauty of Búzios in the 1960s while there with her Brazilian boyfriend. Her trumpeting brought the town's first glitz and glamour crowd that, since then, has adorned its streets.

Enterprising Argentines arrived in town around the early 1970s. They took advantage of their financial leverage to purchase land and build restaurants, hotels, and other bits and pieces of infrastructure for the ever increasing numbers of Argentine tourists. Búzios is still relatively unknown among the U.S. crowd compared to Europeans, but it has caught on with the rich and famous worldwide. Argentines and Brazilians have established a well-greased tourism market in town, and they are responsible for the town's current status as a top-notch beach retreat for foreigners and Brazilians alike. You'll bump into them all in Búzios, from the middle-class stratum all the way up to the ultra-rich.

Getting There

Once you arrive at Rodoviária Novo Rio, in Rio de Janeiro, make your way across the footbridge and to the right at the end of the breezeway. Toward the end of the row, you will see signs for bus line 1001, which runs service to and from Búzios. The ticket will cost you just under $15 each way. Starting at 6:30 a.m., buses run by 1001 leave Rio de Janeiro roughly every two hours until 5:30 p.m. Some buses are "conventional" and don't have air conditioning. The air-conditioned buses normally run during the afternoon hours, at 1, 3, and 5 p.m.

To return to Rio from Búzios, locate the 1001 office just across the street from the bus stop. Starting at 7 a.m., buses leave every two hours until 7:00 p.m. Air-conditioned buses run in the afternoon hours.

The trip is usually about three hours. There is a 15-minute stop at a rest area halfway along the route.

Driving to Búzios is an option if you don't mind fighting Búzios locals for parking. As you leave Rio de Janeiro, cross the Rio-Niterói Bridge and make a left onto RJ-101. The turn is just after the end of the bridge. After 31 miles/50 kilometers on RJ-101, you will pass by a small town called Tanguá. Go 7 miles/12 kilometers from Tanguá and make a right onto RJ-124. This road runs into RJ-106, a secondary state road. Follow RJ-106 for 12 miles/20 kilometers and take a right. By now you should see signs for Búzios. Follow the road for another 9 miles/15 kilometers, and you'll make it to the peninsula. There is a chance, especially on RJ-101, that you will be clocked at least once by electronic surveillance. If you're caught speeding, you will be levied a fine through your rental car company, which will charge the fine plus a service charge to your credit card.

We hate to be killjoys, but we should also alert you to one important WARNING about your travels to Búzios. Along the way, you are likely to encounter at least one **police checkpoint**. As you go through the checkpoint, drive slowly (and remove your sunglasses, so as not to appear shady). The police will scrutinize you and "randomly" choose motorists to stop. If you're one of the "lucky" chosen ones, they will most likely ask you to get out of your car, give you a patdown, and check through your belongings. This invasive process is supposedly to interdict drugs and other contraband transported from Rio to

Búzios. However, Brazilian police are very, very poorly paid, and it is not beyond them to use this opportunity to coerce travelers into paying small fees for inane or even fabricated automotive infractions. We were once required to pay about $25 for being unable to furnish the receipt for tires that the officer believed to be new! Of course, the transaction was made discreetly behind a small police hut. Our best advice is to never give the police a real reason to detain you (i.e., don't *ever* carry drugs to Búzios), and don't get too worked up over this very Brazilian practice. Yeah, it sucks, but you can deal.

The entire trip, from the Rio-Niterói Bridge to the beaches of Búzios, should not take more than an hour and a half. With heavy traffic at the Rio-Niterói Bridge, the trip can often take up to two and a half or even three hours. At peak holiday times, you're looking at more than four hours.

On the Way to Búzios: Saquarema, Cabo Frio, and Arraial do Cabo

Although Búzios is the big draw among all the beach towns east of Rio, there are a few other options to consider. As you head toward Búzios, you will pass by Saquarema, Cabo Frio, and Arraial do Cabo. Saquarema has a few quiet and clean beaches but is known mostly as a surfing destination; Cabo Frio is kind of grubby but offers a base from which to scuba dive; and Arraial do Cabo has several very pretty beaches that some folks say rival those of Búzios (although we still prefer the Búzios beaches). If you're interested in checking out these beaches, the best way to get there would be on 1001, the same bus line that takes you to Búzios. From the bus station in Rio, look for destinations to Saquarema, Cabo Frio, or Arraial do Cabo.

Itaúna Beach in Saquarema is the surfing destination for anyone willing to take a bus outside Rio de Janeiro to surf. If you're into catching waves, you might want to give this beach a visit before heading on to Búzios. Another well-known beach in Saquarema is **Praia da Vila**, which many consider to be the town's most popular beach. With the normal fare of kiosks and beachfront mom-and-pop shops, this beautiful beach can be considered just as nice as any of the beaches in Búzios, though quite a bit less busy. While in Saquarema, consider sleeping at the **Maasai Hotel** at Praida Itaúna (17 Travessa Itaúna, 22-2651-1092), located right on the beach at Praia Itaúna.

Praia do Forte is Cabo Frio's principal beach, but among the wind surfers and kite surfers, **Praia do Foguete** is the place to be. Cabo Frio is perhaps the best area in the state for kite surfing (with a windy day at Rio's Barra da Tijuca Beach coming in a close second for intermediate to expert kite surfers). Cabo Frio is also known for decent **scuba** diving and snorkeling, probably the best in that part of the state. Check out **Cabo Frio Sub** (www.cabofriosub.com.br) for more information. Your best bet is to make a trip to Cabo Frio from nearby Búzios, where accommodation is considerably more professional.

We can't find much difference in natural beauty between Búzios and Arraial do Cabo, except for the fact that Búzios has better options for sleeping, dining, and partying. There is one unique activity that Arraial do Cabo has over Búzios, however—dune buggy rides. **Praia Grande**, in Arraial do Cabo, is more than 24 miles/40 kilometers long and is a great place to take a dune buggy at low tide and rip and roar through the sand. Taking a bus over from Búzios to do a dune buggy "tour" might be a nice way to break up your time in Búzios, but we recommend that you make it a day trip, since Búzios is not too far away.

Getting Around

Once you step off the bus to Búzios, turn left and walk across the main *avenida* and down the cross street toward the center of town. You will run into the main drag, Rua das Pedras, at the Methodist Church in less than five minutes.

Nearly all the beaches on the northern end of the peninsula can be reached by foot from the center of town. All the restaurants, bars, boutiques, hotels, and *pousadas* are tightly clustered around the Rua das Pedras, its extension to the north along Praia da Armação, called Orla Bardot, and around Praça dos Ossos, in the historic part of town at the end of Orla Bardot and over the hill just before the small church.

Bike, buggy, and car rentals are certainly another option, especially if you're interested in covering more ground or would like to explore the full extension of the peninsula, including Geribá. From the Praça Santos Dumont, follow Rua Travessa de Pescadores toward the water to find a small rent-a-car office at number 50. The locally owned tourist shop will give you all the information you need to make a good choice on car, bike, or buggy rentals.

A taxi stand located on the southeastern corner of Praça Santos Dumont has prices posted in plain view. Taxis line up along the length of the Praça, all waiting to take you to any beach. Many will offer to come to pick you up at a prearranged time. You can reach any beach in Búzios for under $10. Prices are inflated, but that's Búzios!

Focus on Búzios: Beaches (and Some Fun Nightlife)

Búzios is synonymous with beaches and nightlife. You don't come to Búzios unless you're looking for at least a full day on the beach—or in the water—followed by a good meal and some fun listening to live music, dancing, or chatting it up in the street with a good-looking local.

Take the time to stroll down Rua das Pedras by day and again by night. Some stores open early and close early; others open only after sunset and don't lock the doors until after midnight. Still others, much like those in Rio, don't get going until well after midnight. All the shopping, eating, and boozing you want to do can be found on or near Rua das Pedras. More of this is discussed in the "Going Out" section.

Beach life is the big draw in Búzios—it dominates the day. Either you take a schooner trip or you take a cab to any number of beaches. Schooner trips cost $10 to $15, take three hours, and give you a tour of the protected side of the peninsula. You pass by two islands, make two beach stops, where you may choose to eat lunch or simply stay until the next boat comes through, and can have all the drinks and fruit you want while on board. For the money, it's a pretty good deal. The only real bother is the beach stop for lunch and snorkeling. The moment you get off the boat, you're bombarded with locals trying to sell trinkets. There's even competition among the restaurants for clients. The excellent boat ride, however, dilutes this minor annoyance.

You don't actually need a schooner to get to the beaches. From Praça Santos Dumont, take a cab to one of several beaches. Go to **Praia João Fernandes** if you want a scene adorned with beautiful Brazilian

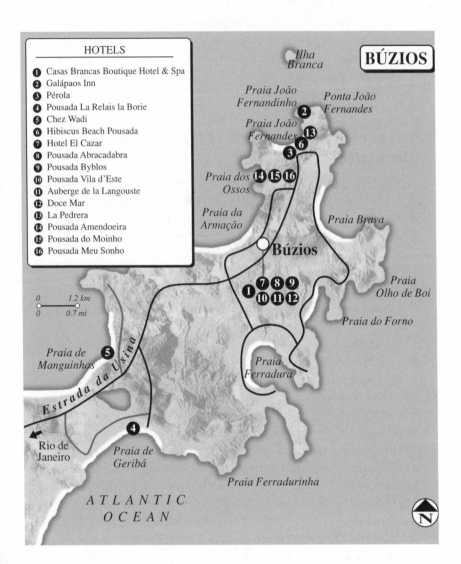

HOTELS

1. Casas Brancas Boutique Hotel & Spa
2. Galápaos Inn
3. Pérola
4. Pousada La Relais la Borie
5. Chez Wadi
6. Hibiscus Beach Pousada
7. Hotel El Cazar
8. Pousada Abracadabra
9. Pousada Byblos
10. Pousada Vila d'Este
11. Auberge de la Langouste
12. Doce Mar
13. La Pedrera
14. Pousada Amendoeira
15. Pousada do Moinho
16. Pousada Meu Sonho

BÚZIOS

Ilha Branca

Praia João Fernandinho
Ponta João Fernandes
Praia João Fernandes
Praia dos Ossos
Praia da Armação
Praia Brava
Búzios
Praia Olho de Boi
Praia do Forno

0   1.2 km
0   0.7 mi

Praia de Manguinhos
Estrada da Usina

Praia Ferradura

Rio de Janeiro
Praia de Geribá

Praia Ferradurinha

ATLANTIC OCEAN

N

families and couples. This is also where you're most likely to spot celebrities. **Praia Brava** is much mellower, peoplewise, but it has less beach and is full of surfers and surfing groupies. It is worth the time, however, to walk along the well-worn trail that winds from Praia Brava to **Praia Olho de Boi** ("Bull's Eye Beach"), where you'll find naturists and those seeking to eliminate tan lines. Even if you don't descend to this small nudist colony, the view from the ridge on the easternmost point of the peninsula is spectacular. Both **Praia Azeda** and **Praia João Fernandinho** are very protected and ideal for snorkeling and easy swimming.

Praia Ferradura has crystal-clear water and is excellent for snorkeling. **Praia de Geribá** is perhaps the nicest beach on the peninsula—it's very reminiscent of Ipanema. The beautiful folks check in around 11 a.m. and filter toward the southern end of the beach. By noon, the place looks like *Posto* 9 in Ipanema, only without the skyline in the backdrop. Geribá is the best spot for a low-key surfing experience, as opposed to Brava Beach, where territorial locals often rule the roost.

Finally ⊛ **Praia da Tartaruga** is a little-known, out-of-the-way beach that, other than having one of the prettiest sunsets around, is more appropriate for a very relaxed day and a nice lunch at the **Pousada Praia da Tartaruga**'s seaside restaurant. Ask for the grilled seafood platter for two. It's perfect with cold beer.

Where to Stay

From elegant to dirt cheap, you can find almost anything you want for a hotel experience in this beach town. Búzios caters to Brazil's richest as well as most modest travelers. There are more *pousadas* than hotels, but the hotels in the area are luxurious, sophisticated, and resplendent, with well-thought-out designs that will leave a good impression of your trip to Brazil.

The choicest hotels are clustered at Praia da Armação and on Morro Humaitá (recommended), which is a hill that overlooks a small harbor. Near Praça Ossos, you will find a tight cluster of more modest *pousadas*. Generally speaking, *pousadas* in this area rarely have rooms with a view and are thus much more economical. On the other side of the peninsula, hanging off the hills overlooking Praia João

Fernandes and Praia João Fernandinho, there is a gaggle of some excellent hotels and *pousadas*. All boast immaculate ocean views and *suh-weet* sunsets. *Pousadas* are not limited to these three areas, however. Walk just 10 feet in Búzios and you will find yet another *pousada*; last we heard, there were more than 200 *pousadas* on the peninsula. Here are a few you might want to consider.

⊛ **Casas Brancas Boutique Hotel & Spa**, 10 Rua Alto do Humaitá, Armacão, Búzios, RJ, Brazil. ℭ 55-22-2623-1458, ✆ 55-22-2623-2147, ⌨ www.casasbrancas.com.br, info@casasbrancas.com.br

▪$ **Pricey** and up ⑪ **CP** Ⓒ Ⓒ 32 rooms and suites

Walking into Casas Brancas, we immediately sensed a level of taste and tradition. This is the oldest *pousada* in Búzios, and its pride shows through the excellent service and attention to detail. Every room is decorated differently, with pieces of furniture and fixtures brought from all over the world — Africa, Asia, Indonesia, and the Mediterranean, mostly — by one of the owners, who loves to travel. Everything else is handmade locally, from the couch covers to the woven chairs used in the dining area, where you can look out over the bay while enjoying your meal from any table. The recently installed ⊛ spa is one of the peninsula's main attractions and a favorite weekend getaway for Brazilian actresses Cleo Pires and Priscilla Fantin. The spa offers a number of unique massages — Bambu from France, Tui Na from China, and Ayurveda from India top the list, apart from more typical methods like Shiatsu, Swiss, and Thai (without the happy ending). Our only real problem with the spa's layout is that it's easy to get lost in the incongruous network of narrow stairwells and right-angled halls that give you a feeling of being in a never-ending whitewashed adobe maze. Fortunately, there always seems to be an attendant or a maid nearby to point you in the right direction. If you're looking for a romantic place to stay, Casas Brancas is it.

Galápagos Inn, Praia João Fernandes, km 3, Búzios, RJ, Brazil. ℭ 55-22-2623-6161, ✆ 55-22-2623-2297, ⌨ www.galapagos.com.br, galapagos@mar.com.br

$ **Pricey** and up 🍴 **BP** CC 37 rooms and suites

The Galápagos sits on a ridge overlooking one of the most beautiful lagoons in Búzios. Every room has a deck; some are bigger than others, but all offer the privacy of your very own sunset. The Spanish tile in the restaurant area and rooms is a refreshing break from the whitewashed walls of the reception area. The wicker chairs are a nice touch. The restaurant and piano bar combine within a spacious, open-air room under a thatched roof. Every inch of the pool deck, bar, and restaurant offers an excellent view, which brings a feeling of relaxation and luxury. Rooms are decorated with a "Galapágos" theme that tries a little too hard, but the nice woodwork more than makes up for the laughable bed covers. The last time we visited, the service was below par, but every room comes with an ocean view, so we were quick to overlook any service issues once we were comfortably settled in our rooms.

Pérola, 222 Avenida José Bento Ribeiro Dantas, Armacão, Búzios, RJ, Brazil. 📞 55-22-2620-8507, 📠 55-22-2623-9015, 🖳 www.perolabuzios.com.br, reservas@perolabuzios.com

$ **Pricey** and up 🍴 **BP** CC 60 rooms

The one real problem with this Mediterranean-style establishment is the absence of beach access or even a decent beach nearby. Perhaps this is why guests are welcomed with a glass of champagne when they arrive. The hotel is focused around a central pool area that matches the decidedly relaxed and cool atmosphere. Poolside chairs have been replaced with slightly raised wooden platforms, complete with brilliantly white padding and a flowing, thin curtain for those who'd like a little more privacy. The rooms are divided into five different subsets, and all come with Internet, a minibar, a/c, and a safe. The style is a mix of Spanish villa and Greek island. We especially like the raised sinks and home-style touch in the bathrooms. The executive suite and the loft are ideal for small families. The superior garden actually has a well-manicured garden, perhaps the first thing you'll see when waking up in the morning (or afternoon, as the case may be). Both the master suite and the loft have raised platforms and specific sleeping areas, and the deluxe and presidential suites are the only ones with a Jacuzzi.

Elsewhere in the hotel, you will find exceptional service, because all the employees have been whipped into shape by an American owner with high expectations. If you want to be close to the beach, this is not your spot, but if you crave privacy, style, service, and close proximity to the Rua das Pedras and all the action in Búzios, it would be hard to beat Pérola.

Pousada Le Relais la Borie, 1374 Rua dos Gravatás, Praia de Geribá, Búzios, RJ, Brazil. ℂ 55-22-2623-1498, 📧 55-22-2623-2303, 🖥 www.laborie.com.br, laborie@mar.com.br

🛍 **Pricey** and up 🍴 **CP** ⒸⒸ 38 rooms

Tucked up against one of the nicest beaches (Praia de Geribá) in Búzios, La Borie is closer to a resort experience than any other place listed. There are two bars, a restaurant, a hot tub, a sauna, hammocks in the gardens, and a walkway that leads directly to white sands and warm south Atlantic waters. The rooms are decorated in a loose-fitting Mediterranean style, everything is a shade of off-white, and the bathrooms are tiled in a light-brown marble. You could never leave the grounds and still have all you need for a well-rounded vacation.

Chez Wadi, 11 Rua Pixiguinha, Manguinhos, Búzios, RJ, Brazil. ℂ 55-22-2623-1296/9999-7698, 🖥 www.chezwadi.com, wadi@chezwadi.com

🛍 **Not So Cheap** and up 🍴 **BP** ⒸⒸ 10 rooms

Even though there's not much here in terms of amenities (just a small pool and a restaurant), we love the Chez Wadi because it's like staying at the house of an old friend. The home-style feel was created by the owner, Waldyr Abifadel, who decorated the whole place with a mixture of Arab and Brazilian tastes. His charisma and genuine friendly nature makes you feel at home within minutes of arrival. His two Labrador retrievers are just as welcoming, if a bit energetic at first. Wadi, as he is known, cooks a number of Arab dishes and has taken care to maintain well-manicured grounds and very comfortable rooms. Situated on the oldest beach in Búzios, Manguinos, Chez Wadi is a great spot to stay if you're not interested in all the glitz and glamour of the Humaita Hill hotels like Casas Brancas or the crowds associated with Geribá or João Fernandes.

Hibiscus Beach Pousada, 22 Rua 1, Quadra C, Praia João Fernandes, Búzios, RJ, Brazil. ℭ 55-22-2623-6221, ✆ 55-22-2623-6221, ⌨ www.hibiscusbeach.com.br, reservas@hibiscusbeach.com.br

💲 **Not So Cheap** and up ⑪ **BP** ⒸⒸ 14 rooms

Tucked into a fold between two hills overlooking João Fernandes Beach, the recently renovated Hibiscus Beach Pousada offers a little more privacy than you'll normally receive in most other *pousadas* in Búzios. Featuring Polynesian-style bungalows with private deck, it's the perfect place for a romantic getaway. The surprisingly spacious bungalows have all been built into a lush green forested area, and, as the name suggests, there are hibiscus flowers everywhere that enhance the tropical feel. The interior design is simple but smart. All come with a minifridge, a/c, a safe, and a private deck with a view of the ocean. There is Wi-Fi throughout the *pousada*. The poolside bar is a nice touch, and the breakfast offers hot items rather than just the usual spread of fruit and juice. Finally, the private parking is a nice addition for those who choose to rent a buggy.

Hotel El Cazar, 6 Rua Alto do Humaitá, Armação, Búzios, RJ, Brazil. ℭ 55-22-2623-1620, ✆ 55-22-2623-1620, ⌨ www.buzioselcazar.com.br, reservas@buzioselcazar.com

💲 **Not So Cheap** and up ⑪ **BP** ⒸⒸ 21 rooms

Perhaps the grandest place to stay in Búzios, this Moroccan-owned establishment offers a very rich, visually stimulating atmosphere and smooth design with deeply hued, well-polished wooden features. An impressive bar and restaurant area, complete with grand piano, present a fluid entry to the suites, most of which open onto a small deck overlooking Armação Beach and the bay in the distance. Each suite presents a subtle feel of Arab grace and comfort. Care and attention have been put into the design and fixtures in all of them. Earth tones complement hues of firebrick, midnight blue, goldenrod, sepia, and burnt sienna, conveying an immediate sense of deep relaxation. Expect an impeccable presentation and the light fragrance of burning incense.

Pousada Abracadabra, 13 Rua Alto do Humaitá, Armacão, Búzios, RJ, Brazil. 𝄐 55-22-2623-1217, 🖥 www.abracadabrapousada.com.br, info@abracadabrapousada.com.br

💲 **Not so Cheap** and up 🍴 **CP** Ⓒ🅒 16 rooms

On par with some of the most sophisticated and plush *pousadas* in Búzios, the Abracadabra maintains pace with our favorite, the Casas Brancas. It has a little less style than Casas Brancas, but it might have more value. The Mediterranean-style rooms are all whitewashed and have various shades of stained wood, from a beautiful wood-paneled floor in the deluxe suite to wooden fixtures and furniture in the standard and superior rooms. The focus on design, however, is secondary to what is clearly a focus on maintaining a well-trained staff. The deck offers a decent-size pool with a nearby bar and is genuinely one of the best lookout spots in Búzios. We could spend hours on the deck, sunning, drinking, and taking in the view. As with many *pousadas* in this part of Búzios, you pay for what you get—great service, an excellent view, and a good night's rest.

Pousada Byblos, 14 Rua Alto do Humaitá, Armação, Búzios, RJ, Brazil. 𝄐 55-22-2623-1162, 🖥 55-22-2623-2828, 🖥 www.byblos.com.br, byblos@byblos.com.br

💲 **Not So Cheap** and up 🍴 **BP** Ⓒ🅒 21 rooms

We think the Byblos makes an interesting first impression, a mix of a brothel with style, a surfer's den, and an elegant furniture outlet. The lobby extends onto an outside deck with a small bar, a pool, and an excellent ocean view, the same one you get from Casas Brancas (next door) or Abracadabra. Nearly all the rooms have an ocean view, and they are priced accordingly. Each has a/c, a minibar, and a decent-size TV. A range of decoration styles, from sun and coral to *etoile*, sea, and *pigionier* (we're not so sure about that one) will greet you, maybe even surprise you. We recommend that you snag a room with an ocean view—the garden view rooms are clearly second rate and overpriced.

The *pousada* has staked an ideal location between Ossos Beach and the center of town. Expect to meet anyone from Mick Jagger to a random porn star in the eyebrow-raising atmosphere conjured by Byblos's style and staff. Although it's a cut away from the luxury and class of places like Pérola or Casas Brancas, we think Byblos is a decent selection if you'd prefer to spend more money on going out at night and other daily activities while saving money on lodging.

Pousada Vila d'Este, 11 Rua Alto do Humaitá, Armação, Búzios, RJ, Brazil. ℂ 55-22-2623-6431, 📠 55-22-2623-1546, 🖥 www.viladeste.com.br, pousada@viladeste.com.br

💲 **Not So Cheap** and up 🍴 **CP** ⓒⒸ 14 rooms and suites

We love the Vila d'Este. This beautifully designed *pousada* looks out over the bay from a distinct height advantage. Slate stone tiles the floor from the reception area to the restaurant out back. In the two sitting areas, Arab rugs with deep hues of blue and red complement comfortable couches of an international style you rarely find in Brazil. The rooms are gracefully and tastefully decorated with hanging mosquito nets that look more fashionable than functional—every room offers a different design, however. The *pousada* now has an infinity pool that overlooks the bay, complete with an underwater tunnel to the Jacuzzi-bar area.

Auberge de la Langouste, 3 Rua Alto do Humaitá, Armação, Búzios, RJ, Brazil. ℂ 55-22-2623-1273, 📠 55-22-2623-1273,

🖳 www.aubergedelalangouste.com.br,
pousada@aubergedelalangouste.com.br

💲 **Cheap** and up ⑪ **BP** (CC) 20 rooms

The Langouste more than makes up for its lack of ocean view with a splendid array of flora that's so thick and lush it attracts fauna from all over the peninsula. It's a jungle just outside your door. Each room is decorated differently with French furniture and design. The master suite has a large deck and is the only room with a view. Inside, a hand-painted mural complements the soothing color tones and comfortable furniture. A pool deck with ample space complements one of the few pools we've seen in which you could actually do laps. There is foosball and a pool table in the game room, whose wooden floor and struts might have come directly from an old schooner or other sailing vessel. Bottom line, the Langouste is quiet, secluded, and very, very lush.

Doce Mar, 4 Rua Alto do Humaitá, Armação, Búzios, RJ, Brazil.
📞 55-22-2623-6181, 📠 55-22-2623-6181,
🖳 www.buziosdirect.com/hoteldocemar,
hoteldocemar@mar.com.br

💲 **Cheap** and up ⑪ **CP** (CC) 19 rooms

The sheer amount of tile work in this hotel is amazing. The feeling is very spartan with a touch of comfort and subtle style —very Mediterranean. We were not surprised to learn that the owners are Italian. A thick slab of stained wood that almost looks like marble adorns the bar area, complete with a row of elegant stools and a selection of top-shelf liquor to match. With more attention to detail than most hotels we've seen, the restaurant and pool area are very well kept and comfortable. The rooms are simple and straightforward with a wall-mounted, wooden headboard and contemporary furniture. All the colors and designs are blended within the spectrum of the white you see along the coast of Spain or Greece. Unfortunately, the Doce Mar (Sweet Ocean) has no ocean views, sweet or otherwise.

La Pedrera, Rua 4, Quadra C, Praia João Fernandes, Armacão, Búzios, RJ, Brazil. ☎ 55-22-2623-4753, ✆ 55-22-2623-4694, 🖳 www.lapedrerabuzios.com.br

💲 **Cheap** and up 🍽 **BP** 🆑 28 rooms

It's rare to find a boutique hotel where even the standard rooms have a private balcony and a spectacular view of the ocean. With what appears to be a details-oriented approach to service and décor, La Pedrera creates an original design we haven't seen before in Búzios. The iron-wrought bed frames, for example, come to mind. Some even have mosquito nets, reminiscent of a time when people poured water from a large ceramic jar into a larger, wide-rimmed bowl to wash their faces in the morning. Don't expect luxury, but comfort with a twist of rustic will await you. All rooms are colored with light earth tones, with similar or matching colors used in the bedding and towels, making for a relaxing atmosphere that's easy on the eyes.

Of particular appeal is the great view from the hotel's top deck and pool area. The pool itself is almost an infinity pool, if it were not for the dark wooden railing that blocked our view. We especially liked the soothing music that seemed to be always within earshot but never too loud. In short, La Pedrera is a great value for the view and the comfort, but it's not as luxurious as others we've listed here. Shuttles to the beach downhill and to the center of town run day and night.

Pousada da Amendoeira, 1449 Rua João Fernandes, Ossos, Búzios, RJ, Brazil. ☎ 55-22-2623-2613, 🖳 www.amendoeira.com.br, pous.amendoeira@uol.com.br

💲 **Dirt Cheap** and up 🍽 **CP** 🆑 6 rooms

Run by a friendly mother-daughter team, this simple *pousada* attracts large numbers of European and U.S. students looking for a good rate and a good location. The rooms are simple and airy, but the walls are thin—shoot for an upstairs room for more peace and quiet, especially during festive weekends. The owners offer a $5 per night discount for guests staying more than two days.

Pousada do Moinho, 1324 Avenida José Bento Ribeiro Dantas, Ossos, Búzios, RJ, Brazil. ℭ 55-22-2623-3719, ✆ 55-22-2623-3719, ⌨ www.pousadadomoinho.com.br, reservas@pousadadomoinho.com.br

💲 **Dirt Cheap** and up ⓘ **CP** ⓒⓒ 4 rooms

The Brazilian owners of the Moinho, Sebastão and Elisa, are worldly, talkative, and engaging, and they will welcome you into their small family for as long as you stay. We have enjoyed many conversations on politics, education, history, and culture with Sebastão. Elisa chimes in when she thinks he's talking too much or simply wrong. The *pousada* is small, and the lobby and seating area are more like extensions of the owner's house than a separate structure. There are only four rooms, and two are much smaller than the other pair. A sundeck on the second story overlooks Praça dos Ossos and is perfect for catching early morning rays while you take your time to wake up after a long night in Rua das Pedras. Expect complete relaxation, good conversation, and excellent service.

Pousada Meu Sonho, 1289 Avenida Jose Bento Ribeiro Dantas, Ossos, Búzios, RJ, Brazil. ℭ 55-22-2623-0902, ✆ 55-22-2623-0902, ⌨ www.meusonho-buzios.8k.com, meusonho@alohanet.com.br

💲 **Dirt Cheap** and up ⓘ **CP** ⓒⓒ 6 rooms for two to four guests

This Argentine-owned *pousada* is more like an international calling center and Internet quick stop than it is a *pousada*. The rooms out back seem to be an afterthought, but their design smacks of typical Argentine style and attention to detail: expensive wood, tile floors, and sturdy bed frames. The upstairs rooms have an ocean view. Don't expect great service. As the name suggests (Meu Sonho means My Dream), this place is more about the owner's dream than it is about your vacation.

Where to Eat

Thanks to the Argentine invasion of this Brazilian beach town, you can always find a decent dish of grilled meat or fish. Seafood is the best option, and, not surprisingly, the top place for restaurants in town can be found along Rua das Pedras.

$ **Chez Michou**, 90 Rua das Pedras, 2623-2169
This crepes bar cooks your order, *doce* or *salgado* ("sweet" or "savory"), in an open-air kitchen. The atmosphere is laid-back but efficient. The *chopp* is very cold, and the televisions are tuned to either *futebol* or surfing. Bands play live music on stage at the back of the restaurant, especially during festive weekends. At night, sons and daughters of upper-class *cariocas* and the local Argentine crowd hang out here. Want to see just how many Argentines there are in Búzios? Come to this joint when the Argentine national soccer team is playing Brazil, or any other team, really. You should get a pretty good idea because the place will be packed with Spanish-speaking Argentines dressed in blue and white. You'll be transported to Buenos Aires without ever having left Brazil!

$$ **Conversa Fiada**, 233 Rua das Pedras, 2623-0308
One of our favorite Rio de Janeiro bars has finally scored a perfect slot in Búzios. Cold beer and decent food are never a bad call, especially along the hottest strip in this little beach town. It's not ideal for a decent meal, but expect this place to fill quickly after the usual dinner hour. It keeps pumping out cold beer and slightly drunk visitors until the early morning. This bar is a stop-off spot for those who are into a late, late night offered by the clubs just a little ways down the road, toward the Orla Bardot.

$$$ **Deck Casas Brancas Bar & Bistro**, Orla Bardot (no number), 2623-1458
Our first impression was that this lounge, bar, and low-key restaurant was a haunt for older people. Man, were we wrong. After the sunset crowd heads off to bed, this hip joint turns off the bossa nova, swapping it for low-level lighting, scantily clad waiters and waitresses (where did *they* come from?), and a rotation of DJs, often on a small break from working the Rio scene. What is better known as a decent spot for food and late-afternoon fun is clearly an up-and-coming hot spot on the

Búzios night scene. It's run as part of the Casas Brancas brand, so expect nothing short of perfect.

$$$ **Favela Chic**, 151 Rua das Pedras, 2623-2697
Favela Chic has a nice beachside deck, right on the water. This is an ideal sunset spot, with an excellent view and decent food and service. The restaurant also keeps a streetside dining area, which usually collects a nightly crowd of young adults in the summer.

$$$$ **Parvati**, 144 Rua das Pedras, 2623-1375
A *trés chic* restaurant in the most polished part of town, Parvati offers inside and outside fine dining where you can see all the action on the main drag, and, more important, it can see you. The clientele is composed of mostly self-important Brazilians and Argentines looking for good food to complement their good looks.

$ **Pizza Cool**, 2 Manuel Turíbio, Loja 11, 2623-4648
The name says it all. This dive has best pizza in Búzios. It opens late and closes early to cater to the late-night crowd and is a venerable dining establishment in the center of town.

$$$ **Restaurante Aquario**, 233 Rua Manoel Turíbio de Farias, 2623-4685
Just down from the Praça Santos Dumont, the Aquario offers some of the best seafood dishes in town. The menu is excellent, and you receive a free *caipirinha* with your meal (how 'bout that!). The open-air dining area is comfortable and classy. The food is excellent, prepared with a practiced hand and an eye for presentation.

$$$ ✪ **Tartaruguinha**, 443 Orla Bardot, 2623-6978
Owned by our *carioca* friend Carlos and managed by an affable, if somewhat strict, Argentine restaurateur, the Tartaruguinha is our favorite space to dine and catch a sunset in Búzios. Seated by the spotless window, which is often closed due to the chilly breeze at night, you're a level off the street and, as such, once-removed from the street-level activity. Perfect for a drink

or a romantic dinner, the Tartaruguinha is a supreme seafood restaurant with impeccable taste, an impressive menu, decent wine selection (mostly Argentine, of course), and a pleasantly surprising design twist, with the combination of very clean lines and rustic, wooden tables and chairs. Visit at least once.

Going Out

The place to be is **Rua das Pedras**. Just head straight for the steady stream of nighttime crawlers and jump into any restaurant or bar that lines this street. It gets crowded here, but the people are the best show — the energy created by the pedestrian traffic alone provides the bulk of the evening scene. Things usually don't peak until after 11 p.m.

Generally speaking, you can move from **Conversa Fiada** and the **Pátio Havana**, a Cuban-style restaurant and club that often has live music on the weekends, toward the Orla Bardot and not miss a spot. The **Casas Brancas Deck** (or just Deck) is a decent place to start, unless you'd prefer to hole up in the Conversa Fiada until the late-night clubs open. **Anexo's Bar** is a laid-back lounge that takes on a more mischievous vibe after sunset. Perhaps the best established club is **Zapata**, just down the road from Deck. It attracts a bouncy, younger crowd, even if the Mexican theme is a bit cheesy. Farther down the road is **Devassa**, the venerable beer brewery and a perfect spot to take a late-night date or a recent acquaintance for great beer and decent food. Finally, we had often heard rumors of beach raves at the **Praia da Tartaruga**, and after our first rave there, we realized we had been missing out. Sometimes on Geribá Beach you will find one or two people handing out cheap-looking flyers for a Tartaruga rave. Don't be fooled by the skimpy flyer — it's worth the visit! It's tough to beat dancing in the sand with excellent music, a bonfire, and an endless source of liquid libation.

Don't Miss

Schooner trip
For a mere $10–$15, this all-inclusive three-hour trip takes you on a boat ride resplendent with all the *caipirinhas* you want to drink and

all the fruit you can hold. Trips that leave later in the afternoon will net you a nice sunset on the way back to port.

Rua das Pedras
After sunset, Rua das Pedras overflows with promenading tourists looking for a deal on shoes or sunglasses, dropping down for dinner, or swinging through for a drink or two or three. The people-watching is top-notch.

Hike from Praia Brava to Praia Olho de Boi
Apart from all the other beaches you should consider visiting, Praia Brava delivers a hike you shouldn't miss. The view from the top of the ridge gives you all the bang for the buck you could want, considering how easy it is to actually get up there.

Dinner at Tartaruguinha
If you're looking for a romantic spot to have a nice seafood dish, served with the perfect wine, don't miss out on our favorite restaurant.

A full day on any beach
You shouldn't come to Búzios unless you're looking for some serious beach time.

Ilha Grande

TOURISTO SCALE

👤 👤 👤 👤 👤 👤 (6)

WHAT USED TO BE BRAZIL'S VERSION OF ALCATRAZ (complete with prisoner escapes by helicopter and fly-by-night drug-smuggling escapades) has become one of Rio's most coveted tourist destinations. This was definitely one "Alcatraz" from which we never wanted to escape. Ilha Grande (Big Island) boasts beauty, tranquillity, and one of the largest protected Atlantic rainforests in Brazil. Naturalists will enjoy a number of trails that lead into the dense jungle. Those intrepid enough to make the trek to the island's peak (Pico do Papagaio) will be rewarded with a magnificent view.

Due to the increased amount of tourism over the years, the islanders and the mainland inhabitants of nearby Angra dos Reis have invested in infrastructure and transport, creating a small village, **Vila do Abraão**, with all the amenities you'll find on the mainland (although the Internet is not too common). A number of *pousadas* offer spectacular service and waterfront accommodations, whereas others provide a simple place for outdoor enthusiasts to crash for a few nights. Some *pousadas* are frequented by Rio's best-known authors, who use the island's nooks as an escape for writing.

In our conversations with locals and visitors alike, we found that Ilha Grande's beaches are what keep people coming back. **Praia Lopes Mendes**, accessible only by a 45-minute walk along a foot trail, is one of the most magnificent beaches in the whole country. At the right time of year, and if you arrive early enough in the morning, it's still possible to be the only human on the sand. Of course, you'll have to share space with the small white-faced monkeys, always looking for a handout (but don't feed them!), as well as a myriad of other fauna that you're not likely to find as easily on the mainland. Apart from soaking in the rays, you can arrange for jungle treks, a private boat trip, snorkeling, scuba diving (see more on scuba diving in the

Ilha Grande: Key Facts

Location	93 miles/150 kilometers west of Rio de Janeiro
	219 miles/354 kilometers northeast of São Paulo
Population	Around 1,200 year-round inhabitants and another 13,000 "floaters"
Area Code	24
Beer to Drink	*Chopp*
Rum to Drink	*Cachaça*
Music to Hear	Whatever is live
Tourism	There is no tourist office that we know of on the island. There were also no ATM machines the last time we checked. Some restaurants and *pousadas* do not accept credit or debit cards, so be sure to bring a secret stash. The best resources we've found are those individuals who eagerly meet the ferry with flyers in hand and the hope of bringing you to a *pousada* of their choice. Unless you're in a hurry, let them take you on a quick tour. For more information, visit www.ilhagrande.com.br.

"Focus" section, below), or simply hang out. Hammock time is "required" here—there are probably enough for everyone on the island, and then some. Once we managed to get our butts out of our hammocks, we still thoroughly enjoyed ourselves on this island. We strongly recommend that you make it a priority to spend a weekend here during your stay in Rio. In fact, we know many people who have come here for a weekend, with plans to return, and when they did, they stayed for a *month!*

One caveat: If you come here during the rainy season of May to September, be sure to pack some bug spray—Vila do Abraão can become Mosquito City at these times, especially in parts of town where the locals tend to store large amounts of water in open vats.

The Briefest History

Five days after André Gonçalves discovered Guanabara Bay, he discovered Ilha Grande. At first, he did not realize it was an island; he expected it to be a peninsula because of its large size. Arriving at the site of modern-day Angra dos Reis, the expeditioners realized their mistake and added the island of Ilha Grande to their claim on the coastal lands they had "baptized" along with Angra dos Reis. The island was generally left alone, apart from small groups of fishermen who had started fishing outposts there, until the young government in Rio de Janeiro decided to construct a prison in 1903. Called Colônia Penal Dois Rios, it served to house those guilty of common crimes. In 1940, the prison was reformed and renamed Cândido Mendes, which eventually became the prison of choice for Brazil's political prisoners during World War II. Cândido Mendes, and by extension, Ilha Grande, reached its height of notoriety during the latter half of Brazil's third military dictatorship, in the late 1970s and early 1980s, when bank robbers, political prisoners, and other hardened criminals were all imprisoned together. After democracy was restored in the mid-1980s, the island's prison population diminished—a number of escapes had occurred despite the prison's location. In 1994, the prison was closed and demolished. Since then, Ilha Grande has become a haven for Rio's island-hopping elite, tourists, and university backpackers from Brazil and beyond.

Getting There

The easiest way to get to Ilha Grande is to take a bus to Angra dos Reis, followed by a quick boat trip to the island.

At the Rodoviária Novo Rio, in Rio de Janeiro, keep a lookout for Costa Verde (2270-5743) bus lines. Buses leave Rio de Janeiro at 4:15, 5:30, 6, 6:40, 7:40, 8:30, 9, 10, and 11 a.m. and at 1, 2, 3, 3:30, 4, 5, 6, 7, and 10 p.m. Arriving at the Rodoviário Nilton Barbosa in Angra dos Reis, you'll be about 1.5 miles from the center of town and the docks where you'll catch the ferry. We've made the walk, but we arrived sweaty, so we recommend that you grab a cab. There are always cabs around the bus stop. The boat for Ilha Grande is run by Barcas SA, which runs one ferry out to the island's Vila do Abraão, Monday through Friday at 3:30 p.m. The ferry docks at the island overnight and returns Monday through Friday at 10 a.m. On Saturday, Sunday, and holidays, the ferry leaves Angra at 1:30 p.m. and returns from the island at 10 a.m.

Returning to Rio, simply backtrack to the Angra dos Reis bus station and catch a Costa Verde bus. Buses leave for Rio every hour from 4 to 11 a.m. and then at 12:20, 1, 2, 3, 5, 6, 8:10, and 10:45 p.m.

On the Way to Ilha Grande: Angra dos Reis

Angra dos Reis is considered a playground for Rio's multimillionares. Semiretired soccer star Romário, whom you might recall from the 1994 World Cup and who recently marked his 1,000th career goal, spends time in Angra, and so do a number of Soap Opera stars. As a result of more attractive destinations like Búzios and Paraty, however, this coastal waypoint does not stick out as a destination in its own right for foreign travelers.

We do think that Angra is worth a night's stopover if you're heading to or from Ilha Grande. Besides, limited boat schedules will force you to stay overnight stay if you miss the afternoon boat. Should that be the case, we recommend that you check out **Portogalo Suite Hotel** (55-21-2292-8405). Located in a high bluff overlooking the bay that separates Angra from Ilha Grande, this midsize hotel offers great value and supurb views from every room (with the exception of some rooms in block 3). If you prefer something smaller, with a little less polish, check out the **Pousada Mandarina** (55-24-3365-3156). This midsize house turned *poudasa* feels like you're staying in someone's home. Squeezed between thick green jungle and the sea, you'll get a taste of what's to come on Ilha Grande if you're on your way there, and the lush green will remind you of where you've been if you're on your way back. Accommodations are simple but comfortable.

Getting Around

We don't recall seeing any cars. There were a few bikes, but probably not too many air pumps or smooth trails. So, like everyone else, your only option is to walk. Around the ferry dock in Vila do Abraão, you might find off-duty fishermen or other entrepreneurial locals willing to give you a boat ride to a specific spot on the island.

Focus on Ilha Grande: Beaches and Jungle (and Maybe Some Scuba Diving)

Praia Lopes Mendes has been named one of the 10 most beautiful beaches in the world, according to a vote in *Vogue* magazine. Clearly, Vogue has a lot of readers, because the beach attracts quite a crowd. Access is only by foot, and it will take you about 45 minutes to get there from Vila do Abraão. You'll be happy to know that other beaches along the island are not as well known and are almost as beautiful. **Santo Antônio Beach**, for example, is a surf haven that's next to Lopes Mendes, but it is also a very good option if there are simply too many people at Lopes Mendes.

Considered a secret spot up until a few years ago, **Praia Caxadaço** is a small bay some distance from Lopes Mendes. Accessible only by boat, you may consider hiring a boat to take you here for a magical afternoon in the sun, swimming in the calm waters of one of the island's most beautiful minilagoons. **Praia Dois Rios**, a beach bordered by a river at both ends, is the site of the old prison. It's a long trek from Vila do Arbaão (at least an hour), but it's possible to make it there and back in a day. Because of its distance from the village, there are few who venture out this far from civilization, so if you want daytime beach privacy, consider a visit to Dois Rios. A boat taxi from the village is also an option, and so are private captains. However, the captains will usually make the 45-minute ride only in the morning, when the seas are calm. You'll probably have to hoof it on your afternoon return. Some of the other beaches worth a visit, and accessible only by boat taxi, are **Praia da Parnaióca**, **Praia de Provetá**, **Praia Vermelha**, and **Praia de Itaguaçú**.

The island's jungle is thick and full of plants you've never seen and animals you've likely only seen in a zoo or a picture book. Setting out from Vila do Abraão, a number of trails wind around the island, and some lead to the **Pico do Papagaio**, the large rock face visible from the village. Apart from the trails that lead you to Lopes Mendes beach and Dois Rios, some of the jungle trails can be confusing. We recommend you ask about a guide at the front desk of your *pousada* or boutique resort.

⊛ Scuba Diving off Ilha Grande

Ilha Grande has dozens of spots for diving, many of which (like the **Parnaióca** shipwreck) are excellent wreck dives for advanced divers. There are also beginner areas, such as **Ponta dos Meros**, on the southwestern tip of the island, which is practically an underwater city of tropical fish.

Although the price per head usually starts at US$85, this is considered cheap in the diving world. For rookies with little more experience than an underwater somersault in your local YMCA pool, you're in luck. Brazilian dive companies are known for bending the rules when it comes to certification and are always happy to give you a "baptism," as they call it.

For more serious divers, the same companies offer top-flight professional service and rental gear if you left your Buoyancy Compensator (BC) at home, and they are available for private dive trips — for an added price, of course! The best months to dive in Ilha Grande are November to February.

The **Elite Dive Center** (3361-5501 or 9991-9292; www .elitedivecenter.com.br) is PADI certified, run by master scuba diver trainer Daniel Gouvea, and keeps a small outpost in Vila do Abraão. Daniel and his instructors speak English. **Océan** (2557-7037; www .ocean.com.br) is another top-flight diving center. With an outpost in Vila do Abraão as well, Ocean is PADI certified and was the first certified dive operation on Ilha Grande. Océan has arguably the best equipment, but the feeling is that it's a little too organized and too touristy. You're sure to get great service from Océan, but for a more personalized experience you might want to consider the smaller, more versatile Elite Dive Center.

Where to Stay

When the boat from Angra pulls into the dock, you'll probably be accosted by any number of locals looking to make money by referring you to their *pousada* of choice. As the island has grown up over time, the accommodations have managed to keep pace. The good-natured locals may be persistent, so a quick mention that you already have a place to stay will get them off your back. There are now dozens of lodging options in the village, most of which are located away from the beachfront road and along the sandy interior streets. We don't recommend that you stay there—these places are less comfortable and are so closely packed together that you're more likely to be "treated" to a nighttime chorus of barking dogs than singing birds or rustling monkeys. There are some choice spots along the beachfront road, but we'd prefer to focus on the following out-of-the-way waterfront spots that are less known and well worth the extra price.

⊛ **Sítio do Lobo**, Ponto do Lobo, Ilha Grande, RJ, Brazil. ✆ 55-24-2227-4138, 🖳 www.sitiodolobo.com.br

💲 **Wicked Pricey** and up 🍴 **MAP** 🆑 6 rooms

> Accessible via a 15-minute boat (or helicopter) ride from Vila do Abraão, this exclusive boutique resort is tucked away in a pristine and otherwise undisturbed corner of Ilha Grande's Atlantic rainforest. One of the island's top luxury accommodations, it has excellent service; above all, expect to be left alone —due to the *pousada's* small size, silence is a given, and the sounds of nature surround. Whether it's the splash of the waves against the deck while you're swinging in one of the locally handmade hammocks, or the swish of branches in the wind while you're napping in your room, this resort is the pefect place to disappear and relax. Each room has different decorations, but all adhere to a rustic yet comfortable style. Earth tones and dark wood are contrasted nicely with white bedding and lampshades. In addition to its waterside location, Sítio do Lobo offers a spa, restaurant, sea kayaking, snorkling, and a spectacular deck with equal parts in the shade and sun. Hop in a kayak and paddle for 20 minutes to reach Enseada das Estrelas Beach, where you will find any number of sea stars and clear, calm waters for swimming. Make your resevations well in advance and ask for options for transfers from Rio and back. In most cases, the resort staff will pick you up in Rio and bring you back, so there's no worry about making the ferry connection in Angra. We're not surprised that *Condé Nast*

Johansens listed Sítio do Lobo as one of Brazil's top luxury accommodations in 2006. We couldn't agree more — it's our top pick for Ilha Grande.

Sagú Mini Resort, Praia Brava, Vila do Abraão, Ilha Grande, RJ, Brazil. ℂ 55-24-3361-5660, 📧 55-24-3361-9530, 🖥 www.saguresort.com

💲 **Not So Cheap** and up 🍴 **CP** ⓒⓒ 9 rooms

Built in the colonial Portuguese style, with a blend of tile work and rock that are typical of Ilha Grande, the Sagú Mini Resort was opened in 2002 and boasts some of the most modern accommodations on the island. The Italian owner has put significant effort into the resort's restaurant, which is considered the only real restaurant on the island. We have two favorite things about this miniresort. First, we love the space and relaxed feel of the architecture. The layout and design of the resort lends itself to capturing the island's cool breeze in just about any spot. The extensive deck overlooking the water invites you to sit around doing nothing for hours, and the Jacuzzi tucked away under a rainforest canopy is the perfect way to kick back with your significant other. Our second favorite point about this resort is the ecofriendly mindset of the owner. The resort's water, for example, is naturally filtered and heated with sun panels. Sagú is just a cut below the luxury of the Sítio do Lobo; this resort's rooms all have private balcony, a/c, minibar, mosquito nets, and Wi-Fi. The simple, elegant style incorporates a fine blend of tropical color in its décor. Some rooms are also decorated with a less vibrant classic Mediterranean feel. Built on 20 acres of land, the resort boasts its own trails. Open-air massage, sea kayaks, snorkling, and boat trips are all on the list of things to do if you decide to get active. Finally, Sagú is located a short distance from Vila do Abraão, so you get the best of both worlds — the feeling of being in the middle of the forest along with easy access to the village. The trail is not lit, so forays into the village at night should be done with a flashlight.

Pousada Naturália, Praia do Abraão, Vila do Abraão, Ilha Grande, RJ, Brazil. 🕜 55-19-3455-0986, 💻 www.pousadanaturalia.net
💲 **Cheap** and up 🍴 **CP** 🆑 12 rooms

> You want nature? You got it. This very simple and very rustic little *pousada* sits on a bluff at the far end of Abraão Beach. Each of the rooms faces the ocean and comes with a small balcony and a hammock. Minibar, a/c, and safe are included in the clean and comfortable rooms, which are most appropriate for a young couple or single travelers. We were impressed by the common room where breakfast is served — a hallmark of simplicity in harmony with nature. A minimum two-day stay is required with every reservation.

Where to Eat

The restaurants in Vila do Abraão are simple, offering mostly seafood, with fried, grilled, baked, or raw variations of that day's catch. All are of similar quality and none really stands out in the crowd. If you choose to stay in a resort, we suggest that you stick to your restaurant there, where the food and wine menu are likely to be better. Otherwise, pick one of the options below or walk down the beach from the ferry dock and follow your nose.

$$ **Adega do Corsário**, 90 Rua Alice Kury, 3361-9624
This simple restaurant specializes in fresh grilled seafood. Like most other restaurants on the island, the décor and seating is simple, it's washed by years of sea spray, and there is open-air dining. Open from about midday to the last customer or when the food runs out.

$ **Lua e Mar**, Praia do Abraão, 3381-5113
Located a little way down the beach from the center of town, this seaside restaurant is a good option for a candlelight dinner. Don't expect exquisite food or well-trained service, but you'll get a nice, simple meal on a beautiful island.

Going Out

Ilha Grande is not known for its late-night scene. Most who visit the island spend long days in the sun, whether they are hiking or drinking on the beach. By nightfall, the highlight is a decent meal, and little else. The area around the dock in Vila do Abraão is your best bet for some spark of life after sunset.

Don't Miss

Praia Lopes Mendes

From Vila do Abraão, you're about a 45-minute walk from one of the most beautiful beaches in the world. If you get there early enough, you might have the chance to enjoy it all to yourself. Of all of our suggested spots not to miss in the state of Rio de Janeiro, this ranks near the top.

A considerable amount of leisure time

You shouldn't come to Ilha Grande unless you're looking for some serious leisure time.

Paraty

WE TOTALLY FELL FOR THE HISTORICAL TOWN OF PARATY (ALSO spelled "Parati"), which has lasted for centuries, tucked away like a jewel in the elbow of a crooked peninsula that juts out into the Atlantic. Walking around in the colonial part of town is an experience in time travel that we rarely found elsewhere in Latin America. Paraty boasts an interesting and eventful history that's unparalleled in the state of Rio de Janeiro. The port here has hosted a trade of goods, people, and fish nearly two centuries longer than Brazil has existed as an independent nation. Over time, gold and slaves, then sugar and its *cachaça* (which is still known throughout the country), and now tourists have passed through this town with little resistance.

Despite weathering hordes of Brazilian, European, and Latin American tourists, Paraty manages to retain the feeling of a quaint colonial port town. It is therefore no surprise that artists, actors, writers, and musicians (Mick Jagger made it a celebrity haunt) flog its shores looking to be inspired by this town's subtle beauty and stunning surroundings.

Paraty is also a pretty good jump-off point to more than 60 small islands and 300 beaches — most are isolated and are best accessed by boat. We were amazed at how many beautiful remote beaches exist in this region. Our only gripe was that many of them require quite a bit of effort to reach. There are a few mainland beaches that are decent (like **Praia do Jabaquara**, which is a large beach with good scenery, and **Praia do Pantal**, which has more vibe but is less attractive). However, most of the better beaches (like the three mentioned below) require at least a one-hour boat ride for which your best approach is to hire a small-boat captain (see *Private Boat Trip* in the "Focus" section, below). Depending on the size and speed of the boat and the cooperation of

Paraty: Key Facts

Location	162 miles/261 kilometers east of Rio de Janeiro
	188 miles/303 kilometers northeast of São Paulo
Population	29,700
Area Code	24
Beer to Drink	*Chopp*
Rum to Drink	*Cachaça*
Music to Hear	Bossa nova
Tourism	The tourist office is located on Avenida Roberto Silveira, across the street from Praça do Chafriz at the beginning of Rua da Lapa. Just up Roberto Silveira, two more tourist shops offer free maps and information. Check out www.paraty.com.br for more information.

the seas, these trips can take as long as two hours. In the Brazilian winter months, the seas are often rough and the captains will refuse to make the trip. If you do decide to invest the time, you'll find that **Praia Vermelha** is a narrow strip of beach that separates the calm waters of a small bay from the encroaching rainforest. It's an ideal peaceful setting. **Praia Saco da Velha** is another small tranquil beach, where you're more likely to find fishermen than tourists. **Praia da Lula** is somewhat more frequented by tourist boat trips from Paraty's docks, so if you're interested in hanging out with an energetic and diverse group of beachgoers, this is your beach.

Some of the other good beaches can be found on the way to Trindade (Praia do Sono) or in Trindade (Praia do Rancho, Praia do Meio, and Praia do Cachadaço), each of which is discussed in the section on Trindade, below.

Paraty's surrounding mountains are covered with Atlantic tropical rainforest, which boasts a variety of flora and fauna that are tough to find elsewhere in the Western Hemisphere. In town, the cobblestone roads, churches, historical buildings, and architecture have been impeccably maintained. Together they are like a work of art. It speaks of an age when life was simpler and people worried less about making money and meeting deadlines.

Those who visit Paraty will soon recognize that the locals have maintained a laid-back approach to just about everything. Don't expect service to be crisp, food to come quickly, or people to rush themselves at your request or desire. Do expect to find fishermen, bartenders, and merchants ready to tell you a story or share a moment in the sun. We found it very easy to relax here, so we think that anybody who is searching for a calming escape from the fast pace of Rio city should plan a weekend in Paraty.

The Briefest History

Guainá Indians preceded Portuguese colonists, who took advantage of the Indians' advanced network of footpaths through the mountains to establish trade routes to the coast. By the early 1600s a trade connection with São Paulo centered Paraty as a port for goods flowing north to Rio de Janeiro from São Paulo and the interior beyond.

When the mines in Minas Gerais began producing loads of gold and precious gems, Paraty became a major stop along the famous "path of gold," or *caminho de ouro*—the trade route of gold moving from Minas Gerais, through the mountains to Paraty, and then north to Rio de Janeiro. Authorities secured the future economic growth of Paraty when they mandated that all gold heading toward Rio must flow through Paraty. The economic tide produced a building boom in Paraty that is well preserved today.

By the 1700s, Paraty had become a regional center of the sugar and *cachaça* markets. At the markets' peaks, there were hundreds of sugarcane farms and distilleries. Paraty even became famous worldwide for its excellent *cachaça*. However, sugarcane was replaced by coffee farming, and Paraty experienced a small growth spurt, largely propelled by the African slaves who worked for coffee bean barons on farms in the mountains.

A railroad that connected São Paulo to Rio de Janeiro in the mid-1800s effectively knocked Paraty from its position of thriving success. When the Brazilian government finally abolished slavery in 1888, Paraty fell into rapid decline as most of its population moved away. By the 1950s Paraty was home to some 600 fishermen and their families, a significant drop from its peak of nearly 20,000.

Culturally aware Brazilians in the government declared Paraty a historical site in 1966, and a coastal road, which connected Paraty to the rest of the country, opened car and truck access to the sleepy little beach town, thus paving the way for tourism. Since the 1970s, Paraty has steadily developed its tourism industry to handle the increasing numbers of annual visitors. After the ages of gold and *cachaça*, Paraty is catching its third wind and seems none the worse for wear.

Getting There

At Rio de Janeiro's Novo Rio bus station, Costa Verde bus line (windows 86 and 87) sells tickets for about $15. Buses leave for Paraty every three hours from 4:15 a.m. to 10 p.m., except on Sunday, when the last bus leaves at 10:30 p.m. Buses from Paraty to Rio leave every three hours from 3:30 a.m. until 9:15 p.m. The trip is just over four hours each way.

Driving to Paraty allows stops along the way, where the beauty of the Atlantic rainforest might inspire you to get out of the car and take a look around. From downtown Rio, get on RJ-101. Once you leave the city, which takes some time, you'll begin to twist and turn along the Rio de Janeiro state coast. We consider this to be one of the most beautiful drives in the whole state. After 135 miles/219 kilometers of stunning coastline and small villages, such as Angra dos Reis, you'll arrive in Paraty. Driving time from Rio to Paraty should not be more than three hours.

Getting Around

Walk. The cobblestone streets of the colonial section of town are inaccessible to cars. There are no taxis. Bicycle rentals are available from the tourism office, but we recommend that you skip this option, spare your spine and butt, and avoid the hazards of navigating over large, irregularly shaped stones.

Private boats can be rented by the hour for about $12 if you haggle. The captains will take you anywhere you want to go (seas permitting), will wait as long as you like, and are happy to tell you a little about the surrounding area along the way. Generally they don't leave any earlier than 7 a.m., and they like to be back by sunset.

Focus on Paraty: Walking Through History

The modern-day section of Paraty has little more than *pousadas*, hotels, and cheap restaurants to offer. You will want to spend most of your time wandering the narrow streets of the historic part of town. Locate Rua da Lapa, which begins at Praça Macedo Soares by the main tourism office, and start walking east, toward the ocean. You will pass numerous merchants, restaurants, Internet centers, cafés, and many other sights and sounds of interest. This street is the main entrance and an artery of the colonial section of town.

Morro do Forte

Cross the canal, which runs alongside the biggest church in town north of Rua da Lapa, and make your way up the hill to the old fort. The ruins are nothing spectacular, but the view overlooking the bay and colonial part of town is worth the walk. A short hike through the Atlantic rainforest is a refreshing respite from the heat in the streets below.

Private Boat Trip

By walking down Rua da Lapa and winding your way through the colonial part of town, you will eventually hit the water. The boats moored along the dock are fishing vessels and commercial schooners. The latter fill up with tourists interested in squeezing together for a five-hour preplanned trip around the surrounding area. Avoid this trap by hooking up with one of the private fishing-boat captains docked along the sea wall at high tide. To find them, walk past the fish market and toward the modest church just beyond. This church is old and historical in its own right, but we use it as a landmark for where the best private-boat operators dock and offer their services once the day's catch is in. These captains are more expensive, but they will make your day. Most will want to give you a three-hour tour, but if you insist, you can hire them for the whole day. At low tide, they will be moored along the dock, so you must pass through the chaos of all the haggling as you find your way to a small-vessel captain. Keep in mind that all boat trips can be subject to changes in schedule based on ocean conditions. We recommend that you look for the captain of a boat called

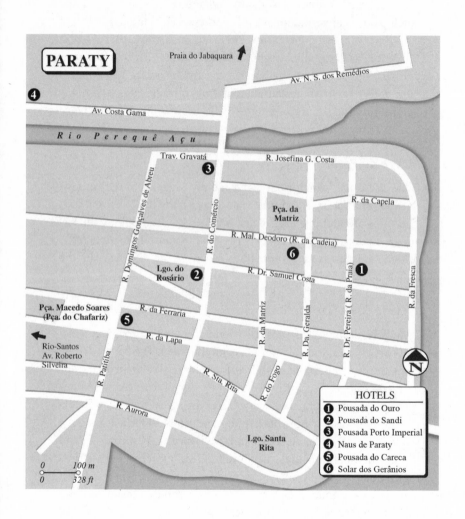

PARATY

Praia do Jabaquara ↑

Av. N. S. dos Remédios

Av. Costa Gama

④

R i o   P e r e q u ê   A ç u

Trav. Gravatá

R. Josefina G. Costa

③

R. Domingos Gonçalves de Abreu

R. do Comércio

R. da Capela

Pça. da Matriz

R. Mal. Deodoro (R. da Cadeia)

⑥

Lgo. do Rosário

②

R. Dr. Samuel Costa

R. Dr. Pereira (R. da Praia)

①

R. da Fresca

Pça. Macedo Soares (Pça. do Chafariz)

⑤

R. da Ferraria

R. da Matriz

R. Da. Geralda

R. Dr. Pereira (R. da Praia)

R. da Lapa

Rio-Santos
Av. Roberto Silveira

←

R. Parititba

R. da Lapa

R. Sta. Rita

R. do Fogo

R. Aurora

N

Lgo. Santa Rita

HOTELS

❶ Pousada do Ouro
❷ Pousada do Sandi
❸ Pousada Porto Imperial
❹ Naus de Paraty
❺ Pousada do Careca
❻ Solar dos Gerânios

0 ——— 100 m
0 ——— 328 ft

Giovanna Netta. His knowledge of the coastline is extensive. (These are the same boats that can be rented to take you to various distant beaches and islands.)

Where to Stay

For such a laid-back port, Paraty is nearly overflowing with *pousadas*. There are no real hotels to speak of, but the *pousadas* offer every level of décor, service, and ambiance. You will find establishments oriented to backpackers, families, and even the rich and famous. None is too expensive; we were left with the impression that some should charge more!

⊛ **Pousada do Ouro**, 145 Rua da Praia, Paraty, RJ, Brazil.

    ℭ 55-24-3371-4300, 55-24-8117-6116 (English or German)

    55-24-3371-1378, 🖳 www.pousadaouro.com.br, reservas@pousadaouro.com.br

    💲 **Pricey** and up ⑪ **CP** ⒸⒸ 26 rooms

Pousada do Ouro has been a hideaway for the famous who are looking to get away from cameras and fans. (Mick Jagger was a regular here.) It occupies two buildings on either side of Rua da Praia. As you walk toward Praça da Matriz, the reception area is on the right. Since our last visit, the *pousada* has entered the Internet age with Wi-Fi access—in case you've just *got* to surf the Net. The rooms are quaint, designed with class, and make use of what looks like antique wooden furniture, giving them a feeling of self-importance, if not a little fragility. The rooms across the street from the reception area have private garden areas. If you'd like to spend a little more than the regular room rate, opt for one of the upstairs suites. Somehow these rooms combine eloquence and comfort in a space that we think might have once been an overstuffed attic. The views from these upstairs suites are spectacular. In some rooms, it's possible to lounge in bed while looking out at a shimmering bay beyond your window—a view worth the extra cost if you're looking for some inspiration. A pool, antique bar, sauna, and well-kept social area bring the *pousada* together and make us realize why the prices here, though well worth it, are a little steep. They're not too steep, though—it would be a shame to price out returning guests like Tom Cruise and Anthony Hopkins.

Pousada do Sandi, 1 Largo do Rosario, Paraty, RJ, Brazil. ℂ 55-24-3371-2100, 🖋 55-24-3371-1236, 🖳 www.pousadadosandi.com.br, info@pousadadosandi.com.br

💲 **Pricey** and up 🅨 **CP** ⒸⒸ 26 rooms and suites

We find this *pousada* to be one of the most deluxe places to stay in Paraty. Built into a complex that once housed a school big enough for the whole town, Pousada do Sandi is immense. It has two bars, one by the pool, a separate building for the suites, and three levels of rooms within the main building. Attached to the main building is a large wing that holds even more rooms and a restaurant—fine dining, with even a private room for "special" guests who want extra privacy. Each room is uniquely decorated, and the suites on the third floor have small indoor balconies that overlook the pool and the mountains beyond. Like the Solar dos Gerânios (listed below), Pousada do Sandi is nearly all wood, but a fine polish and finishing touches have been applied throughout. It is Paraty living at its most fancy, if not a tad overdone.

Pousada Porto Imperial, s/n Rua Tenente Francisco Antônio, Centro Histórico, Paraty, RJ, Brazil. ℂ 55-24-3371-2323, 🖳 www.portotel.com.br/PortoImperial/index2.asp

💲 **Pricey** and up 🅨 **BP** ⒸⒸ 44 rooms

Perched on the perfect corner, Pousada Porto Imperial faces the bay, the major colonial churches, and opens up right onto Paraty's (in)famous cobblestones leading to all the shops and restaurants. Although the narrow hallways remind us of the labyrinth-like interior of a Brazilian navy ship, they surround a beautiful tropical tree- and bird-filled common area—perfect for late-night chats or afternoon leisure. As with nearly all lodging in Paraty, the maritime theme runs strong, with model colonial ships, paintings of sea adventures, and the colors of Brazilian patriotism. Pick one of the rooms on the second floor, each one adorned with a plaque describing a famous Brazilian. (We stayed in Clarice Lispector's quarters.) The rooms are nothing to write home about, other than the sheets and the comforter, which are so soft you might get lost in them and lose a day of vacation sleeping away.

Naus de Paraty, 12 Rua das Acácias, Caboré, Paraty, RJ, Brazil. ℭ 55-24-3371-1825, 🖥 www.nausdeparaty.com.br/index.htm, pousada@nausdeparaty.com.br

💲 **Cheap** and up ⑪ **CP** ⓒⓒ 15 rooms

If you've broken one or two heels (or your nose!) from walking on the rough cobblestone streets of the historical district, venture out to the Caberé neighborhood, where the endless bubbling of late-night voices will be substituted by singing birds. Naus de Paraty is a perfect, affordable substitute for the downtown *pousadas*. It is a refuge within a refuge. You can choose to snooze by the palm tree–surrounded pool or in a hammock that offers a spectacular view of the green mountains nearby. Reserve one of the second-floor rooms with a balcony facing the mountains if you'd prefer to wake up to views of the Atlantic rainforest. There is also a suite with a Jacuzzi, or "hydromassage," as they call it in Brazil. The head manager, Antônia, is a gracious host and will set up any number of historical or nature tours in the area. Though short in the services offered in the upscale *pousadas* downtown, Naus de Paraty more than makes up for a lack of posh with hospitality and tranquillity.

Pousada do Careca, s/n Praça do Chafariz, Paraty, RJ, Brazil. ℭ 55-24-3371-1291, 🖥 www. paraty.com.br/pousadadocareca, pousadadocareca@hotmail.com; pousadadocareca@backpacker.com.br

💲 **Dirt Cheap** ⑪ **CP** ⓒⓒ 22 rooms

Our friend Samuel is Paraty personified. He is relaxed, good-natured, and living the easy life. He offers a solid breakfast and good conversation for all his patrons, mostly Brazilian travelers. Even though the *pousada* is perfectly located in the middle of all the action, most foreigners overlook the place. We can't figure out why. Maybe it's because there's no air conditioning or Internet access. However, the rooms are simple, with comfortable bedding. The rooftop widow's peak is a generous fringe benefit, if you manage to get past the drying laundry. From up there you can see the whole town, the mountains behind, and the port in front. You pay about $20 for a good night's sleep and are treated like royalty. For that price, it doesn't get much better.

Solar dos Gerânios, s/n Praça da Matriz, Paraty, RJ, Brazil. ℭ & ◉ 55-24-3371-1550, ⌨ www.paraty.com.br/geranio

💲 **Dirt Cheap** and up 🍽 **CP** 12 rooms

Old, old, old. We found ourselves taking a liking to this backpacker-cruncher hotel, which actually has a working carpenter shop behind the reception area — we assume it's there to keep up permanent maintenance on this very old building. More wooden pegs than modern-day nails hold the place together. The aged wooden stairs are bowed from time and use, and, yes, they creak. The elderly receptionist appears to be just as old, and her quick wit and animation remain strong. On the whole, this hotel is simple, cheap, and a beautiful relic from Paraty's colorful history.

Where to Eat

For such a small town, Paraty offers an unexpectedly wide range of gastronomic options, and it's still not polluted by fast-food joints. Thai, Indian, Arab, Italian, and, of course, Brazilian food are all available. We're surprised there's no sushi bar in town. Most of the best restaurants are clustered between Rua da Lapa and Praça da Matriz in the colonial part of town. Many of the restaurants offer live music, which is often good bossa nova or samba, but sometimes it's not worth the automatic cover charge you'll find on your bill at the end of the night.

$–$$ Café do Canal, 709 Avenida Octavio Gama, 709, in front of
Ponte Nova, in the Caberé neighborhood, 3371-1040
Café do Canal was the best-kept secret of our Paraty dining
experience. Even if you're not lodging in one of the Cabaré *pousadas*, it is worth the five-minute taxi ride from the historic center. We kept waiting for the catch but found none. Offering an
unbelievable variety of delicious pizzas for next to nothing, a
diverse selection of tropical mixed drinks, and an exciting cap-
puccino, this place kept getting better as the meal went on.
Patrons can choose to dine at the intimate tables tucked in the
back or the patio tables next to the brick oven. During the day,
there might be a crowd screaming at a soccer match on a large
TV, whereas the night brings couples and families who take
to the charming interior.

$$ Café Paraty, 253 Rua Comércio, 3371-0128
Café Paraty differs from other establishments that offer
music and food by displaying a more jazzy feeling and cater-
ing mostly to the non-Brazilians who visit Paraty. One of the
only restaurants with a dark beer on tap, the café has a broad
menu that moves from salads to crepes to meat and fish dish-
es, as well as a variety of sandwiches. Service is generally slow
and requires active participation on your part to get a menu,
order, and ask for the check. But hey, you're in Paraty, re-
member? And with some of the best music around, you'll
quickly understand why the waitstaff is often distracted.

$$$ Margarida Café, Praça do Chafariz, 3371-2381
Have an itch for top-shelf imported liquor? Want a first-rate
pizza? Do you love an excellent wine collection? If you answered yes to any or all of these questions, the Margarida is a
must. This restaurant is separated into four dining areas: the
main dining room and stage, the lounge, the bar, and the
indoor garden room. There is an in-house wine cellar, so your
cabernet or merlot is pleasantly at the right temperature.
Preparation, presentation, and excellent service complement
the nightly offer of locally "brewed" bossa nova and light

samba favorites. The tile floor and marble-top tables add a touch of class to this eclectically decorated restaurant, where the owner still makes rounds to each table to chat with guests. You'll leave satisfied, especially if you try the brownie dessert.

$$ **Refúgio**, 1 Praça de Bandeira, 3371-2447
Our friend Samuel at the Pousada do Careca recommended the Refúgio as the best place for seafood in his hometown. He was right. The fish and lobster melted in our mouths. Side dishes that are nearly impossible to pronounce are worth an experiment, too. Everything on the menu is tempting. You can't miss! The smiling waitstaff is unobtrusive but efficient. This small, local spot is off the tourist-trap map. We like to think our friend Samuel tells only a few people, so pay it a visit before he's told too many!

$$$ **Restaurante Banana da Terra**, 198 Rua Dr. Samuel Costa, 3371-1725
We like this restaurant because it doesn't waste time misleading you with the name (well, the food's great, too). This place is banana everything: banana leaves on the walls, banana-based dishes, and banana place mats. Hordes of cachaça bottles stand at attention above the bar. Who knows, maybe there's banana cachaça. The dining area is historic, tropical, and rustic, yet it also provides a cosmopolitan air, with the occasional Brazilian soap opera star chatting it up with randoms over wine at the bar. Locals cite it as one of the best restaurants for regional dishes, even though the menu boasts house recipes not found elsewhere. We agree with the locals, especially after tasting the stuffed crab shell with succulent mussel- and-eggplant appetizer plate. Everything that followed was just as good. You're not going to find this kind of food anywhere else!

$$$ **Restaurante Paraty**, under Pousada do Careca, Rua da Lapa, 3371-2651
Perhaps the first thing you'll notice in this restaurant is the display of ancient guns on the wall. They are remnants from

when it was necessary to defend the tiny port town from 19th century ne'er-do-wells. Depending on what time in the evening you arrive, you'll notice that the small dining area is packed with a rainbow of colors worn by the patrons — pastels and black socks for the Euros, earth tones and solid-colored Izod shirts for the older Brazilian couples, and black on black for the young urban crowd from São Paulo. The food is well flavored, but not quite as much as the people.

Nearby Destination: Trindade

While you are in Paraty, the town of Trindade, just 15 miles/25 kilometers south on RJ-101, is a great place to see. This small fishing village, which is much more laid-back and less crowded than Paraty, is off the beaten path for most foreign tourists but is a widely recommended destination by many Brazilians. To get there by car from Paraty, head toward the coast and follow the signs to Trindade. Along the way, you'll have to leave the main road (keep following the signs to Trindade) and drive up and over the coastal mountains that guard access to Trindade. At the peak of the pass, you'll arrive at a fork in the road. Head right to arrive at Trindade. (Note that you can also take a nice detour by heading left at this fork toward Condomínio Laranjeiras, which is where a trail head will lead you toward **Praia do Sono** — a beach dreamer's pot of gold. Praia do Sono can also be accessed from Paraty by boat, but only if the captain deems the seas calm enough to make the one-hour crossing. Taxi is another option for reaching Praia do Sono, but be sure to negotiate a price and arrange for a return pickup ahead of time.) If you want to travel to Trindade by public transportation, vans leave the Paraty Rodoviária every hour, and buses leave every half hour.

Two of Trindade's best beaches are Praia do Rancho and Praia do Meio. **Praia do Rancho** has a protected swimming area, small restaurants that serve excellent food for nearly nothing, and a white-sand beach that stretches into the distance. It begs you to find a spot, sit, and start really relaxing. To get to this beach, park along the main drag (in that classic haphazard manner that only Brazilians seem to have mastered) and ask somebody to direct you toward the bus stop at the far end of town. Right near this bus stop is a trail that cuts through a horse pasture and leads to the beach. Also within walking distance from town is the popular (sometimes too popular, for our tastes) **Praia do Meio**. It is small, with calm waters that make it great for swimming (but don't get too close to the rocks!). The beach has several thatched-roof restaurants that serve grilled seafood and cold beer to sunning tourists splayed in plastic chairs balanced in the sand. At low tide, you can climb to the top of Praia do Meio's boulders, from which there is a cool view of many other beaches and the open ocean. If you continue farther along the same trail that brought you to Praia do Meio, you can reach the nearby **Praia do Cachadaço** (also sometimes called Praia de Trindade), which is known for its natural pools—great for snorkeling or for just floating around.

Where to Stay and Eat: Trindade

Services and infrastructure for lodging range widely along this tiny town's only main road, which is really just a strip of poorly maintained asphalt. It is on this main drag that you will find plenty of restaurants and *pousadas*. All its *pousadas* can be characterized as rustic, though mildly comfortable, and all are within a stone's throw of the beach. A common theme among these *pousadas* is the combo deal—in the front there's usually a restaurant that offers a variety of seafood and cold beer, and in the back there are rooms that face the sea. When in Trindade, we tend to choose our lodgings based just as much on the seafood as on the comfort of the rooms. Some places serve a wonderful white snapper, but the sheets feel like sandpaper, whereas other places will offer the opposite. Either way, Trindade is a town worth a quick visit—spending the night is not always necessary.

Brancas Restaurante/Pousada and **Pousada Larica's** offer both lodging and full-service restaurants. We confirmed what the locals tipped off: These are two simple spots, with no Internet and certainly no saunas. However, the rooms are clean and comfortable, and the fresh ocean air wafts in off nearby waves. If you're up for more than a cold beer after a day on the beach, be sure to request a *caipirinha* made with strawberries or kiwis from the restaurant.

A more upscale option than the aforementioned *pousadas* is the **Hotel Garni Cruzeiro do Sul** (www.hotelgarnicruzeirodosul com br). In addition to a delicious breakfast on a beachside deck, you'll find many of the services that spoiled you in Paraty: a sauna, a freshwater pool, and, yes, the Internet. Anyway, what we most like about the Garni Cruzeiro is that you can stare at the sea from your table and then from your bed. It's one of the best, little-known spots for a well-priced beachfront existence.

After hitting the beach for the day, drop by **Bar Tequila** on the main street. Don't let the name fool you—this tiny coffee and smoothie shop is both a perfect morning or afternoon refresher, serving creamy cappuccinos and bowls of deep purple *açaí* topped with fruit. And, of course, there's tequila.

Don't Miss

Private boat trip

Taking the time to visit the islands and beaches around Paraty is a must when you are in town. Avoid the larger schooners unless you want to get sweaty with a horde of tourists, listen to music you might not like, and be hassled to leave the beach just when you've gotten comfortable.

The colonial part of town

This part of town has three churches, street fairs, loads of interesting stores, art galleries, and excellent restaurants. It is the source of Paraty's charm.

The fort

A quick walk to the fort awards you with one of the best views to be had in Paraty.

Trindade

Take a day trip to this small town to avoid foreign tourists while scoring huge on beautiful beaches and excellent, cheap seafood. Spend the night, or take two, if you'd like to withdraw completely from the hustle and bustle of the life you left at home.

Petrópolis

PERCHED IN THE MOUNTAINS, JUST NORTH OF RIO DE Janeiro, the city of Petrópolis is a quick escape, but it's a large contrast from the hustle and city beat of Rio city. From our standpoint, Petrópolis serves two purposes. First, it is a monument to Brazilian history as the final home of Brazil's greatest emperor, Dom Pedro II. Second, the area's beautiful peaks, cooler climate, and fresh air attract tourists on day trips and *cariocas* for a day, a weekend, or even a week of respite from the searing heat in Rio de Janeiro during the summer. Petrópolis also attracts loads of elderly folks — it's kind of like Rio's version of Florida, only with hills in place of beaches. There are many wealthy *carioca* families who have staked claims on many of the homes that pepper the hills outside town. Although Petrópolis isn't our favorite spot in the state, it presents the easiest way to get a quick taste of Rio's mountainous splendor while also providing an enormous perspective on Brazilian history and Rio's place in it.

Like most things in this small city, nightlife in Petrópolis is mostly history. You will find pleasant walks along canals, historical monuments, cathedrals, museums, and cafés. You will also encounter classic old hotels. Some are in need of a touch-up, but all are in proper order and possess some charm. Bus trips to nearby destinations might serve to extend a trip to Petrópolis to two or more days, but the city is only about an hour away from Rio. You could easily cover it in less than a day, allowing you to be back in Rio in time to party that night (should you really need that) and enjoy the beach the next morning.

If you do stay overnight in Petrópolis, consider visiting **Itaipava**. It's a small village built to cater to the rich, who live in mansions tucked into the hills. Although it is basically one long strip mall, filled with shopping centers, restaurants, bars, a couple discos, and the occasional

Petrópolis: Key Facts

Location	42 miles/68 kilometers north of Rio de Janeiro
	229 miles/369 kilometers from Belo Horizonte
	263 miles/425 kilometers from São Paulo
Population	287,000
Area Code	24
Beer to Drink	Itaipava and Bohemia, both locally brewed
Rum to Drink	*Cachaça*
Music to Hear	*Chorinho, forró*
Tourism	Petrotur has an office at Praça Dom Pedro, across the park from the obelisk. It's open from 9 a.m. to 5 p.m. daily. For more information, visit www.petropolis.rj.gov.br.

hardware store, it does offer an alternative to the lack of nightlife in Petrópolis.

Also, **Teresópolis**, which is the outdoor activities center of the state of Rio de Janeiro, lies about an hour farther from Petrópolis into the mountains. There you will find trekking, camping, white-water rafting, and climbing. See the Teresópolis chapter for more information.

The Briefest History

While scouting around for help to support his young revolution and Brazilian independence in 1822, Dom Pedro I found himself in the thick forests that cover the hills north of Rio de Janeiro. He liked the area so much that he purchased a ranch here and initiated plans to turn it into his summer retreat and country palace.

After inheriting the ranch from his father, Dom Pedro II founded the city of Petrópolis in 1843, just two years before builders and designers broke ground on the palace. Construction was completed in 1862. Soon after, the young city of Petrópolis became known as the Imperial City because it was the favorite retreat of the emperor and his court traveling from Rio de Janeiro.

A road and railway that connected the mines in Minas Gerais to Rio de Janeiro passed through Petrópolis, making the city a suitable stopping point before descending to the coast to the ports in Rio, which ensured its permanence as an important urban center. One of the first paved roads in the region connected Petrópolis to Rio de Janeiro, befitting the city's importance to the political elite residing in Rio de Janeiro.

True to its history, Petrópolis today is the summer retreat of Rio's rich and famous. They flock to their mountain homes to escape the heat in Rio. The city is also considered a historical and cultural mainstay in Brazil due in large part to its Imperial Museum, which is the preserved summer home of Dom Pedro II—a museum of true national pride.

Getting There

From Rio de Janeiro, the Novo Rio bus station, or *rodoviária,* has buses leaving every 30 minutes for Petrópolis. From anywhere in the city, a city bus with Rodoviária written across its "forehead" will get you to the Novo Rio bus station for around 75 cents. From Zona Sul, the private line run by Real will take you to the station for $1.50.

Across the bridge from the entrance, down the steps and to the left, you will find the bus line Facil Unica (at store numbers 83 and 84). It is the best company that runs buses to Petrópolis from Novo Rio. A ticket will cost about $6 each way. The same company has a store at the bus station in Petrópolis with similar prices. It is a slightly faster trip back to Rio. Buses leave as early as 6 a.m. and as late as 9 p.m. each way. The trip by bus between Rio and Petrópolis takes about an hour and 20 minutes.

Should you decide to spend time in Itaipava, the bus from Petrópolis to Itaipava leaves from the Petrópolis bus station about every 15 minutes. Just get in line at the back of the bus; it costs $1 each way. Itaipava is not the first station at which you'll arrive, but it takes less than half an hour.

Driving to Petrópolis from Rio is an easy trip and takes about an hour, depending on weekend traffic. Take BR-040 north out of town. Some 19 miles/31 kilometers later, the road will split. Stay to the right and follow the signs for Petrópolis. Chances are you will pass by many buses on the way. If you feel confused or lost, just follow a bus with the "Petrópolis" banner.

Getting Around

The best option is to walk. The parts of the town you will explore are focused around and up the canal from an obelisk, positioned halfway down the main drag from the cathedral, and located right next to the bus station. Along the main drag, Rua do Imperador, you will find nearly all of Petrópolis's hotels, restaurants, and stores.

If you prefer to ride in taxis, you will wait. Taxis are few and far between in Petrópolis. Most buses operate direct routes to nearby towns or back to Rio, but not within the historical part of town, which is where you will spend most of your time.

Focus on Petrópolis: A Cultural Trip to Rio's Imperial Past

You should consider making Petrópolis a day trip, so purchase a ticket back to Rio before leaving the bus station. Outgoing buses tend to fill up quickly in the afternoon and early evening.

Set out toward Rua do Imperador. With your back to the bus station, the street is to your left. You can't miss the promenade, with a cathedral at one end, a canal that splits the road, and an obelisk halfway along the stretch. Once you reach the obelisk, turn right and head toward the Imperial Palace Museum. When you see the horse-drawn carts, you're getting close. Look right, and you'll see the gardens. Walk to the end of the fence and past the gate to purchase your tickets.

You'll want to take at least half an hour to wander around the museum. Electronic guides are available in Portuguese or English. The art, sculptures, preserved clothing, and personal grooming devices are all interesting and well-preserved pieces of another time. It's the crown jewels, however, that might keep you staring the longest. Oh, and don't be surprised if you're asked to wear big coverings over your shoes when you enter the building; the details-oriented curators are forever worried about preserving the beautiful wood floor.

Leaving the museum, turn right and follow the canal as it turns to the left down Rua Tiradentes. You'll see the cathedral to the right—

this is your second stop. Climb the steps to the upper level. As you enter the cathedral, just before you enter the main worship chambers, look to the right—Dom Pedro II lies next to his wife, front and center (to the right and left are their daughters).

Head back toward the obelisk and Rua do Imperador to find some lunch. At this point, you have the option of relaxing and enjoying the gorgeous mountainous setting for a couple hours or possibly an evening. We suggest you opt for the former and return to Rio in time for another night out on the town.

Where to Stay

Although our advice is to not bother spending a night here unless you're staying with friends, the places listed here will get the job done. They lack many of the comforts and services found in the Rio hotels, but they do possess an appealing, older style.

Pousada Tankamana Eco Resort, s/n Estrada Júlio Cápua, Vale do Cuiabá, Itaipava, RJ, Brazil. © 55-24-222-9181 or 222-9182, 🖳 www.tulum.com/nhotels/pousadatankamana

💲 **Very Pricey** and up 🍽 **CP** CC 15 chalets

Located some 21 miles/34 kilometers beyond the city's historical center, the Tankamana has been ranked as the region's most charming hotel by *Guia Quatro Rodas*, one of Brazil's leading guidebooks. It is our favorite eco resort in the state. It's hard to imagine roaring fireplaces, steaming hot tubs, and cozy blankets when you think about Rio de Janeiro, but if you happen to travel during South America's winter months, you might find Rio rainy and cold. Make a spontaneous change of plans and go for an eco-retreat. The rustic look and feel of this getaway in the middle of the forest blends seamlessly into an interior décor that reminds us of a mountain lodge in Aspen. The wooden bathtubs really took us aback! We were assured they don't leak. Along with omnipresent (24-hour) but not in-your-face room service, the lodge contains a sauna, a steam bath, massage services, a game room, and an award-winning

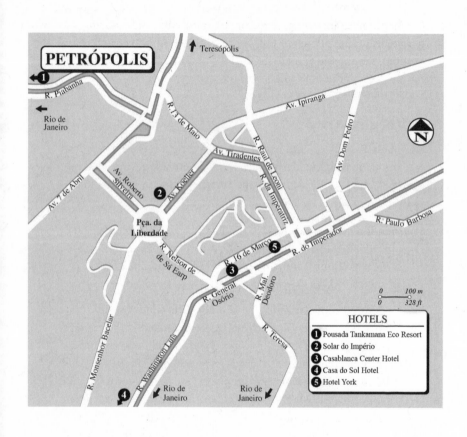

restaurant that uses trout from its own trout farm in many of its dishes. There's quite a unique twist at the *pousada*'s restaurant: Windows have been installed in the floor, making for an interesting display of fish swimming in the natural pool beneath the establishment. Each chalet is complete with a minibar, cable TV, DVD player, Jacuzzi, and fireplace.

Solar do Imperio, 376 Avenida Koeler, Petropolis, RJ, Brazil. ℰ 55-24-2103-3000, 💻 www.solardoimperio.com.br, atendimento@solardoimperio.com.br

💲 **Not So Cheap** and up 🍴 **CP** (CC) 16 rooms

Kill two birds with one stone: Sleep in Princess Isabela's palace for the history lesson *and* receive the royal treatment at the same time. Since reopening in 2005, the palace has preserved its period-specific furniture and has added all the modern amenities to satisfy the needs of its new guests. Since the rooms and prices differ based on space (not treats), we suggest sticking with the smaller imperial suite. You'll still get to roll around on a king-size bed and sink in the cloudlike down comforter and pillows. You don't have to move a finger to do anything—laundry service is a mere phone call away, and so is the weekend 24-hour room service. The rooms also have cable TV, Internet, and a minibar. But don't get too spoiled in your room —check out the restored reading room, and then walk out to the veranda and surrounding garden. There is also a heated pool and a sauna. This place will make you want to raise a glass to the trappings and luxury of monarchy.

Casa do Sol Hotel, 115 Avenida Ayrton Senna, Petrópolis, RJ, Brazil. ℰ & 🌐 55-24-2243-5062, 💻 www.casadosolhotel.com.br, casasol@compuland.com.br

💲 **Cheap** and up 🍴 **CP** (CC) 32 rooms

Set along the bank of the lake in front of the Quitandinha Palace, Casa do Sol displays its own postcard view of an Imperial City landmark. With the surrounding tree-blanketed hill and winding paths, you might think you have been transported to the heart of Bavaria. Walk among the various sculptures and other works of art on long and lulling afternoon or morning walks to completely forget the sterilized light of your office (or whatever other cage you have run from). You'll find that your room also caters to your escapist cravings — the luxury apartments have a panoramic view and a Jacuzzi. Other conveniences and treats are laundry service, cable TV, Internet, a heated pool, a playground, a sauna, tennis courts, a game room, and a sport court. It's all about you, almost — the restaurant's room service closes before midnight. But you're not in Rio, so you'll probably be tired from being outside all day. The utter lack of nighttime agitation here will probably have you rising with the sun. Don't forget to jump in a canoe and paddle around the little lake. It'll make the "chunky soup" of Rio's Lagoa a pleasantly distant memory.

Casablanca Center Hotel, 28 Rua General Osorio, Petrópolis, RJ, Brazil. ℭ 55-24-2242-2612, ✎ 55-24-2242-6298, 🖳 www.casablancacenterhotel.com.br, info@casablancacenterhotel.com.br

💲 **Cheap** and up 🍴 **EP** (CC) 70 rooms and suites

The Center Hotel is well named — you couldn't find a better location in the middle of town. The retro-designed lobby matches the dapper but laid-back reception team. No one is in a hurry here. The rooms are spacious and come with cable TV, minifridge, and safe. Dark-color hues and thick curtains are reminiscent of forgotten times. Aged class wins out over simple comfort yet maintains a modern tweak with Internet and fax services, a 200-person event room, laundry service, and a game room. The clincher, though, is the property that's offered to all guests, located 25 minutes outside downtown at Casablanca Center's other hotel, **Vale Real** (www.valereal.com .br). It's an adult and kid playground set in the wooded foothills, with a large pool, tennis courts, volleyball courts, soccer fields, saunas, Jacuzzis, game rooms, and a home theatre. Nature walks are also available. No joke, this place is awesome. You might just end up staying at the Vale Real property instead.

Hotel York, 78 Rua do Imperador, Petrópolis, RJ, Brazil. ℂ 55-24-2243-2662, ✈ 55-24-2242-8220, 🖳 www.hotelyork.com.br, info@hotelyork.com.br

💲 **Cheap** ⑪ **CP** 32 rooms

A stone's throw from the bus station, on the main drag, Hotel York offers nothing special. It is close and convenient for arrival and departure. Restaurants are just down the street, and the city's cultural monuments are less than a 10-minute walk. The subtle class of this very old hotel is a nice touch, however. The bed might not be too comfortable, the blankets are worn a little thin, and the flower motif is a bit much, but we didn't mind the older style displayed in the rooms. The rooms have minifridge, safe, and Internet. The bottom line: This place has a great location and a good bang for the buck.

Where to Eat

Dining in Petrópolis is nothing eventful. *Kilogramas, churrascarias, suco* bars, and coffee stands punctuate the center of town. They all offer a good rate for decent food, but don't expect to have the meal of your life. Many *cariocas* who visit this town host barbeques at their mountain homes with family and friends. As a result, there is less demand and therefore less support for dining establishments.

$ **Fuka's**, 23 Rua Nilo Peçanha, 2231-7798 or 2243-7280
Pronounced "FOO-kas" (so stop laughing), this *kilograma* is perfect for a quick lunch with friends after you've walked around town enough to build up an appetite. The salad bar is stocked with an assortment of fresh legumes and vegetables. The meat dishes are similar to what most *kilogramas* offer — beef stroganoff, filet mignon, or chicken curry. The service is surprisingly charming. *Cafezinhos* (tiny cups of strong coffee) are free.

$$ **Majórica Churrascaria**, 754 Rua do Imperador, 2242-2498
For more than 45 years, Majórica has served meat dishes to *carioca* families interested in a long, comfortable lunch after a day of sightseeing in the center of town. The atmosphere is

homey and, not surprisingly, family oriented. The grandfather clock at the entrance adds a special touch of aged class that seems to permeate most establishments in this town.

$$ **Massas Luigi**, 185 Praçada Liberdade, 2244-4444
Built into a renovated house on the edge of a peaceful plaza, this Italian restaurant is the best family dining atmosphere you'll find in Petrópolis. The main dining room is spacious enough for large groups, and the smaller dining areas are perfect for smaller families and couples. The wooden floor and high ceilings complement each other and create an atmosphere of eating in an old colonial home.

Don't Miss

Cathedral São Pedro de Alcântara

The resting place of Dom Pedro II, his wife, and their daughters is a must-see if you're walking around town. The tomb is nothing spectacular—rather simple, actually—but you should not leave town before making a short walk to the cathedral. Admission is free, and the cathedral is open for a quick peek of the tombs on weekdays from 11 a.m. to 5 p.m.

Imperial Palace Museum

Formerly the summer home of Dom Pedro II, this museum is a well-preserved piece of historical architecture. In fine detail, it presents the living quarters and lifestyle of Brazil's most beloved emperor. The display of the crown jewels is perhaps the highlight of the tour. Admission is $7, and the museum is open Tuesday through Sunday from 11 a.m. to 5 p.m.

Teresópolis

AFTER ABOUT A WEEK OF LATE NIGHTS (WHICH, OF COURSE, turned into early mornings) in Rio, we knew it was time to cleanse ourselves of the urban world for a while. Petrópolis was a nice diversion, but Teresópolis really did the trick. It lies about an hour farther into the hills from Petrópolis (or about an hour and a half from Rio) and is the rock-climbing and outdoor sporting center of the state of Rio de Janeiro. There is also ✪ hiking, camping, and white-water rafting. More important for us, it was an ideal destination for a retreat from the city and the world—the mountainous splendor serves as a great environment for those who prefer to just relax (in this case, that was us!). Tucked away in one of the many luxurious chalets, we found that our days just slipped by with little more than bird songs in the morning and the occasional chill breeze around sunset to remind us of the time.

If you want to really take advantage of the outdoors, at the top of your list should be a visit to **Serra dos Órgãos National Park**. Some of the tallest peaks in Rio de Janeiro can be found here, as well as a range of mountain-climbing routes and hiking trails. Difficulty levels range from beginning to expert. The **Mirante do Soberbo** is another attraction. On a clear day you can see greater metropolitan Rio de Janeiro, Guanabara Bay, and the valleys and hills that surround it.

Aside from the traditional mountaineering endeavors, a number of ranches dot the area, offering horseback riding and zip-line canopy tours—something we haven't found elsewhere in the state. For a less strenuous activity, consider visiting the city's famous *feirarte* ("arts and crafts fair"), held at Praça Higino da Silveira. The word is that this fair harbors more than 700 merchant stands, which seemed to be an accurate number, although we lost count at about 15 (remember, we were here to relax).

Teresópolis: Key Facts

Location	56 miles/91 kilometers north of Rio de Janeiro 269 miles/434 kilometers from Belo Horizonte 341 miles/550 kilometers from São Paulo
Population	138,081
Area Code	21
Beer to Drink	Itaipava and Bohemia, both locally brewed
Rum to Drink	*Cachaça*
Music to Hear	*Chorinho, forró*
Tourism	The Teresópolis tourism secretariat has two offices, open daily from 9 a.m. to 5 p.m. They are located at Avenida Rotariana, Soberbo, and Plaza Olímpica Luiz de Camões. Alternatively, you can access tourist information at www.teresopolis.rj.gov.br.

Finally, this destination is close enough to Rio to offer a brief overnight escape from its fast-paced, loud, and sweaty existence (perhaps we're exaggerating a bit here for effect, but you get the picture). If history and a quick day trip is your thing, go to Petrópolis, but if you want natural beauty, and bounds of it, then head an extra hour up the road to Teresópolis.

The Briefest History

Teresópolis was founded in the late 1700s as a *quilombo*—an indigenous village that became a place where former slaves, non-Brazilians, marginalized Portuguese, and other personae non gratae gathered. In 1855, the village became incorporated and was named Freguesia de Santo Antonio de Paquequer, but the locals continued to call the place Therezopolis in homage to Portuguese Empress Tereza Cristina, the wife of Emperor Dom Pedro II. The small village eventually benefited from being located near the summer retreat of Portuguese royalty in Petrópolis when Princess Isabel, the daughter of Dom Pedro II, visited in 1868. In 1870, the emperor himself visited. He was duly impressed. In 1891, the village was upgraded to a municipality. Since the early 1900s, the small town has slowly become known for its mountains and highland climate, separating itself from Petrópolis as an adventurer's travel destination and favorite climbing location for mountaineering in Brazil. Finally, when the road from Rio de Janeiro was opened in 1959, it became a regular destination, thereby growing quickly from a backwater town to the small city it is today.

Getting There

From Rio de Janeiro, the Novo Rio bus station, or *rodoviária*, has buses leaving for Teresópolis every 30 minutes from 4:45 to 8 a.m., and every hour from 8 a.m. to 10 p.m. Look for the Viação Teresópolis window to purchase tickets. Buses returning to Rio from Teresópolis leave every hour between 6 a.m. and 10 p.m. and then at midnight, seven days a week. Tickets for Rio can be purchased at Teresópolis's Viação bus station. The cost is about $10 each way, with the return trip being slightly cheaper. The bus trip from Rio to Teresópolis should take about an hour and 40 minutes. The return trip is a bit shorter because you're going downhill.

If you are traveling to Teresópolis from the Petrópolis bus station, the first bus leaves at 5:45 a.m. (Monday through Friday). The next buses are at 7 a.m., 9 a.m., noon, 3 p.m., 5 p.m., and 7 p.m. The return bus to Petrópolis leaves Teresópolis at 6 a.m. (Monday through Friday), then at 7 a.m., 9 a.m., noon, 3 p.m., 5 p.m., and 7 p.m. The bus trip between these two mountain towns takes approximately an hour and costs about $5.

Driving to Teresópolis from Rio is an easy trip and takes less than an hour and a half, although it can take quite a bit longer on weekends and holidays. Take BR-040 north out of town. Once you leave the outer reaches of Rio de Janeiro, you will see signs for BR-116 and Teresópolis. Follow BR-116 until you arrive in town. Chances are you will pass by many buses on the way. If you feel confused or lost, just follow a bus with "Teresópolis" written across its "forehead." To return to Rio, follow BR-116 to BR-040 and head south into Rio. Again, the return trip should take a bit less time since you're traveling downhill.

If you happen to be coming to Teresópolis from Petrópolis, follow BR-485 through Itaipava. Driving time between Teresópolis and Petrópolis should be about an hour each way.

Getting Around

In the town center, everything you might need is nearby, so the best option is to walk. If you prefer to spend time in the park or to roll around the surrounding area, we recommend that you rent a car in Rio (better rates) and drive up to the mountains.

Focus on Teresópolis: A Mountainous Playground and Retreat

You have two options in Teresópolis: challenge Mother Nature or disappear. Some of the highest peaks in Brazil surround this mountain town. As in Itatiaia, trails and climbing routes abound. Although you don't need a guide, we recommend that you hook up with one so that you neither get lost nor miss out on any of the sweet spots along the route. Some trail heads start right from the area's hotels, so just after breakfast you can simply take off for a day in the wilderness. Other hotels are tucked within the folds and valleys of the high peaks. Surrounded by the thick Atlantic forest and the sounds of nature, you'll quickly forget about the city of Rio or what you left back home. Much as in Petrópolis, some of the boutique chalets around Teresópolis are perfect for getting through that stack of books you have always wanted to read or for finally writing that novel. If you're in Rio de Janeiro for less than a week, it's probably not worth it to come here, but if you've planned a longer stay and appreciate peaks, valleys, and nature, you should consider at least a long weekend in Teresópolis.

Where to Stay

These listings range from downtown and modern to in-the-sticks and simple. All should suffice for a long weekend.

⊛ **Hotel Le Canton**, Estrada Teresópolis-Friburgo, km 12, Vargem Grande, RJ, Brazil. ℂ 55-21-2741-4200, ✆ 55-21-2741-4029, 🖳 www.lecanton.com.br

💲 **Very Pricey** and up 🍴 **CP** CC 106 rooms and suites

Hotel Le Canton is a source of pride for those who choose to live in Teresópolis year-round. Considered the primary attraction for business conventions, golf tournaments, horseback-riding competitions, and honeymoon getaways, this hotel simply offers it all. This Swiss-style establishment is our favorite pick for the classic hotel experience in a small city that normally offers a more rustic choice of accommodations. Le Canton boasts a spa that rivals many found in Rio de Janeiro, a selection of dining experiences that bring old-world Europe to your dinner table, and options for sports that you won't find in Rio. Complete with its own stables and paddocks, Le Canton offers horseback-riding classes, not just tours. The nearby golf course is considered one of the best-groomed courses in Rio's mountains region. The hotel has a children's play area, which is perfect for wearing out the kids before nap time. Telephone, safe, DVD, cable TV, and air conditioner/heater are standard in all rooms. Master suites in the tower come with your own private mezzanine and wine cooler and, like the hotel's Lugano Restaurant, have an Old Europe feel. The superior luxury suites have a private sauna and modern décor. The superior rooms (as opposed to the luxury suites) are not our favorite — they have a Comfort Inn–style, so we don't recommend them.

Hotel Alpina, 837 Rua Cândido Portinari, Teresópolis, RJ, Brazil. ℂ 55-21-2741-4999, 📧 55-21-2742-5490, 🖳 www.hotelalpina.com.br, alpina@hotelalpina.com.br 💲 **Pricey** and up 🟡 **CP** ⒸⒸ 83 rooms

The Hotel Alpina might not be as luxurious as Le Canton, but its centralized location brings you closer to the city action. If you're interested in spending serious time at the town's arts and crafts fair or just want to enjoy a smaller city atmosphere, we recommend that you stay here. We admit that the room décor is rather unattractive, but hey, you're only sleeping here, right? The rooms have all the necessities: phone, safe, and a/c. The master and junior suites have a balcony overlooking the golf club, but only the master suites have a hydromassage in the bathroom. We were impressed with the workout center as well as the heated pool. There is also a playground that's ideal for kids. This hotel maintains a relationship with Sorte Turismo, a company that offers a number of guided tours to some of Teresópolis's natural attractions—from lazy walks to pristine waterfalls to challenging hikes, or even more demanding climbs.

Hotel Fazenda Vida Boa, Estrada Teresópolis-Friburgo, km 34, Vieira, RJ, Brazil. ℂ 55-21-2641-0279, ✈ 55-21-9461-0156, 🖳 www.hotelboavida.com.br, boavida@terenet.com.br

💰 **Not So Cheap** and up 🍴 **CP** ℂℂ 12 apartments, 9 chalets, 4 bungalows

The Fazenda Vida Boa (Good Life Ranch) is the most rustic of our listings. Although its design seems to have been an afterthought and the sheets are scratchy, we haven't found other accommodations in Teresópolis with more to offer. Like other mountain retreats here, there are heated pools, barbecue pits, a sauna, and a kids' playground. However, the Fazenda Vida Boa also offers horseback tours, a zip line from treetop to lake, and a treetop platform tour (called *árvorismo*) that is similar to what you might find in Costa Rica. The bungalows sleep six, complete with television (forget cable) and a fan. Yeah, we said rustic. The chalets are ideal for families, and the apartments are best for couples. The chalets and apartments are just as rustic as the bungalows, offering little more than a place to sleep. Another option would be to sleep elsewhere and visit the ranch for a day trip, but given its relatively remote location, it's probably best to weather the rough sheets and enjoy the *árvorismo*.

⊛ **Vrindávana Pousada & Spa**, Estrada Teresópolis-Friburgo, km 6.5, RJ, Brazil. ℂ & ✈ 55-21-2644-7362, 🖳 www.vraja.com.br, contato@vraja.com.br

💰 **Not So Cheap** and up 🍴 **CP** ℂℂ 8 rooms, 2 chalets

This place redefines peace. The sounds of nature here are louder than those of humanity. Situated on well-organized and spacious grounds, this *pousada* and spa is complete with natural pools and some of the most amazing views we've seen from private property in Teresópolis. The rooms are minimalist, with smooth, dark-stained wooden floors and great vistas of their own. The Vrindávana maintains an ongoing number of yoga and religious retreat classes, which can be booked in advance of your arrival (a schedule is listed on the *pousada*'s Web site). Open-air yoga, rose-petaled Jacuzzis with a view, and professional massages await you here. There is a small creek that leads to a natural pool. The property also has tennis courts and a swimming pool. This retreat is ideal for nature enthusiasts who might enjoy some Eastern spiritual influence (and maybe a little incense).

Hotel Holandes, 5800 Estrada Isaias Vidal, Canoas, RJ, Brazil. ℭ & ✆ 55-21-2644-6475, 🖳 www.hotelholandes.com.br, contato@hotelholandes.com.br

🛍 **Cheap** and up ⑪ **All-Inclusive** ⒸⒸ 22 rooms

This all-inclusive resort is a cut above the Vida Boa Ranch in terms of décor and comfort. It has nearly as many daytime activities, and the package includes live music and a "tropical night" (which seems a bit out of place, given the surroundings). The hotel is close to the center of town, so there are evening options like a theatre performance, a movie, or simply a romantic meal. In general, Hotel Holandes's manicured lawns, spacious pool setting, and quiet atmosphere make for an ideal spot to take a break from the heat and fervor of Rio de Janeiro without spending too much.

Where to Eat

We recommend that you first try the restaurants or dining options offered by your hotel, because dining in Teresópolis comes second to the beautiful surroundings. It's as if restaurateurs are interested in getting their work done as quickly as possible so they can spend more time outside. However, we have managed to uncover a couple of good restaurants, where it appears that the owners are just as interested in delivering a good meal as they are in running around outside. In addition to these two restaurants, there are also *kilogramas, churrascarias, suco* bars, and coffee stands.

$$$ **Crémérie Genéve**, Estrada Teresópolis-Friburgo, km 16, 3643-6391
This working cheese factory added a restaurant 10 years ago and continues to maintain a hard-earned reputation as one of Teresópolis's top dining establishments. Bleached white tablecloths contrast nicely with darkly stained wooden tables and chairs. The French cuisine is light and refreshing, and we were pleased with the wine list. Try the trout with Roquefort and almonds—it's great with sauvignon blanc. Open Friday to Sunday and holidays for lunch and dinner.

$ **Têmpero com Arte**, 262 Rua Prefeito Sebastão Texeira, 2724-1299
What was once someone's mountain escape has become a simple pizzeria with decent pies and service. We like to think of this place as a great spot for lunch before or after you hit the fair or as a place to grab a quick meal while you're in town shopping.

Don't Miss

Serra dos Órgãos National Park

In 1817, Austrian mountaineers discovered this mountainous region after arriving in Rio de Janeiro to explore the little-known reaches of the state. After this discovery, the locals began to realize the area's potential. Over the years, the mountain peaks in this park have attracted climbers from all over the world, primarily from the old continent. This park has the highest peaks in the state as well as easygoing trails for nature lovers interested in a hike without risking their necks. Although you can certainly show up at the doorstep of the park, we recommend that you ask your hotel to make advance arrangements with a guide.

Mirante do Soberbo Lookout

Don't forget your camera if you plan to stop along this scenic lookout, located along BR-116 at kilometer marker 89.5. Just step out of your car and look down the valley at Guanabara Bay and the greater Rio metro area. Then look in another direction and take in the beauty that surrounds you. On a clear day, the view can be so spectacular that you might feel no need to continue. Heck, this view is so hard to beat that at this point you might even consider turning around and heading straight back to Rio!

Feirarte (arts and crafts fair)

This high-altitude version of Ipanema's Hippie Fair is worth a quick stop. Even if you're just interested in grabbing some trinkets before heading back to the coast, we recommend that you stay at least an hour or so. In the middle of 700 different booths, there's no telling what you might find to decorate your living room.

Itatiaia

TOURISTO SCALE

👤 👤 👤 (3)

WHEN WE TOLD OUR FRIENDS BACK HOME THAT WE WENT to Itatiaia, their response was "Huh?" This was due partly to our butchering of the name (pronounced *ee-tah-chee-EYE-a*) and partly because almost nobody outside Brazil has heard of this place. True, this is not the most popular spot for gringos, but it certainly possesses great natural charm. The focus of the Itatiaia region, located in the far southwestern corner of the state, near the border of São Paulo state and Minas Gerais, is Itatiaia National Park—the oldest national park in Brazil. Founded on June 14, 1937, by the president of Brazil, Getúlio Dornelles Vargas, the 46-square-mile park is located in the **Mantiqueria Mountain Range**, which separates the states of Rio de Janeiro and Minas Gerais. Now in its 70th year of operation, the park remains a playground for rock-climbing enthusiasts, a waterfall lover's dream come true, and a reprieve from the city for nature lovers from both Rio and São Paulo.

The park is separated into two sections. The **Sede do Parque**, or lower section, is formed around the small town of Itatiaia and has a visitor's center (see below) as well as some beginner hiking trails. The **Planalto**, or high section, is known for sheer rock faces and some of the highest mountains in Rio de Janeiro state. Capped by **Pico Agulhas Negras** (Black Needles Peak), which stretches to 9,158 feet/2,792 meters above sea level, this section of the park is definitely the most

Itatiaia: Key Facts

Location	98 miles/159 kilometers west of Rio de Janeiro
	157 miles/253 kilometers northeast of São Paulo
Population	21,216
Area Code	24
Beer to Drink	Whatever's around
Rum to Drink	*Cachaça* — most likely in a small shot form, called a "dose"
Music to Hear	Nature's call
Tourism	The park's visitor's center is located in the small town of Itatiaia. Open from 8 a.m. to 5 p.m. daily, 3352-1461. See www.parquedoitatiaia.com.br for more information.

rugged mountain experience you're going to find in the state. High altitude (well, relatively high) trails and attainable peaks present incredible views that might make you forget you're even in Brazil.

Beyond the national park, the Itatiaia region contains two other locales of interest: Penedo and Visconde de Mauá. Each of these places offers similar activities to Itatiaia National Park, and they are discussed in more detail below.

The Briefest History

During Brazil's precolonial era, the land was occupied by Tamoios, Puris, and Coroados Indians, who were eventually forced out by Portuguese settlers looking for a route from Minas Gerais to the ports of Rio de Janeiro for the passage and eventual export of gold. The route that was formed here eventually extended to Paraty and Angra dos Reis, but it quickly lost its importance when a railroad was built through Petrópolis to the city of Rio de Janeiro.

As miners moved away from the land, it was quickly purchased by some of Brazil's first capitalists, who saw an opportunity to use the land for fruit and coffee exports to the new world. In the 1850s, the land was purchased by Irineu Evangelista de Sousa, a.k.a. the Visconde of Mauá. Known at the time as a political leader and capitalist, the Visconde sought to turn the modern-day park into a coffee bean–producing ranch, thereby preserving most of the land. He fell into financial troubles in the late 1800s, however, and was forced to sell his land to the state, which soon declared the land *belo campo* or "beautiful country," and by law elevated it to the status of a "district." He gave it the name of Itatiaia (meaning "many pointed rock") on December 31, 1943. Four years later, the area formerly owned by the Visconde of Mauá was declared a national park by President Getúlio Vargas.

Getting There

From the Rio de Janeiro bus station, look for Cidade de Aço Bus Company at windows 76 and 78. A ticket for Itatiaia will cost around $15. The trip will last between two and three hours, depending on traffic. Buses leave Rio for Itatiaia at 5:30, 6:15, 9:15, and 10:30 a.m., and at 1:35, 2:15, 6:05, 7, and 9:45 p.m. The early morning bus and early afternoon buses are direct, whereas the others make a brief stop in Resende.

The return trip to Rio from Itatiaia costs around $15. Buses leave at 2:10, 6:20, 6:45, 9:20, and 10:30 a.m., and at 12:40, 2:55, 3:10, 5:10, and 5:40 p.m. There are no direct buses to Rio—all pass through Resende along the way.

If you are driving, head out of Rio de Janeiro in the direction of São Paulo via Avenida Brasil (BR-101), which will take you to Rodovia Presidente Dutra (BR-116, a.k.a. Via Dutra). Once on Presidente Dutra, continue until kilometer marker 316, just past Resende, and you will see an exit for Itatiaia. This will take you to the lower portion of the park, the town of Itatiaia, and the park's visitor's center. Just 12 kilometers up the road, at exit 330, you will see signs for highway BR-324 and Rio-Caxambú. Take this exit to head into the upper portion of the park. Once the road turns from pavement to dirt, you'll know you're in the park itself.

Getting Around

Walk. It's why you're there, right? Guided tours will most likely get you to the trail head in an old rickety jeep. From there, however, it's up to your own two feet!

Focus on Itatiaia: Nature Walks

Whether you're in the upper or lower section of the park, the thing to do here is get out and enjoy nature. A number of waterfalls, peaks, and valleys await your discovery.

Pico Agulhas Negras (Black Needles Peak)

This is the tallest peak in the state and the seventh tallest in the country, so reaching the top of this beauty should be your number one priority in Itatiaia. There are various routes to reach the top, from beginning to difficult. We don't recommend, however, that you go at it on your own. Any of the hotels in the region have trained guides who will ensure that you make it to the top safely.

Mirante do Último Adeus (Last Goodbye Lookout)

From here you can see the whole park and one of the best views the region has to offer.

Cachoeira Poranga (Poranga Waterfall)

A 30-foot waterfall with a large volume of water cascades into a refreshing pool. An ideal spot to visit in the summer months, this is just one of several waterfalls that await hikers for a refreshing dip after a long walk. Other waterfalls include: **Cachoeira Véu da Noiva** (Bride's Veil Waterfall) **Cachoeira dos Flores** (Waterfall of the Flowers), and **Cachoeira Camapuã** (Camapuã Waterfall).

A Hike to Três Picos (Three Peaks)

Three summits at about 5,900 feet/1,800 meters, all within a close walk of one another, are accessible via a steep 3.7-mile/6-kilometer trail. Not a hike for beginners, this trail is considered one of the richest in terms of bird sightings and plant life. Talk to the reception for a guide to this marvelous viewing point.

Where to Stay

You're not going to find five-star luxurious resorts like your hotel on Ipanema Beach, but there is enough comfort to make a two- or three-night stay at the park a memorable "trip within a trip" to Rio.

Hotel do Ypê, 96 Estrada do Maromba, Parque Nacional do Itatiaia, RJ, Brazil. ✆ 55-24-3352-1453, ✉ 55-24-3352-1453, 🖥 www.hoteldoype.com.br, hoteldoype@hoteldoype.com.br

💲 **Not So Cheap** and up 🍴 **FAP** 🆑 8 rooms and 15 cabanas

This mountain retreat has the pointed roofs of a Swiss hotel that you might have seen in an old James Bond movie, complete with wooden shingles and stone sidings. We didn't find a need for the outdoor pool, but we loved the breathtaking view of the national park from the hotel's deck. As a result of its high altitude, this hotel has one of the best mountain views in the whole state of Rio. Guests can select from rooms or cabanas (perhaps a better choice for a small family or a group of friends willing to split the price and share floor space). Nothing special here—just your normal log cabin feel with a bit o' dust. It's comfortable but simple. Guided tours of the park are available, but if you want to just hang out, you'll be happy to know there is a pool table, Ping Pong tables, and an outdoor playground for the kids. With steam room and sauna, an indoor heated pool, a workout room, and an indoor soccer court, this hotel has a range of indoor activities. We're happy about the indoor options because the weather at this altitude can actually be quite unpredictable and, yes, cold. Bring your sweater.

Hotel Donati, Estrada do Parque Nacional, km 9.5, Itatiaia, RJ, Brazil. ✆ 55-24-3352-1110, ✉ 55-24-3371-1378, 🖥 www.hoteldonati.com.br, donati@hoteldonati.com.br

💲 **Not So Cheap** and up 🍴 **FAP** 🆑 26 rooms

The Hotel Donati is basically a collection of chalets placed randomly around a central lodge building. We found it to be ideal for a long weekend retreat with a maximum of privacy. The simple rooms give off a distinct log cabin feeling, with wooden walls and rustic furniture that keeps you in the mountain frame of mind. The charming lodge is surrounded by tall pines and provides a number of indoor amenities, including a sauna, heated pool, game room, and reading room. Trails leading into the forest can be accessed from the grounds, and guided trips are available at the front desk.

Where to Eat

Almost all the dining options in Itatiaia are located within the hotels and *pousadas*. Thus, it's best to visit just about any hotel in the area or stick with the complete meal plan wherever you are staying. Otherwise, the nearby town of Penedo has several options.

Nearby Destinations: Penedo and Visconde de Mauá

Penedo

A historic ranch was founded by Finn immigrants seeking to live at peace with nature. Their tradition has become the modern-day town of around 5,000 that looks more European than perhaps any other pocket of Rio de Janeiro. In the center of town you'll find the Santa Claus House. It's the focal point of the whole Finn-built town and is its major tourist attraction. If you're into chocolate, you should stop by the **Chocolate House** as well as a number of other chocolate stores. We also recommend that you check out **Koskenkorva** restaurant, the only Finn-specific menu in the state! Other restaurants, such as the **Vikings**, **Wein Stüble**, and **Casa do Fritz** (where they serve meat sautéed in beer) all offer Scandinavian or German food. Like the nearby national park, Penedo has beautiful views from the **Pico do Penedinho**, as well as refreshing waterfalls such as **Cachoeira das Três Quedas** (Three Falls Waterfall), **Cachoeira de Deus** (Waterfall of God), and **Cachoeira das Três Bacias** (Waterfall of the Three Basins). To reach Penedo by car, take the exit for RJ-163 just after Resende and follow the road into town.

Visconde de Mauá

Off the same road that takes you to Penedo, you will find access to Visconde de Mauá, another region near Itatiaia National Park that contains a range of waterfalls, outdoor hikes, pleasant views, and tucked-away chalets for a romantic evening. Located not far from the regional center (we can't even call it a town) is the **Pousada Recanto da Serra** (3387-1498). It's made up of three cozy chalets, one of which has an African theme with an outdoor bathtub for long soaks after a day of hiking. We also like the **Pousada Jardim das Aguas** (3387-1547), where from any one of the five chalets, you will fall asleep to the sound of a running river. Ask for Zezinho when you call. One of the region's main attractions is the **Cachoeira Santa Clara**, a waterfall with an impressive slide of water cascading down a rock surface in the middle of the forest. Another waterfall, called **Cachoeira Escorrega** (Slippery Falls), is popular with the younger crowd that likes to ease out into the water at the top of the falls and slide down into the pool below.

Don't Miss

Pico Agulhas Negras (Black Needles Peak)
This is the summit to reach. It is the reason we all go to Itatiaia. Would you go to Rio de Janeiro and not see the Christ statue?

Portuguese
Survival Guide

IT HAPPENS SOMETIMES WHEN WE TELL PEOPLE WE'RE going to Rio. First we hear "awesome!" Then we're asked if we have brushed up on our *Spanish*. As a result of Rio's increasing popularity as a tourist destination, however, more travelers are tuned in to the fact that they speak *Portuguese* in Brazil. In fact, due to Brazil's bulging population of 186 million, Portuguese is the most widely spoken language in all of South America.

We're not saying that your high school Spanish classes won't be of some help. Indeed, many speakers of Portuguese can understand a fair amount of Spanish. Unfortunately, it doesn't work so well in reverse. It's harder for speakers of Spanish to understand Brazilian Portuguese because of the Brazilians' unique pronunciation.

In order to best understand this beautifully melodic language, one should first comprehend some of its many sounds. We like to think of Portuguese as Spanish made difficult. Although Portuguese includes Spanish's rolling *R*, it also combines French nasal sounds with Arabic guttural sounds. (This Arabic influence is a result of the Moorish invasion of Portugal in the early eighth century). The Brazilians take the language one step further than the continental Portuguese by softening several of the consonants (more on this later), and, thankfully, speaking a bit more slowly. (Keep in mind that although many people think that Brazilian Portuguese is music to the ears, the continental Portuguese maintain that Brazilians have butchered their language, much as the British might say about American English. This is a war of which we best stay clear.)

We're sure you'll enjoy listening to the many sounds of Brazilian Portuguese. One sound you will rarely hear is that of the English language—it is not commonly spoken here, as it is in Europe or even the other Latin American countries. As a result, it's a good idea to give yourself a fighting chance and buy a *Brazilian* Portuguese (not continental Portuguese) language tape, phrasebook, and dictionary.

To get you started, here are some helpful words and pronunciation tips to aid in your survival. Remember, don't be shy—Brazilians are extremely appreciative of your efforts to speak their language. In addition, they are surprisingly adept at understanding our brutal attempt at pronunciation (we are testimony to that). No matter how poorly you talk, someone will always tell you how well you speak Portuguese. You'll know they are lying, but it still feels good to hear the compliment.

To begin the winding tour of Brazilian linguistics, let's start with the first three words you will need: "yes," "no," and "thank you," or *sim, não,* and *obrigado,* respectively. Sounds easy, huh? Unfortunately, they're not. You see, *sim* consists of a nasal *N* sound at the end of the word. Thus, the correct sound for *sim* is "seenh," where the *nh* is really the nasal sound of shoving the *N* through your nose. (If only it were a simple "see" sound, like the Spanish *si!*) Any time you see a word ending in *M* that's preceded by a vowel, it should be pronounced with this nasal *N* sound.

Similarly, we encounter a nasal sound with *não,* pronounced "nownh." Anytime we see *ão,* it is to be pronounced with a heavy nasal "ow" sound finished off by a touch of the aforementioned *nh* sound of shoving the *N* through your nose. To illustrate the importance of the nasal sound, consider the following example. The word for "bread" is *pão,* pronounced "pownh." The word for "stick" is *pau,* pronounced "pow," where *au* has a non-nasal "ow" sound. In Brazilian slang, *pau* also means "penis." (Can you see where we're going with this?). Clearly, *pão* and *pau* have similar sounds (except for the nasal ending in *pão*), but largely different meanings. Thus, you are forewarned that if you ask your waiter if he has "pow" (*pau*/stick) instead of "pownh" (*pão*/bread), you will be asking him if he has a penis!

But we digress. Moving to *obrigado* ("thank you"), we say "oh-bri-GAH-doo." Note that we want to roll the *R* (good luck!), and pronounce the final *O* with an "oo" sound, as in "toot." (This is the case every time we encounter an *O* at the end of a word.) As an interesting change of pace, only male speakers say *obrigado.* If you are female, you say *obrigada* (note the final *O* is replaced by an *A*), spoken "oh-bri-GAH-dah."

Now back to R. Any R found in the middle of a word has a similar sound to R in English, but try to throw in a little tongue roll when you say it. However, in the case of the double R, a guttural H sound is made. Thus, *barraca* ("tent" or "beach umbrella") is pronounced "bahr-HAH-cah," where the "HAH" sound should be expressed as if you were trying to clear phlegm from your throat. More important, an R at the beginning of a word always has an H sound. So when luck is on your side and you meet the beautiful Renata or the handsome Ricardo, please call her "hay-NAH-tah" and him "hee-CAR-doo," not "ray-NAH-tah," or "ree-CAR-doo," or you'll blow your chance with them. This means that all those times we've pronounced the word *Rio* as "REE-oh" we really should have been saying "HEE-oo." (By the way, the *I* is always pronounced "ee.")

Speaking of Rio, or the *Cidade Maravilhosa* (Marvelous City), here are several more linguistic twists. For example, the word *cidade* is pronounced "see-DAH-jee" as a result of the *de* being "softened" to a "jee" sound in Brazilian Portuguese. This same "jee" sound is made in the event of a *di* combination. Similarly, a *te* or a *ti* is softened to a "chee" sound. Hence, *vinte* ("twenty") is "VIN-chee," and *tio* ("uncle") is pronounced "CHEE-oo." Of course, there are several exceptions, but let them be part of your language adventure.

Other sounds of note are the following. The *lh* combination takes on a quick L sound followed by a Y (as in "yellow") sound. Thus, *ilha* ("island") is said "EEL-yah." An S usually has the same sound as in English, but sometimes sounds like the Z in "zebra." So when proposing marriage to your girlfriend in Portuguese, pronounce *casar* ("to marry") "ca-ZAHR." If you were to mistakenly say "ca-SAHR," or *caçar* ("to hunt"), you'd be offering an exciting yet much less romantic offer. Whenever this *Ç* with the little dangling appendage (known as a cedilla) appears, it signifies the standard S sound, as in "save." Yes, please save me! In all other cases, C takes on the same sounds and properties as in English. Just to make things difficult, those in Rio speak with a *carioca* accent, which makes the S have an *sh* sound, as in "bush." Therefore, *português* is pronounced "por-too-GAYSH" in Rio.

Meanwhile, the Brazilian *J* is pronounced like the S in "confusion." Confused yet? Well, just make sure you get it right when ordering the always important *cerveja* ("beer"), which is pronounced "sayr-VAY-zjha." The *ei* combination, as well as the *ê*, always sounds like *A* as in "way." If you master these sounds, we'll say *Você é um rei*, spoken "voh-SAY eh oonh HAY," which means "You are a king." The *ai* combination sounds like the word "eye." So, continuing with the royalty theme, *rainha* ("queen") is said "HINE-ya." A *ch* has the same sound as our *sh*. So when the Brazilian heat is getting to you, and you feel the urge to call your travel partner a *chato* ("annoying person"), make sure you say "SHAH-too." *X* will also usually mark the spot with an *sh* sound, such as *xícara* ("cup"), which is pronounced "SHE-kahrah." However, sometimes *X* has the typical *Z* sound. Thus *exame* ("exam" —yes, there will be a test on this later) is pronounced "ay-ZAH-mee." Finally, the letter *L*, preceded by a vowel, is probably the signature sound of the Brazilian accent. In this case, the *L* will sound like a very soft *W*, as if you were speaking like the famed *Saturday Night Live* character Baba Wawa. Therefore, "Brazil" is actually pronounced "brah-ZEE-oo."

OK, we are now finally armed and ready to roll. So let's speak Portuguese: *Rio de Janeiro, Brasil—a cidade maravilhosa.* All together now: "HEE-oo jee zhah-NAY-roo brah-ZEE-oo—ah see-DAH-jee mah-rah-veel-YAWH-zah." Easy!

Assuming that you do speak Portuguese with some degree of clarity, don't be surprised if you receive the common Brazilian sign of approval—a thumbs-up. The thumbs-up sign is often given after completing a pleasant transaction or encounter. The double thumbs-up is twice as good. However, if you return the favor, don't do so with an OK sign, as this is their equivalent to the American middle finger.

In the "dictionary" below, capital letters indicate the correct syllable of emphasis. Pronunciations in parentheses indicate the *carioca* or Rio accent.

Greetings and Other Basics

ENGLISH	PORTUGUESE	PRONUNCIATION
Hi/Hello	*Oi*	oy
Goodbye.	*Tchau.*	chow
	Até logo.	ah-TAY LOH-goo
How are you?	*Como você está?*	COH-moo voh-SAY es-TAH? (esh-TAH)
	Como vai?	COH-moo veye

	Tudo bem?	TOO-doo bainh
I'm fine.	*Vou bem.*	voh bainh
	Tudo bem.	TOO-doo bainh
	Tudo bom.	TOO-doo bonh
	(colloq.) *Tudo legal.*	TOO-doo LAY-gow
	(colloq.) *Tudo jóia.*	TOO-doo ZJOY-ah)
So-so	*Mais ou menos*	mize oh MAY-noos (meyesh oh MAY-noosh)
Please	*Por favor*	por fah-VOHR
Thank you	*Obrigado* (male speaker)	oh-bri-GAH-doo
	Obrigada (female speaker)	oh-bri-GAH-dah
You're welcome	*De nada*	jee NAH-dah
Yes	*Sim*	seenh
No	*Não*	nownh
Good morning.	*Bom dia.*	bohnh JEE-ah
Good afternoon.	*Boa tarde.*	BOH-ah TAR-jee
Good evening.	*Boa noite.*	BOH-ah NOY-chee
Excuse me.	*Com licença.*	conh lee-SEHN-sa
I'm sorry.	*Desculpe.*	jess-COOL-pee (jesh-COOL-pee)
May I?	*Posso?*	PAW-soo
Nice to meet you.	*Prazer em conhecê-lo/la.*	prah-ZAYR aynh con-yes-SAY-loh/lah
	(or *Muito Prazer*)	MWEENH-too prah-ZAYR.
	(or just *Prazer*)	prah-ZAYR
Where?	*Onde?*	ON-jee
When?	*Quando?*	KWON-doo
How much?	*Quanto?*	KWON-too
What?	*O Que?*	oo KAY
How?	*Como?*	COH-moo
	(Often used as "What?"when you didn't hear something.)	
Why?	*Por quê?*	por KAY
because	*porque*	por-KAY
for	*por*	por
with	*com*	cohnh
without	*sem*	sainh

thing	coisa	KOY-zah
My name is...	Meu nome é...	MAY-oh NOH-mee eh...
What is your name?	Qual é o seu nome?	Kwahw eh oo SAY-oh NOH-mee
I	eu	AY-oh
you	você	voh-SAY
he/she	ele/ela	AY-lee/EH-lah
we	nós	naws (noysh)
they (masc.)	eles	AY-lees (AY-leesh)
they (fem.)	elas	EH-lahs (EH-lahsh)

On the Move

Do you speak English?	Você fala inglês?	voh-SAY FAH-lah een-GLACE (een-GLAYSH)
I speak English.	Eu falo inglês.	AY-oh FAH-loo een-GLACE
I don't speak English.	Eu não falo inglês.	AY-oh nownh FAH-loo een-GLACE.
I speak Portuguese.	Eu falo português.	AY-oh FAH-loo por-too-GACE (por-too-GASH)
I don't speak Portuguese.	Eu não falo português.	AY-oh nownh FAH-loo por-too-GACE
How does one say... in Portuguese?	Como se fala... em português?	COH-moo see FAH-lah... aynh por-too-GACE
I want to go to...	Eu quero ir para...	AY-oh KEH-roo ear pah-rah...
How do I get to . .?	Como eu chego a ...?	COH-moo AY-oh SHAY-goo ah
What is the address?	Qual é o endereço?	Kwahw eh oo ehn-deh-RAY-soo
Where is...?	Onde é...?	ON-jee eh
the airplane	o avião	oo ahv-ee-OWNH
the airport	o aeroporto	oo air-oh-POR-too
the bank	o banco	oo BAHN-koo
the bar	o bar	oo bahr
the bathroom	o banheiro	oo bahn-YAY-roo
the beach	a praia	ah PREYE-ah
the boat	o barco	oo BARH-koo
the bus	o ônibus	oo OH-nee-boos (OH-nee-boosh)

the bus station	a rodoviária	ah hoh-doh-vee-AH-ree-ah
the church	a igreja	ah ee-GRAY-zjha
the currency exchange office	a casa de câmbio	ah CAH-za jee CAHM-bee-oo
downtown	o centro (da cidade)	oo SEHN-troo
the drugstore (for medicine but not prescription drugs)	a drogaria	ah droh-gah-REE-ah
the Embassy (American)	a Embaixada Americana	ah aim-bye-SHAH-dah ah-mehr-ee-CAH-nah
the Embassy (Australian)	a Embaixada Australiana	ah aim-bye-SHAH-dah ow-strahl-ee-AH-nah
the Embassy (British)	a Embaixada Britânica	ah aim-bye-SHAH-dah bree-TAHN-ee-kah
the Embassy (Canadian)	a Embaixada Canadense	ah aim-bye-SHAH-dah can-ah-DAIN-zee
the ferry	a balsa	ah BAHW-sah
the hospital	o hospital	oo oh-speet-OWH
the hotel	o hotel	oo oh-TAY-oo
the Inn	a pousada	ah poh-SAH-dah
the lake	o lago (or a lagoa)	oo LAH-goo, or ah lah-GOH-ah
the pharmacy	a farmácia	ah farm-AH-see-ah
the post office	o correio	oo kor-HAY-oo
the restaurant	o restaurante	oo hest-oh-RAHN-chee
the square	a praça	ah PRAH-sah
...Street	Rua...	HOO-ah
...Avenue	Avenida...	
the supermarket	o supermercado	oo soup-ehr-mehr-CAH-doo
the tourist information office	o posto de informação turística	oo POHS-too jee in-for-mah-SOWNH tur-EES-chee-kah
the train	o trem	oo trainh
I'd like to change some money.	Eu gostaria de trocar dinheiro.	AY-oh gohst-ah-REE-ah jee troh-CAHR jeen-YAY-roo
I need a taxi.	Eu preciso de um táxi.	AY-oh preh-SEE-zoo jee oonh TAHK-see
Could you tell me?	Você poderia me dizer?	voh-SAY pod-ehr-EE-ah mee jee-ZEHR

I am looking for a...	*Eu estou procurando um/uma...*	AY-oh ehs-TOE proh-cor-AHN-doo oonh/oomah
I understand.	*Eu entendo.*	AY-oh ehn-TEHN-doo
I don't understand.	*Eu não entendo.*	AY-oh nownh ehn-TEHN-doo
Could you repeat that, please?	*Você poderia repetir, por favor?*	Voh-SAY pod-ehr-EE-ah hay-peh-CHEER, pohr fah-VOHR
exit	*saída*	seye-EE-dah
entrance	*entrada*	ayn-TRAH-dah
map	*mapa*	MAH-pah
left	*esquerda*	ehs-KEHR-dah (ehsh-KEHR-dah)
right	*direita*	jeer-AY-tah
straight	*em frente (or direto)*	aynh FRAIN-chee, or jee-REH-too
here	*aqui*	ah-KEE
there	*lá*	lah
east	*este*	EHS-chee
north	*norte*	NOR-chee
south	*sul*	soohw
west	*oeste*	oh-EHS-chee
birthplace	*local de nascimento*	loh-COWH jee nah-see-MEHN-too
birth date	*data de nascimento*	DAH-tah jee nah-see-MEHN-too
female	*feminino*	fehm-ee-NEEN-oo
male	*masculino*	mahs-coo-LEEN-oo
name (first)	*nome*	NOH-mee
name (surname/family name)	*sobrenome*	soh-bree-NOH-mee
nationality	*nacionalidade*	nah-see-on-ahl-ee-DAH-jee
passport	*passaporte*	pahs-ah-POR-chee
ticket	*passagem*	pahs-AH-zjainh

Restaurants, Hotels, Shopping

English	Portuguese	Pronunciation
I would like...	*Eu gostaria de...*	AY-oh gohst-ah-REE-ah jee
Could you bring me the check, please? (formal)	*Você poderia me trazer a conta, por favor?*	voh-SAY paw-deh-REE-ah mee trah-ZEHR ah CON-tah por fah-VOHR
The check, please (colloq.)	*A conta, por favor.*	ah CON-tah por fah-VOHR
a little	*um pouco*	oonh POH-coo
bill/check	*conta*	CON-tah
breakfast	*café da manhã*	ca-FAY dah mahn-YAH
closed	*fechado*	feh-SHAH-doo
cup/glass	*copo*	COH-poo
dessert	*sobremesa*	soh-bree-MAY-zah
dinner	*jantar*	jahn-TAHR
drink	*bebida*	beh-BEE-dah
food	*comida*	coh-MEE-dah
fork	*garfo*	GARH-foo
knife	*faca*	FAH-cah
lunch	*almoço*	ow-MOH-soo
menu	*cardápio*	car-DAH-pee-oo
napkin	*guardanapo*	gwar-dah-NAH-poo
open	*aberto*	ah-BEHR-too
plate	*prato*	PRAH-too
spoon	*colher*	cohl-YAYR
table	*mesa*	MAY-zah
waiter	*garçom*	garh-SOHNH
waitress	*garçonete*	garh-sohn-EH-chee
Do you have...?	*Você tem...?*	voh-SAY tainh
How much is it?	*Quanto é?*	KWAHN-too eh
How much does it cost?	*Quanto custa?*	KWAHN-too COOS-tah
Can I see...?	*Posso ver...?*	PAW-soo vehr
I am looking for a...	*Eu estou procurando um/uma...*	AY-oh ehs-toh proh-koor-AHN-doo oonh/oomah
I'm just looking.	*Só estou olhando.*	so ehs-toh ohl-YAHN-doo
I like...	*Eu gosto de...*	AY-oh GOHS-too jee

I don't like...	Eu não gosto de...	AY-oh nownh GOHS-too jee
Do you like...?	Você gosta de...?	voh-SAY GAWS-tah jee
Do you accept credit cards?	Você aceita cartões de crédito?	voh-SAY ah-SAY-tah car-TOYHS jee CREH-jee-too
Where is the bathroom?	Onde é o banheiro?	ON-jee eh oo bahn-YAY-roo
I need a room for tonight.	Eu preciso de um quarto.	AY-oh preh-SEE-zoo jee oonh kwahr-too
single bed	cama de solteiro	CAH-mah jee sohw-TAY-roo
queen bed	cama de casal	CAH-mah jee cah-ZOWH
What is the daily room rate?	Quanto é a diária?	KWAHN-too eh ah jee-AH-ree-ah
bathing suit (men)	sunga	SOON-gah
bikini	biquíni	bee-KEE-nee
bikini (thong)	fio dental ("dental floss")	FEE-oo dayn-TOW
CD	CD	say-DAY
coat	casaco	cah-ZAH-coo
color	cor	kohr
condom	camisinha	cah-mee-ZEEN-yah
dress	vestido	vehs-CHEE-doo
jewelry	jóias	ZJHOY-ahs
music	música	MOO-zee-cah
pants	calças	COW-sahs
sandals	sandálias	sahn-DAH-lee-ahs
shirt	camisa	cah-MEE-zah
shoes	sapatos	sah-PAH-toos
size	tamanho	tah-MAHN-yoo
socks	meias	MAY-ahs
suntan lotion	protetor solar (em loção)	proh-teh-TOHR (ainh loh-SOWNH)
towel	toalha	toh-AHL-yah
watch	relógio	hay-LAWH-zjhee-oo

Food

bean/beans	feijão	fay-ZJHOWNH
beef	carne de boi	CAR-nee jee boy
beer	cerveja	sayr-VAY-zjha

beer (draft)	*chopp* (or *chope*)	SHO-pee
bread	*pão*	pownh
cheese	*queijo*	KAY-zjhoo
chicken	*frango*	FRAHN-goo
coconut	*côco*	COH-coo
coffee	*café*	ca-FAY
coke	*coca-cola*	CAW-cah-CAW-lah
crab	*caranguejo*	cahr-ahn-GAY-zjhoo
egg	*ovo*	OH-voo
fish	*peixe*	PAY-shee
fruit	*fruita*	FROO-tah
gin	*gim*	zjheenh
ice	*gelo*	ZJHAY-loo
juice	*suco*	SOO-coo
lobster	*lagosta*	lah-GAWS-tah
meat	*carne*	CAR-nee
milk	*leite*	LAY-chee
nut	*noz*	nawz
onions	*cebolas*	say-BAWL-ahs
orange juice	*suco de laranja*	SOO-coo jee lah-RAHN-zjah
pepper	*pimenta*	pee-MEHN-tah
pizza	*pizza*	PEET-zah
pork	*carne de porco*	CAR-nee jee POHR-coo
rice	*arroz*	AH-hoze
rum	*rum*	hoonh
salad	*salada*	sah-LAH-dah
salt	*sal*	sowh
shrimp	*camarão*	cah-mah-ROWNH
steak	*bife*	BEE-fee
(could be beef, pork, or chicken steak)		
sugar	*açúcar*	ah-SOOC-ar
tea	*chá*	shah
vegetable	*legume*	lay-GOO-me
vodka	*vodka*	VAWJ-kah
water	*água*	AH-gwah

water (carbonated)	água com gás	AH-gwah cohn gahs (gueyesh)
water (still)	água sem gás	AH-gwah sainh gahs (gueyesh)
whiskey	uísque	oo-EES-kee
wine (red)	vinho tinto	VEEN-yoo CHEEN-too
wine (white)	vinho branco	VEEN-yoo BRAHN-coo

Numbers

0	zero	ZEH-roo
1	um/uma	oonh/OO-mah
2	dois/duas	doyce (doysh)/DOO-ahs (DOO-ahsh)
3	três	trace (traysh)
4	quatro	KWAH-troo
5	cinco	SEEN-coo
6	seis	sace (saysh)
7	sete	SEH-chee
8	oito	OY-too
9	nove	NAW-vee
10	dez	dehs (dehsh)
11	onze	AWN-zee
12	doze	DOH-zee
13	treze	TRAY-zee
14	catorze	cah-TOHR-zee
15	quinze	KEEN-zee
16	dezesseis	JEE-zeh-sace (JEE-zeh-saysh)
17	dezessete	JEE-zeh-seh-chee
18	dezoito	jeh-ZOY-too
19	dezenove	jeh-zeh-NAW-vee
20	vinte	VEEN-chee
21	vinte e um	VEEN-chee ee oonh
30	trinta	TREEN-tah
40	quarenta	kwah-REHN-tah
50	cinqüenta	seen-KWEHN-tah

60	sessenta	seh-SEHN-tah
70	setenta	seh-TEHN-tah
80	oitenta	oy-TEHN-tah
90	noventa	naw-VEHN-tah
100	cem	saynh
101	cento e um	SEHN-too ee oonh
200	duzentos	doo-ZEHN-tooce (doo-ZEHN-toosh)
300	trezentos	tray-ZEHN-tooce (toosh)
400	quatrocentos	kwah-troo-SEHN-tooce (toosh)
500	quinhentos	keen-YEHN-tooce (toosh)
600	seiscentos	say-SEHN-tooce (toosh)
700	setecentos	seh-chee-SEHN-tooce (toosh)
800	oitocentos	oy-too-SEHN-tooce (toosh)
900	novecentos	naw-vee-SEHN-tooce (toosh)
1000	mil	MEE-oo
one million	um milhão	oonh meel-YOWNH

Colors

beige	bege	BAY-zjhee
black	preto/preta	PRAY-too/PRAY-tah
blue	azul	ah-ZOOH
brown (general)	marrom	mahr-HOHNH
brown (eyes & hair)	castanho	cahs-TAHN-yoo
gold	ouro	OH-roo
gray	cinza	SEEN-zah
green	verde	VEHR-jee
orange	alaranjado/alaranjada	ah-lah-rahn-JAH-doo/ah-lah-rahn-JAH-dah
orange (fruit or color)	laranja	lah-RAHN-jah
pink	cor-de-rosa	cohr-jee-HAW-zah
purple	roxo/roxa	HOH-shoo/HAW-shah
red	vermelho/vermelha	vehr-MEHL-yoo/verh-MEHL-yah
silver	prata	PRAH-tah

| white | *branco/branca* | BRAHN-coo/BRAHN-cah |
| yellow | *amarelo/amarela* | ahm-ah-REH-loo/ahm-ah-REH-lah |

Days and Months

Monday	*segunda-feira*) (or just *Segunda*	seh-GOON-dah-FAY-rah
Tuesday	*terça-feira* (or just *terça*)	TEHR-sah-FAY-rah
Wednesday	*quarta-feira* (or just *quarta*)	KWAR-tah-FAY-rah
Thursday	*quinta-feira* (or just *quinta*)	KEEN-tah-FAY-rah
Friday	*sexta-feira* (or just *sexta*)	SACE-tah-FAY-rah (SAYSH-tah-FAY-rah)
Saturday	*sábado*	SAH-bah-doo
Sunday	*domingo*	doh-MEEN-goo
January	*janeiro*	zjhah-NAY-roo
February	*fevereiro*	fay-veh-RAY-roo
March	*março*	MAR-soo
April	*abril*	ah-BREE-oo
May	*maio*	MEYE-oo
June	*junho*	ZJHOON-yoo
July	*julho*	ZJHOOL-yoo
August	*agosto*	ah-GOHS-too
September	*setembro*	seh-TAYMH-broo
October	*outubro*	oh-TOO-broo
November	*novembro*	noh-VAYMH-broo
December	*dezembro*	deh-ZAYMH-broo

Time

What time is it?	*Que horas são?*	kay OR-ahs SOWNH
It is one o'clock.	*É uma hora.*	eh OO-mah OR-ah
It is two o'clock.	*São duas horas.*	SOWNH DOO-ahs OR-ahs
It is two thirty.	*São duas horas e meia.*) ("There are two and a half hours.")	SOWNH DOO-ahs OR-ahs ee MAY-ah

| It is two forty-five. | *São duas horas e quarenta e cinco* (or *São quinze para três*). ("There are 15 minutes to three.") | SOWNH DOO-ahs OR-ahs ee kwar-EHN-tahee SEEN-coo (or SOWNH KEEN-zee PAHR-ah TRACE) |
| It is twelve o'clock. | *São doze horas* (or *É meia dia*). ("It is midday.") | SOWNH DOH-zee OR-ahs, or EH MAY-ah JEE-ah |

The Vitals

bathroom	*banheiro*	bahn-YAY-roo
Call a doctor.	*Chame um medico.*	SHAH-mee oonh MEH-jee-coo
Call the police.	*Chame a polícia.*	SHAH-mee ah poh-LEE-see-ah
doctor	*médico*	MEH-jee-coo
drugstore	*drogaria*	droh-gah-REE-ah
Help!	*Socorro!*	soh-COHR-hoo
I can't swim.	*Eu não sei nadar.*	AY-oh nownh say nah-DAHR
medicine	*remédio*	hay-MEH-jee-oo
native of Rio city	*carioca*	ca-ree-OH-cah
pharmacy	*farmácia*	fahr-MAH-see-ah
Where is the bathroom?	*Onde é o banheiro?*	ON-jee eh oo banh-YAY-roo
Football (soccer)	*futebol*	foo-chee-BOW

Brazilian Slang

Cheers!	*Saúde!*	sow-OO-jee
Cool!	*Legal!*	LAY-gow
Gosh!	*Nossa!*	NAW-sah
It's worthwhile.	*Vale a pena.*	VAH-lee ah PAY-nah
My God!	*Meu Deus!*	MAY-oh DAY-ohs
Pain in the ass	Pé no saco	PEH noo SAH-coo
Shit!	*Merda!*	MEHR-dah
Thanks (cool and casual)	Valeu	vah-LAY-oh
Whoops!	*Opa!* (or *Ops!*)	OH-pah, or, ahps
Wow!	*Uau!*	oo-OW

More Slang: Carioca Gíria ("Slang")

While in Rio, do as the *cariocas* do, but you'll never learn to speak quite like them. Brazilian Portuguese is one of the most colorful languages you are ever likely to encounter. This Portuguese Survival Guide has taught you some of the basics, but we wanted to make sure you could add a little spice. Practice these sayings, and if you use them at the right time, you're sure to have your Brazilian friends laughing and your travel buddies wondering, "Where did you pick *that* up?!"

Let's start simple and move forward. First, try *enchendo meu saco* (pronounced en-SHEN-doo MAY-o SA-koo). Literally this saying means "filling up my sack." When used by Brazilians, however, it translates into "it's annoying me" or "it's bothering me." It's normally used to describe another person, as in *Ele está enchendo meu saco* (AY-lee es-TAH...), meaning, "He's getting on my nerves."

The opposite would be *puxa saco* (POO-sha SA-koo). Literally this means "pulling a sack," but it's used to describe someone as a brown-noser, or someone who is kissing ass. So, *ele é um puxa saco* (AY-lee EH OONH...) means he's a guy that kisses up to everyone. If you say *Ele esta puxando meu saco*, it means "He's kissing up to me." You could also say, *Não seja um puxa saco!* (NOWNH SAY-dzja...), "Don't be a kiss ass!"

Ok, let's move on to some bar talk. A *copo furado* (KOH-poo for-AH-doo) is a glass with holes. It's used to describe your cup if you're drinking fast, or you could ask your drinking partner if his or her cup is *furado*: *O seu copo está furado?* "Does your cup have holes in it?" In other words, you're pointing out that he or she is drinking fast. Depending on your tone of voice, it could be an invitation or a turnoff, so be careful!

Someone with a *copo furado* may soon become very drunk, or *mais pra lá que pra cá* (MICE prah LAH kee prah KAH). Literally this means "more there than here" and that someone is not present—they're staring at the wall and about to pass out. *Ele esta mais pra lá que pra cá!* "He's about to pass out!"

There's also *conversa fiada* (cohn-VER-sah fee-AH-dah), which means talking about nothing, or a pointless conversation. It's a favorite *carioca* pastime. Maybe that's why there's a famous chain of bars with the same name.

Fofoca (foh-FOH-cah) is gossip. A *fofoqueira* (foh-foh-KAY-rah) is someone who likes to gossip. Someone who is *se acha o tal* (see AH-shah oh TAU), which roughly translates to "he thinks he's a big shot," is full of himself. And *estou nem aí* (es-TOH NAYN ah-EE) roughly translates to "I'm not even there" and means "I couldn't care less." Most people cut off the *es* from *estou* and simply say, *Tou nem aí* (TOH...). This shortened version is also the name of a popular Brazilian song and one of our favorite bars in Ipanema!

A *pé sujo* (PAY SOO-dzjoo), or a dirty foot, is a corner bar that serves cold beer and very unappetizing food. Years ago, these bars were frequented by men only and, more often than not, had dirt floors, thus making the feet of their patrons dirty. Nowadays, some *pé sujos*, like Bracarense, in Leblon, have become modernized and attractive to a younger, hip crowd.

Last but not least is perhaps the most colorful phrase we have to share: *nem fode nem sai de cima* (NAYN FAW-jee NAYN SEYE jee SEE-mah). It literally means "He [or she] neither f—s nor gets off of me." It's a phrase used to describe an unpleasant situation when someone or something is bothersome and is physically blocking the way. Often you'll hear it from taxi drivers who get stuck behind a garbage truck, or from a restaurant patron who's trying to get by someone blocking the door. *Esse aí nem fode nem sai de cima!* (ESS-ee ah-EE...)

INDEX

ABOUT THE AUTHORS

JONATHAN RUNGE is the author of 18 other travel books: *Rum & Reggae's Puerto Rico, Including Culebra & Vieques* (2007); *Rum & Reggae's Caribbean* (2006); *Rum & Reggae's Costa Rica*, co-authored with Adam Carter (2006); *Rum & Reggae's Brazil* (2005); *Rum & Reggae's French Caribbean* (2005); *Rum & Reggae's Grenadines, Including St. Vincent and Grenada* (2003); *Rum & Reggae's Virgin Islands* (2003); *Rum & Reggae's Caribbean* (2002); *Rum & Reggae's Jamaica* (2002); *Rum & Reggae's Puerto Rico* (2002); *Rum & Reggae's Dominican Republic* (2002); *Rum & Reggae's Cuba* (2002); *Rum & Reggae's Hawai'i* (2001); *Rum & Reggae's Caribbean 2000* (2000); *Rum & Reggae: The Insider's Guide to the Caribbean* (Villard Books, 1993); *Hot on Hawai'i: The Definitive Guide to the Aloha State* (St. Martin's Press, 1989); *Rum & Reggae: What's Hot and What's Not in the Caribbean* (St. Martin's Press, 1988); and *Ski Party!: The Skier's Guide to the Good Life*, co-authored with Steve Deschenes (St. Martin's Press, 1985). Jonathan has also written for *Men's Journal, Outside, National Geographic Traveler, Out, Skiing, Boston*, and other magazines. He is the publisher and a partner of Rum & Reggae Guidebooks, Inc., which is based in Boston.

SAM LOGAN is a native of New Orleans and now lives in Rio de Janeiro, so he knows a good party when he sees one. Sam has lived in Rio de Janeiro for five years and has married a Brazilian — now he can't move away even if he wants to. His freelance work for *Rolling Stone, Men's Journal, Maxim, Playboy Brazil*, and Time Out guides has taken him to just about every forest, slum, city, and beach in Latin America. "Mr. Everything," as we like to call him, has done it all, from founding a marketing consulting firm in Chile to exporting organic apples from Argentina and working for Outward Bound and leading white-water kayaking tours in Costa Rica. In addition to working as an investigative reporter for a number of news publications, Sam recently signed a deal with Hyperion Books to author a book on organized crime, human smuggling, and immigration that's due out in the summer of 2009. Whenever he gets the chance, Sam finds time to surf, samba, tango, play guitar, hurtle off raging waterfalls, or sit on the beach doing nothing. He has an M.A. in International Policy Studies. Best of all, he can mix a mean *caipirinha*.

NOTES

NOTES

NOTES

RUM & REGGAE'S TOURISTO SCALE

🌀

1. What century is this?

🌀🌀

2. Still sort of a secret; this place is practically empty.

🌀🌀🌀

3. A nice, unspoiled yet civilized place.

🌀🌀🌀🌀

4. Still unspoiled, but getting popular.

🌀🌀🌀🌀🌀

5. A popular place, but still not mentioned in every travel article.

🌀🌀🌀🌀🌀🌀

6. The secret is out; everybody is starting to go here.

🌀🌀🌀🌀🌀🌀🌀

7. Well-developed tourism and lots of tourists;
fast-food outlets conspicuous.

🌀🌀🌀🌀🌀🌀🌀🌀

8. Highly developed tourism and tons of tourists.

🌀🌀🌀🌀🌀🌀🌀🌀🌀

9. Mega-tourists and tour groups;
fast-food outlets could outnumber restaurants.

🌀🌀🌀🌀🌀🌀🌀🌀🌀🌀

10. Swarms of tourists.
Run for cover!